Shakespeare was Irish!

Corstown – MMXI

Dedicated to my family, the descendants of the Nugents of
Ballina

The paperback edition is:
ISBN 978-0-9556812-1-9

CONTENTS

Preface and Acknowledgements...4

1. Did you ever hear the like..5

2. Irish influences on Shakespeare...11

3. My heritage is mystic speech...22

4. I hope to obtain his head..32

5. This wonder of our Isle..45

6. Conclusion...56

Appendices:

A – Further Interesting References in Shakespeare's works..97

B – Dating Problem FAQ...118

C – Allusions to Shakespeare..124

D – The policy of the Barons of Delvin 1575-1642.............131

E – Calendar of Original Documents...................................171

PREFACE

I use here standard Irish history abbreviations including: NLI – National Library of Ireland, PRONI – Public Record Office of Northern Ireland, CSPI – Calendar of State Papers (Ireland) and DNB – Dictionary of National Biography. The abbreviation 'Cockatrice' refers to the book: Basil Iske [Elizabeth Hickey]"The Green Cockatrice" (Tara, Meath Archaeological and Historical Society, 1978).

I'd like to thank all that have helped me in these historical researches, my parents, extended family including my aunt Sr Claire Nugent, and all at the Public Record Office Northern Ireland, National Library, Cavan County Library, Royal Irish Academy, Gilbert Library Pearse St and the libraries at the following locations:

California: Huntingdon Library, San Marino.

England: Bodleian Library, British Library, the National Portrait Gallery's Heinz Archive and Library, and the Irish Genealogical Research Society Library.

Belfast: Linenhall Library.

Armagh: Armagh Public (Robinson) Library, the Irish & Local Studies Library and the Cardinal Ó Fiaich Memorial Library.

North Midlands: the County Libraries of Meath and Westmeath at Navan and Mullingar respectively, and NUI Maynooth Library.

Dublin: National Archives, Franciscan Library Killiney, the Jesuit Library at the Milltown Institute and the Jesuit Archives Leeson St, Capuchin Archives Church St., Representative Church Body Library Rathgar, Marsh's Library, Central Catholic Library, Royal Society of Antiquaries of Ireland Library, the Central Library Ilac Centre, Blanchardstown and Fingal Local Studies Library, Manuscript Department and Library at Trinity College Dublin, University College Dublin Library, and Dublin City University Library.

Brian Nugent B.A.(Hons), Co. Meath, 9th March 2008.

CHAPTER 1

"Did you ever hear the like?...Did you ever dream of such a thing?"

To cut a long story short there are an increasing number of scholars all across the world who are beginning to question the theory that William Shakespeare came from Stratford-upon-Avon. More and more people feel that while that William certainly existed that he nonetheless did not write the works of Shakespeare, because so little of that actor's life seems to match the sort of political insider and aristocratic background that seems to come across from Shakespeare's plays. If you look at comparable examples of enduring popular works, in say contemporary fiction, you can see how difficult it is for somebody outside a particular profession or political circle to write really convincingly about that chosen field without the sort of insider knowledge that authors like le Carre and John Grisham possess. Look at the life story of these writers for example:

John Grisham writes very popular works on the legal scene in the American South which is actually where he has practiced as a lawyer until recently; John Mortimer, the author of Rumpole of the Bailey, is also a practicing Barrister himself; 'Yes Minister' was written by two authors that used a network of political insiders, including Marcia Williams and Bernard Donoghue;[1] Ian Fleming, the author of the James Bond books, was a member of MI6 and served with them in places like Hong Kong; John le Carre, who's real name is David Cornwell, also served with MI6 and was exposed as an agent by Kim Philby, who he then portrayed as Gerard in 'Tinker Tailor Soldier Spy',[2] Frederick Forsyth was a well traveled correspondent with the BBC before he wrote his books, and one of them relates to a coup in Africa that he was actually involved in the planning for;[3] Jeffrey Archer is famous for hob nobbing with the rich and famous almost all his life, starting with his time hosting the Beatles while he was a student at Oxford etc etc. The moral of the story is that if you want to write your blockbuster book then stick to some field that you have personal knowledge of! And yet Shakespeare's works, which teem with insights into aristocratic life and political intrigue, have endured for some 400 years without any link whatsoever being established between the William of Stratford and court or political life.

This has perplexed many people over the years like even Otto von Bismarck who felt that Shakespeare must have been

"in touch with the great affairs of state [and] behind the scenes of political life."[4]

There are also pretty direct allusions in his plays to people like Burghley,[5] Edmund Campion SJ,[6] and possibly the Duke of Guise,[7] which show him to have had some inside knowledge of these people and their circle. Yet in the very extensive papers of people like Burghley there is again no link whatsoever to Shakespeare of Stratford.

Modern scholarship has also highlighted Shakespeare's accurate knowledge of the geography, and politics, of places like Italy and France,[8] while no evidence exists of the Stratford actor traveling any further than London.[9] Moreover modern scholars who have looked in great detail at the sources for Shakespeare have concluded that he must have been able to read Italian, again no evidence at all that the Stratford William could.[10] Finally Shakespeare's works have been shown to contain an intricate knowledge of the law, as Edmund Malone, the Irish barrister and Shakespearean scholar, remarked:

[Shakespeare's] "knowledge and application of legal terms, seems to me not merely such as might have been acquired by casual observation of his all-comprehending mind; it has the appearance of technical skill; and he is so fond of displaying it on all occasions, that there is, I think, some ground for supposing that he was early initiated in at least the forms of law."[11]

Again needless to say 400 years of research has not yielded any evidence of legal learning, or any formal education, on the part of Shakespeare of Stratford. In fact the surviving documentation on Shakespeare seems to show if anything a money lender, or at least a man of business rather than a poet.[12]

Of course the standard reply to these criticisms of the Stratford story is that this is the 16th century after all and there is only so much surviving evidence on any poet at this time, so it is no surprise that we lack direct documentary references to his education, possible foreign travel etc. But anybody who has read some of the surviving papers will tell you that there is still quite a lot out there, especially if a lot of time by a lot of people is expended in doing the research, and Shakespeare has had thousands of people researching intensively over nearly 400 years. (I concede of course that the intensive body of Shakespearean research dates from the late 18th century, but this still gives you say 220 years of continuous high level research). The fact that there is still so little to go on after all that effort seems suspicious. It is not true either that the same mysterious lack of supporting evidence is true of most of the poets of the time. Far from it, it seems only Shakespeare suffers from this lacuna, at least that was the finding of Diane Price who compared the surviving evidence for all the main Tudor/Stuart writers in a recent book. Her work is summarised here:

"The ten categories used by Price:
1) Evidence of education
2) Record of correspondence
3) Evidence of having been paid to write
4) Evidence of a direct relationship with a patron
5) Extant original manuscript
6) Handwritten inscriptions, receipts, letters, etc., touching on literary matters.
7) Commendatory verses, epistles, or epigrams contributed or received.
8) Miscellaneous records (e.g., referred to personally as a writer)
9) Evidence of books owned, written in, borrowed, or given
10) Notice at death as a writer.
...In category #2, Price found that, of the 25 writers, 14 had left record of correspondence, especially concerning literary matters – but not Shakspere of Stratford.

In category #6, Price found that 15 of the 25 left handwritten inscriptions, receipts, letters, etc., touching on literary matters – but not Shakspere of Stratford.

It must be remembered that these other 24 writers have not been subjected to 300 years of intensive search for relevant documents by an army of scholars equipped with a king's ransom in research funding, as Shakespeare has. If they had been, no doubt their paper trails would be more extensive.

To round out the cumulative impact that Stratfordians must find a way to ignore, here's the gist: of the 10 categories of personal literary paper trails left by the 25 most prominent writers of the day, here's how they fared:

Ben Jonson: 10 for 10
Thomas Nashe: 9 for 10
Phillip Massinger: 8 for 10
Gabriel Harvey: 8 for 10
Edmund Spenser: 7 for 10
Samuel Daniel: 7 for 10
George Peele: 7 for 10
Michael Drayton: 7 for 10
George Chapman: 7 for 10
William Drummond: 7 for 10
Anthony Mundy: 7 for 10
John Marston: 6 for 10
Thomas Middleton: 6 for 10
John Lyly: 6 for 10
Thomas Heywood: 6 for 10
Robert Greene: 6 for 10
Thomas Dekker: 5 for 10
Thomas Watson: 5 for 10
Christopher Marlowe: 4 for 10
Francis Beaumont: 4 for 10
John Fletcher: 4 for 10
Thomas Kyd: 4 for 10
John Webster: 3 for 10

Shakespeare of Stratford........0 for 10."[13]

Hence it is not surprising that so many people are beginning to think that maybe this 'William Shakespeare' is a pseudonym. Amazingly evidence for this idea has actually been floating around since the end of the 17th century, as you can see in this reference from 1687:

> "...there is a play in Mr.Shakespeare's volume under the name of Titus Andronicus, from whence I drew part of this. I have been told by some anciently conversant with the stage that it was not originally his, but brought by a private author to be acted, and he only gave some master touches to one or two of the Principal parts or Characters;"[14]

Maybe going by that reference some scholars felt that this play was a collaboration by Shakespeare with George Peele but now it is felt that the whole play is as much Shakespeare's as any other.[15] This begs the question then that the above reference should really apply to the whole canon.

Here is another quote, this time from the controversial early references to Shakespeare i.e. a quote from those critical references to a new playwright of the period 1585-1592 which some scholars say refer to Shakespeare. This is from Robert Greene of 1591:

> "Others will flout and overread every line with a frump, and say 'tis scurvie, when they themselves are such scabbed Jades that they are like to die of the fashion, but if they come to write or publish any thing in print, it is either distilled out of ballads or borrowed of Theological poets, which for their calling and gravity, being loath to have any profane pamphlets pass under their hand, get some other Batillus to set his name to their verses: Thus is the asse made proud by this under hand brokery. And he that can not write true English without the help of Clerks of parish Churches, will needs make himself the father of interludes."[16]

As you can see then the idea that Shakespeare might be a

pseudonym is by no means a new concept.

CHAPTER 2

Irish influences on Shakespeare

Scholars who are examining this mystery have tried to trace these early references to Shakespeare, like the above quote, by going back through the works of Robert Greene and Thomas Nash and tracing the pattern of complaints they had against some 'upstart' 'crow' from 1585. From these references, highlighted by Richard Simpson and many others, we possibly have our most complete picture of Shakespeare the playwright. Bear in mind the logic applied here. What is happening is that they are taking Greene's famous phrase about the 'upstart crow' (which is a pun on a line from Shakespeare and includes the word 'Shakescene') and showing that this is only the culmination of a long line of literary references which talk about some 'upstart' that has become a prominent figure on the London theatre scene.[17] From these clues we can say a few things about Shakespeare. Firstly he comes from some remote place [18] generally looked upon as a country backward area,[19] where they drink a lot and dance jigs and even have their own language or dialect.[20] Here is a good example of these kind of references (useful as a text book example of how to give an insult if nothing else!):

> "Indeed, it may be the engrafted overflow of some kill-cow conceit that overcloyeth their imagination with a more than drunken resolution (being not extemporal in the invention of any other means to vent their manhood) commits the digestion of their choleric encumbrances to the spacious volubility of a drumming decasyllabon."[21]

Another example is:

> "They which fear the biting of vipers do carry in their hands the plumes of a phoenix."[22]

What catches the eye of course is the 'kill-cow conceit' and 'fear...of vipers' because of the allusion to St. Patrick with Ireland also well known at that time for its cattle raiding. So all these references seem to be consistent with that strange world ...

...which is the twilight zone where Shakespeare is Irish! I suppose you think no, surely people would have noticed phrases or words that would give away that the person was Irish? Well ponder these:

Words
Puck – a 'spirit' in Midsummer Nights Dream (Act II Scene I) from Irish Púca meaning ghost;[23]
kam (same as the Irish) for crooked Coriolanus Act 3 Scene I c.317;
brogue – the Irish for shoe, exactly as used by Shakespeare in Cymbeline Act IV Scene II 269;
bob – to play a trick on someone, much the same in Irish, Troilus and Cressida Act III Scene II 69;
Queen Mab – (as a fairy queen in Romeo and Juliet Act I Scene IV 58-100) Queen Maeve, spelt in Old Irish script as 'Mab' with a dot over the 'b'.
When Prof JJ Hogan of UCD edited his Malone editions of Shakespeare he noted quite a few similarities to Irish diction:

Julius Caesar
"The infinitive is more used [by Shakespeare] than in modern English...Such uses of the infinitive are still common in the English of Ireland."(p.33)
"The double or reinforced negative, banished from literary English since Shakespeare's day, occurs pretty often [in Shakespeare. He doesn't say so but the double negative is very Irish, see http://en.wikipedia.org/wiki/Hiberno-English .] (p.35.)
"Bring, escort, take with one...the Shakespearian sense surviving in our Irish English."(p.36.)
Act I Scene I line 17 ""out" meaning "not friends" is an old English expression still current in this country."
Act I Scene 2 line 59 ""where', that (an old use of the word still current in this country as in 'I saw in the newspapers where he was summoned and fined.')"
Act II Scene II line 67 ""afeard. afraid" Still used in dialects, including the English of Ireland."

Act IV Scene 3 line 97 "'check'd', rebuked...We still keep the word in this sense in Ireland."

Henry IV pt 1
Act IV Scene 1 lines 96-97 "comrades; here stressed on the second syllable, as it often is still in Ireland."

As You Like It
Act II Scene II line 13: "wrestler, here 3 syllables, as it is often pronounced in Ireland."
Act II Scene IV line 42: "found, felt; this sense of find survives in Anglo-Irish use."

Hamlet
Act I Scene I lines 158-164 "A piece of folklore, now forgotten in England, but surviving in this country."
Act I Scene II line 21 "safety; the word here has three syllables, as is still usual in Irish pronunciation."
Act III Scene II line 129 "mich is probably the word still used in Ireland in the sense "to play truant (from school)."""
Act III Scene II line 230 "Tropically, figuratively, so he practically tells Claudius that it is a trap for him. In the pronunciation of the day (as in the present English of Ireland) Tropically made a pun on trap."

<u>Phrases</u>
Agrippa greets Coriolanus (Act II Scene I 185) with "A hundred thousand welcomes";
Hamlet swears "by St. Patrick" (Act I Scene V 132);
"Month's Mind" (Two Gentlemen of Verona Act I Scene II 137) a religious reference very common in Ireland but surely less so in England even then;
"Did you ever hear the like?...Did you ever dream of such a thing?" (Pericles Act IV Scene IV 1).
Pauline McLynn – the actress in Fr Ted – is touring Ireland doing Taming of the Shrew with Irish accents and she claims that "it makes me believe Shakespeare was Irish, it works so well." You can see what she means if you imagine Barry Fitzgerald saying

lines like this from The Merchant of Venice Act II Scene II:
"who, God bless the mark, is a kind of devil;

...

who, saving your reverence, is the devil himself.

...

God bless your worship!

...

Indeed, the short and the long is,

...

His master and he, saving your worship's reverence,
are scarce cater-cousins."

That 'God bless the mark!' phrase is also in Othello Act I Scene I
33 while the similar, and very Irish, phrase 'God save the mark!'
is in Henry IV pt 1 Act I Scene III 58 and Romeo And Juliet Act
III Scene II 56.

Grammar

Shakespeare it is said follows the Irish (and Scottish) use of
'shall' not the English method. One of these differences is described by Judge Barton:

"There is another misuse of the word 'shall' which
is to be found both in Ireland and in Shakespeare,
namely, its use in the first person in acceding to a
request or a command...e.g."We shall, my lord,
perform what you command us."[24]

Pronunciation

Barton again: "The Irish brogue is sometimes betrayed by the
agency of a rhyme e.g. in the time of Shakespeare or even in
much later times, we find 'again' and 'pen' rhyming with 'pin',
'tea' with 'obey', 'drought' with 'youth', 'conceit' and 'receipt'
with 'bait' and 'straight', 'devil' with 'evil'." Similarly a pun here
by Falstaff can only be understood if 'reason' is pronounced like
'raisin': "If reasons here as plentiful as blackberries". The pronunciation can also be seen in the spelling of words like "Macbeth does murther".[25]

Poetry

There is apparently one old Irish poem that Shakespeare seems to have some knowledge of. It is 'Womankind' by Gerald 'the bard' Fitzgerald the 4th Earl of Desmond and here are verses three and six from that poem:

> "Married men with witless wife,
> Fails in strife with foreign foe,
> Bad for hart is belling hind,
> Worse the tongue of Womankind
>
> Wedded wife from altar rail,
> Pious-pale before the priest,
> After feast shows bitter rind –
> Best beware of womankind."[26]

Maybe Touchstone in 'As You Like It' Act III Scene II 102 is alluding to it when he teases the vain Rosalind with these words:

> "If a hart do lack a hind,
> Let him seek out Rosalind
> ...Sweetest nut hath sourest rind,
> Such a nut is Rosalind."

Mythology

Its often said that Shakespeare's knowledge of Celtic mythology, in works like Macbeth, is surprisingly accurate and there is one particular incident in it that has amazed at least one Irish scholar with its accuracy.[27] It is a story in Macbeth that Shakespeare gets from this reference in Hollinshed:

> "Macbeth would not be vanquished till the wood
> of Birnam came to the castell of Dunsinane."

So that's all that Shakespeare has to work on and as you can see its not a very illuminating reference, like how is the wood supposed to move? Imagine you are the playwright trying to draw up a scene based on that line, how would you write it? Maybe you would have an avalanche moving the wood or some such because otherwise it doesn't make any sense! This is how Shakespeare interpreted it in Act V Scene IV 6:

> "Let every soldier hew him down a bough
> And bear't before him: thereby shall we shadow
> The numbers of our host, and make discovery

Err in report of us."

Then Act V Scene V 33:
> "Messenger: As I did stand my watch upon the hill,
> I lookt toward Birnam, and anon, methought,
> The wood began to move.
> Macbeth: Liar and slave!
> Messenger: Let me endure your wrath if't be not so:
> Within these three mile may you see it coming;
> I say, a moving grove."

And this is very accurate according to Irish mythology, as this passage from Measca Ulad indicates:
> [Crom Deroil one of the watchers arguing with Crom Daroil]
> "O Crom Darail what seest thou through the fog,
> On whom rests disrepute after the contest?
> 'Tis not right to contend with me in every way;
> Thou sayst, O stooping man, they are slow moving groves!
> If they were groves, they would be still at rest,
> They would not rise, unless alive to depart.
> ...As they are not trees, ugly their uproar – a fact undoubted –
> Victorious men they, men with shields, their weapons great.
> ...'Visible to us now is the host,' said Crom Darail."[28]

Would anybody have made that kind of interpretation of Holinshed's phrase without knowing more detail of Irish mythology?

Music

W.H. Gratton Flood in his 'History of Irish Music' (Dublin, 1905) devotes a whole chapter to Shakespeare's knowledge of Irish songs. He feels that Shakespeare alludes to 11 Irish songs in his plays:

1. Callino casturame – Mentioned as an Irish tune in 'A handful of Pleasant dities' (1594).

2. Ducdame – a corruption of An d-tiocfaidh from Eileen A Rún .

3. "Fortune my Foe" – (Merry Wives of Windsor Act II Scene III) 'reckoned always an Irish tune'.

4. "Peg a Ramsay" – (Twelfth Night Act II Scene III) This was known as a 'dump tune' and Flood stated that those tunes are so called because they were played on an Irish instrument called a tiompán. It was a kind of a small harp. It referred to the sound the instrument made and is not a reference to a doleful song as you can see from the phrase in Romeo and Juliet where they talk about a "merry dump".[29]

5. "Bonny Sweet Robin" – also an Irish song.

6. "Whoop do me no harm, good man"– (A Winter's Tale Act IV Scene III) better known in Ireland as "Paddy whack" and adapted by Tom Moore to "While History's Muse".

7. "Welladay; or Essex's last Good-Night" – Irish origin as well. It is about the death of the Earl of Essex in Ireland in 1576 and used again when his descendant was Lord Lieutenant in 1601.

8. "The Fading" or "Witha a fading" – ("A Winter's Tale" Act IV) "is, even on the testimony of the late Mr William Chappell (an uncompromising advocate of English music) undoubtedly an Irish dance tune. Also called the 'Rince Fada'."

9. "Light o' Love" – (Two Gentlemen of Verona Act I Scene 2) al-lusion is made to the tune of 'light o'love' another Irish tune.

10. "Yellow Stockings" – undeniably Irish tune. Known in Gaelic as "Cuma, liom" and the reference is to the saffron 'truis' of the medieval Irish. Tom Moore set the tune to his lyric "Fairest put on awhile".

11. "Edgar: Wantest thou eyes at trial, madam? Come o'er the bourn, Bessie, to me." – (King Lear Act III Scene VI) Irish melody again.[30]

Irish Language

Yes believe it or not it is now the mainstream interpretation of Shakespeare to admit that there are a few words of Gaelic used in his works.[31] It is now accepted that the phrase in Henry V Act IV Scene IV 4 "Calin o custure me" is from an Old Irish harp melody called "Cailín ó cois Stúir mé", which means girl from the banks of the Suir (in Tipperary). In English it was written like this:

"When as I view your comely grace
Caleno custurame
Your golden hairs, your angel's face,
Caleno custurame."

When it was published in 1673 it was called 'an Irish tune'.[32] As pointed out Ducdame is also felt to have a similar origin and the interesting thing is that its Irish meaning could be alluded to in the text ('As You Like It' near the end of Act II Scene V). The meaning in Irish of ducdame in Eileen a Rún is said to be '(an) dtiocfaidh (tú)' meaning roughly 'will you come'. Then in the text Shakespeare seems to be saying that it means to come into a circle.[33] A couple more references are of interest here as well. Shakespeare translates the Irish word for whiskey 'uisce beatha' correctly as 'aqua-vitae' in Latin [34] whereas most other writers of the period use some corruption of the Irish word, like 'usquebagh' used by Ben Jonson,[35] possibly because they, unlike Shakespeare, didn't know the true meaning of the original Irish words. Finally Gratton Flood tells us that when Shakespeare mentions "a roundel and a fairy song" he is mentioning types of Irish music with 'fairy song' being a direct, and unusual for the time, translation of Ceol-Sidhe.[36]

Btw on this subject of the Irish language it might be helpful to point out that there is explicit use of Irish in one of the 'apocryphal' plays of Shakespeare called the *Famous History of Captain Stukely* (1605). By 'apocryphal' it is meant that some people claim Shakespeare wrote it but it is not accepted by mainstream scholarship. In the case of this work Richard Simpson examined the story of Stukely and the play in great depth and he feels that Shakespeare wrote the first three acts which is interesting because it is in act two that the Irish references are which include characters responding to the meaning of the word 'eist' in gaelic etc. The question is who could have written this play if not Shakespeare, as in what other playwright operating in London at the time has ever displayed the knowledge of Ireland necessary to write it? None comes to mind which should make people suspect that there was some unknown Irish playwright on the London scene at that time.[37]

Irish History

The list of Talbot's titles in Henry VI part 1 Act IV Scene VII "great Earl of Washford, Waterford and Valence" is taken from an epitaph to this deceased Irish nobleman from Rouen in France and its a mystery how Shakespeare tripped across it while on the other hand it wouldn't be particularly surprising for an Irish person travelling through France to have viewed it.[38]

But the fact is that on the surface at least Ireland is almost anonymous in Shakespeare. There are maybe about three pages of explicit references to Ireland in a thousand pages of his works and this is very unlike the way he treats almost all other countries in this part of Europe. For Wales you have numerous characters and allusions like Owen Glendower, for Scotland Macbeth, for Denmark Hamlet, as well as numerous plays set in Italy and France but for Ireland almost nothing. We get just one brief character called Captain Macmorris (probably Captain James Fitzmaurice, the famous Irish rebel which might show Shakespeare's sympathies) who says:

"Of my nation? What ish my nation? Ish a villaine,
and a bastard, and a knave, and a rascal. What ish
my nation? Who talks of my nation?"
(Henry V Act II Scene II)[39]

While overtly Ireland is absent it seems that more and more mainstream scholars accept that this country is present in a kind of coded and covert way. Here is a few quotes from modern scholars on this like Michael Neill:

"Similarly in Henry V, a play full of conscious allusions to the Irish wars...the many details that reveal Shakespeare's "preoccupation with Irish affairs".[40]

And from Willy Maley:

"Ireland looms large in Shakespeare's work and in
the political culture which produced it, but not in
obvious ways."[41]

Neill refers as well to "this shadowy presence" of Ireland in this literature echoing Andrew Hadfield who's research showed that "the ghostly presence of Ireland haunts many of Shakespeare's works" including even King Lear, Macbeth and Othello.[42] Clearly the question then has to be asked why does Shakespeare allude only obliquely to Ireland, of which he was quietly very knowledgeable, when he is happy bringing forth all these obvious references to the other countries of Western Europe? Why the secrecy? Of course it is obvious that if Shakespeare himself was Irish then he would have a motive to disguise his knowledge of Ireland both because it might give away his identity and because he might wish to be sympathetic to his own country in a way that would scandalise an English Elizabethan audience.

Adding to that there have apparently always being strong traditions in Ireland that Shakespeare was an Irish poet. Specifically it is claimed that he got his account of Hamlet from old Irish folklore, as you can see from this reference in a journal in the 1940s:

"In the province of Munster in Éire one may learn more about Hamlet than from a course in any college. The shanachies or story-tellers there tell their own story of Hamlet, and of how Shakespeare got the material for his play from the Irish tradition."[43]

The curious thing here is that in the mid19th century there were already references to these old traditions:

"There is a tradition common in the north of Ireland that Hamlet's father was a native of that country, named Howndale, and that he followed the trade of a tailor."[44]

One modern scholar also agrees that "Hamlet's name is Irish not Danish", and goes on to say that in Hamlet

"the extent and nature of the allusions to Ireland seem to me to be particularly systematic, and to point directly to a crucial area of interest in the text."[45]

Another persistent tradition is that Shakespeare composed Hamlet while visiting his friend Dowling at Dalkey near Dublin, and that the account of the shore of Elsinore is actually based on the shoreline in Dalkey.[46] They seem to be quite proud of these traditions there and even celebrated it in poetry:

"Along to coast
That makes out "Elsinore",
To the left as you look
Out to sea,
Cross the harbour of old Colimore."[47]

These stories seem to date back some distance judging by the fact that an old 1840s house in Dalkey is called Elsinore.[48] There are also numerous other scattered references to Shakespeare as Irish that I have added to the footnotes.[49]

So all we need now is a champion! Some likely candidate to carry the flag as the brilliant Irishman behind the Shakespeare myth! What most people don't seem to know is that in fact a scholarly book was written in 1978 already putting forward an Irish candidate for Shakespeare. The book is called "The Green Cockatrice" and was written by Elizabeth Hickey who for many decades was probably the most highly respected Meath historian.[50] And the candidate is one William Nugent, a Catholic rebel who lived most of the time at Ross castle (near Lough Sheelin Co. Meath) and Kilkarne near Navan. First of all I will hope to show this person's family background, and in doing so I think I can prove that his circle of family and acquaintances teem with poets and musicians in contrast to the Stratford William, who's parents and children and said to have been illiterate. Of course this doesn't prove anything on its own, but it still seems more likely that the literary genius that is Shakespeare came from and blossomed in this learned background rather than the business orientated atmosphere of Shakespeare's Stratford.

CHAPTER 3

"My heritage is mystic speech"

William Nugent was from an ancient family settled at Delvin Co. Westmeath since the 1170s and ennobled as the Barons of Delvin. His family is frequently mentioned in works like the Annals of the Four Masters. For example Richard Nugent, the Baron who died in 1475, was described there as "an eminent leader of charity and humanity" with a "knowledge of every science".[51] Of course it was quite traditional for those old Irish lords, Gaelic and Norman, to patronise the hereditary gaelic poets and the Nugents were no exception. They employed the O'Coffeys who ran a poetry school at Uisneach Co. Westmeath and it is they who are the authors of the numerous praise poems on the Nugents, the traditional poem recited on the death of a chief.[52] Here is a few quotes from the praise poem on Richard Nugent, William's father:

> "The groups of wits and poets, who will be found to provide for them now since the protecting tree of the Gall is dead? – the leader of warriors and horses.
>
> ...where will the scholars of Ireland, South and North henceforth get support since the chief patron of the poets is in his grave? Cause for keening in the land of Conn – for poets and musicians – is the death of the man who did not hoard wealth: it would be strange if all poets did not mourn him...I will mourn the patron of the poets...Tara and Tailtin of the crafts, Uisneach of Meath of the smooth swords, though sad that they should be as they are, it is not they that have wounded my heart. Cruachan, Kincora of the harbours, Aileach of the cups and horns – I consider more grievous than them is the plight of the poets without the warrior of shields and swords."[53]

...with many more references to his patronage of the poets. Of course in a poem like that a bit of hyperbole goes with the territory but even so you cannot help but think that the poet really does feel that Richard was a great patron of poetry. As you can see poetry as an art was quite prominent and cherished at this time in Ireland, more so I would guess than it was in England.

Moving on then to William's brother Christopher we find a similar character in that he was first and foremost a soldier but also dabbled in the poetic arts. Christopher is the author of a famous manuscript book called a 'Primer' which was a sort of traveller's phrase book in Irish, Latin and English which he presented to Queen Elizabeth c.1583.[54] From his preface to the work:

> "And albeit that few or none of English nation born and bred in England, ever had that gift [of speaking Irish]; yet the same chanced not through difficulty of speech, but only for want of taking the right manner of instruction; for commonly men do learn by demanding the signification of the words; not by the letter, as your Majesty hath here set down unto you, which is the speedier and better way."

Here is a few of the phrases in Irish – Latin – English:

> "Cones ta tu – Quomodo habes – How doe you
> Taim go maih – Bene sum – I am well
> Go ro maih agad – Habeo gratias – I thanke you."[55]

At the same time he wrote a plan to reform the Irish government which obviously reflects some of what he had observed of that government over the previous years:

> "3. The lack of justice in the judges who either for fear or flattery do wrest the laws to the injury of the innocent, as they see the Governor affected...
> 5. The breach of the prince's word in giving protection and defrauding the same again, many times with the murder of the party protected, an occasion of great scandal to the state and mistrust in the Irish.
> ...And lastly the soldier be compelled to answer the Common Law."[56]

Christopher also wrote Latin poetry [57] and even composed music, this is from Lynch writing of him in 1667:

"who as he became melancholy through his long abode in prison, so he sought to soften it a little and cultivated music till he gained a great proficiency in it. We have often heard his celebrated song on liberty lost sung to the harp, the violin and the harpsicord."[58]

Fr. Charles O'Conor writing in the early 1800s mentioned that he heard this song played by the great harpers that frequented Clonalis when he was growing up.[59] Incidentally he seems to have been fond of falconry as well judging by the references in his will to his eerie of hawks.[60] In general Christopher is clearly well educated and there are many mentions of his interest in law, books, history, architecture and theology as well as his ongoing struggles in the military and political sphere.[61] Even Lord Deputy Fitzwilliam begrudgedly had to admit of "the wit wherewith God had endued the Baron of Delvin and the love wherewith the country does affect him."[62]

Secondly there is William's son Richard who was also a poet. He was the author of a long poem called 'Cynthia' that was published posthumously in London in 1604. It is supposed to be the story of a long unrequited romance but it may be an illusion to Richard's troubles with the state in the person of Queen Elizabeth who is often called Cynthia by poets of the age. Richard had gone over to Hugh O'Neill during the period 1597-1600, later fleeing to Holland on the way to Spain, and next we hear of his death c.1603.[63] In the poem he says how he had to flee into exile:

"Coming to take my last leave of my love,
(Oh that I then leave of my life had taken [sic])
I told her, how I now my chance would prove:
Abroad, since home-borne hopes had me forsaken."

I think this poem could be a reference to his rebellion, which went against the wishes of his parents:

"Step forth into the world mine Orphan verse,
Abortive brood, of my deceased hopes,
And dolefully, pursue your parents hearse,
Attir'd in your black stoles, and tawnie copes,
Such mourning weeds, beseems our mournful

24

woes,
And sith [since] revenge, is all your remedy,
With out-cries loud, to coasts unknown disclose,
The dire contriver of my tragedy:
Then prophecy, with holy fury fir'd(?),
And tell fair Cynthia, how the heav'ns on high,
The sun, the stars, the earth have all conspir'd,
To wreak my wrongs, and end her tyranny:
And that the sprights below, and pow'rs above her,
Threaten revenge, for murther of her lover."[64]

He seems to have been as well a good friend of the Irish poet Bonaventura O'Hussey who composed an elegy in his honour addressed to his mother Jenet Marward, here is a few lines from the translation:

"Noble was the young scion that has parted from
thee, no marvel is thy reason for sorrow. His career
was happy, he was wise in conflict, he was a fight-
er, a leader, a scholar."[65]

The poem also alludes to his interest in astronomy which matches with a reference in the state papers where he is reported to have owned a telescope.[66]

Then there is William's nephew Gerald (a brother of the Earl of Westmeath) who wrote 'Fada in éagmais Inse Fáil' while he was homesick in exile in England. First off he was broke! and secondly maybe he did miss those things he mentions in the poem, this is he writing to Cecil in 1607:

"being here in England utterly disfurnished of
means for my maintenance...I humbly crave your
Lordships favorable leave to repair unto my country, being utterly disablest to live here any
longer."[67]

Here are a few verses from his poem:

"Ḟaḋa ı n-éaȝmaıſ ınſe Ḟáıl
ı Saxaıḃ (ḋıa ḋo ḋıombáıḋ):
ſıa an ḃlıaḋaın ó Ḃanḃa a-ḃuſ
('ſ Laḃſa ḋıaṁuıſ aſ nḋúċċuſ)

...

bınne óſ ȝaċ cúıl a ceól;

25

ᵹıᴸе ᴀ húıᵱ ⁊ ᴀ hᴀıеóᵱ...

Ꝛᴀᵱᵹ ᴀ ᴸᴀоıċ ı ᴸó ᵮеᴀᵭmᴀ;
áᴸᴀınn ᴀ mná mínᵭеᴀᴸᵬᴀ;...

Ꭺ hᴀıᵮᵱınn, ᴀ huıᵱᵭ ċᵱáᵬᴀıᵭ,
ᴀ hᴀоᵱ cıúıᴸ (mo ċоmpánuıᵹ)
ᵮıᴸıᵭ cᴸáıᵱ Ꝛᴀᴸᴸ ⁊ Ꝛᴀоıᵭеᴀᴸ,
ᴀnn ıᵴ cᴸáıᵱ ᵭо ċоmmᴀоıᵭеᴀṁ."

"In England, away from Inis Fáil, time passes
slowly (sufficient reason for sorrow). Here, far
from Banbha, the year is longer (my heritage is
mystic speech).
...[Ireland's] music is sweeter than that of any land,
and her soil and air are brighter...Fierce are her
warriors in the day of need: lovely her women with
the gentle visage;...
Her masses, her religious orders, her musicians
who were my companions, and the poets of that
land where Goill and Gaoidhil dwell."[68]

Fr. Robert Nugent SJ (1577-1652) was another famous relative of William's. He was his first cousin (a son of Oliver Nugent
of Ballina) and was the head of the Jesuits in Ireland from 1626-
46 and 1650-52. He has been described by Charles O'Connor of
Stowe thus:
> "The celebrated Fr. Robert Nugent of Kilkea [the
> Countess of Kildare's, Elizabeth Nugent his first
> cousin once removed, house], who was much
> beloved of the Irish, on account of his amiable
> manners, his profound mathematical learning, his
> exquisite compositions on the harp, and his zeal in
> defence of his religion...was equally celebrated for
> his poetical talents...[quoting John Lynch:] his
> modesty, his learning and his virtue are above all
> praise."[69]

The improvements that he made to the Irish harp are elaborately described in Lynch's 'Cambrensis Eversus'.[70] Unfortunately its not clear from the references to him in Lynch which language he was a poet in. It was either Irish, English or Latin but probably Irish because he was a correspondent of the famous poet Bonaventura O'Hussey.[71] He was well known for his learning as you can see and for this reason the Confederation of Kilkenny put him in charge of their printing press in the 1640s.[72]

A brother of this Robert, Nicholas Nugent, was also a Jesuit and also interested in music:

> "In 1616 Fr. Nicholas Nugent, an Irish Jesuit, was taken prisoner at the house of his relative, Lord Inchiquin, and was imprisoned in Dublin Castle for 4 years. During his imprisonment he solaced himself by composing Irish hymns set to old tunes, which, as his biographers tell us, 'became very popular, and were sung throughout Ireland.' "[73]

Still with the same Ballina family a nephew of these Jesuits (a son of their brother William),[74] and a first cousin once removed of our William, was another poet Séamus Dubh Nuinseann. Here is a few lines from his poem Lucht an Mhacnasa (1659) edited and translated by Patrick Fagan:

> "Ní le ceapt a pinnpeipeaċt
> aċ le neapt a láiṁe-
> baoġlaċ iad don Impeipeaċt
> ⁊ do biocáipe Ṁic Ṁáipe.
>
> Tap ṡaċ ní dá n-abpamuid
> a noubpap ní áóbap cáile;
> ir deapb liom ġup rladadap
> Cpíopt pá luaċ a páipe."

> "Not by the right of ancestors but by the strength of their arms,
> they are a danger to the Empire and to the Vicar of Mary's Son.
>
> Let everything we mentioned happen, their black tribe is nothing to be proud of (?);

it is clear to me that they have robbed Christ of the price of His Passion."[75]

Séamus was apparently a frequent correspondent with Fr. Thomas Dease the Bishop of Meath (1568-1651), they used to write poems across to one another, and he is another learned figure who is very much part of this milieu of William's family.[76] The bishop was a second cousin of William's [77] and lived most of the time in the Earl of Westmeath's (William's nephew of course) house at Delvin. As well as that he was a frequent correspondent of the Jesuit Robert Nugent [78] and is described as "perhaps good friends" with the Capuchin Lavallin Nugent.[79] Again a learned figure, he had been President of the Irish College in Paris [80] as well as being the reputed author of "Letters printed from Paris to the persecuted Catholiques in Ireland concerning the presenting of Recusants and other points."[81] No doubt following the tradition that he must have found in the Earl's house he is also famous as an Irish poet.[82] Finally we find that he is described as a musician and: "bequeathed in his will of 1648 a tiompan as an heirloom, he was a timpanist."[83] I think this reference could be to Dease's poem 'Tiomna Thomáis Déis' where he writes a poem on making a will, here is a few lines from it:

"Cinte móra ar an urlár,
corrmán tiompán ir cláirreac,
ó d'imcig rin ir an féile
d'fágbar Éire 'na fárac"

"Great fires on the floor, sound of harp and kettle-drum – since these and hospitality went, Ireland was left a wilderness."[84]

Mind you some people had a go at him for his risque rhymes which contrasted so much with his strict and senior church position, like the author of the 'Aphorismical Discovery':

[Dease] "ever spent his time in jollitie, composing Irish rhymes, more like libels than any exemplary or virtuous myters (as the subject now offered), displaying therein the secret faults or private mis-carriage of either sex, whether right or wrong..."[85]

As pointed out Dease was a friend of the famous Capuchin Lavallin Nugent from Dysert Co. Westmeath who cuts quite a dash in Counter Reformation Europe, never mind Ireland, while never losing sight of his family connections, describing himself for example as a good friend of the Earl of Westmeath.[86] Lavallin had been educated in Irish and English in Ireland [87] before he went to college in Paris after which we find him so learned in Hebrew and Greek [88] that he became lecturer in Philosophy at Louvain before he was 21.[89] After that he joined the Capuchins, founded the Capuchin mission to Ireland and was a leading figure in their missions to Germany and Belgium. It was said that he was an expert preacher in Latin, Flemish, Italian and French as well as obviously his native Irish and English.[90] He is an important political figure as well and in 1623 was involved in the negotiations leading to the marriage of James I's son to a French princess (as opposed to the Spanish match, Lavallin had taught Pere Joseph and so favoured the French government's position).[91] William must have known him quite well and F.X. Martin thinks that it was William who got Lavallin his place in college in Paris in the early 1580s.[92]

Then there is Richard Nugent of Donore who was clearly a good friend of William's. We can see that because he employs him as a trustee of his estate [93] and was the probable source for the inside information that William received from prisoners in Dublin Castle during the court case in the 1590s. (Richard was a prisoner in Dublin Castle at the same time).[94] Its no surprise then to find Richard writing a poem to William's son as recorded in Cynthia. He starts off with a little pun that he holds the same name as the person he is writing to and I wonder too if the romantic troubles referred to are really an allusion to political ones?:

"Mine own dear Dicke, whom I love as my life,
And ever shall, whiles I in life remain,
I thee advise, to leave this lingring strife,
Between thy love, and thy loves hope so vain,
And for those years, wasted so long in vain,
To shed some tears, with full remorse of minde,
And to be rid of thy tormenting pain,
To shun the path, misguided by the blind:

As for to flee the place of thy decay,
I no mislike, (if that may work thine ease.)
Yet better were, this weed to root away,
Which so infects, and fills thee with disease:
For lust it is not love, that doth torment,
Where love is just, there still is found content."

There are a lot of other friends and relations that you could mention in this context, like the Stanihurst family of the Skyrne area who were friends of the family e.g. William's son travels to the continent with Walter Stanihurst, a brother of the poet Richard who wrote the Irish entries in Holinshed's Chronicles (a frequent source for Shakespeare);[95] and the Barons of Howth. The Baron in 1590, who was William's first cousin and heavily involved with the Nugents in the famous court cases, was the owner of an important work on Pale history which had been compiled by his father known as the 'Book of Howth'. It draws on sources like Hall's Chronicle which is another favoured source of Shakespeare's.[96]

To sum up then William's father was noted for his 'wit'[97] and patronage of poets, his son was a poet, his brother was a songwriter for the harp as well as a Latin poet and the author of two well known and much admired works on language and politics, his nephew was a poet, his first cousin was celebrated for his great learning in mathematics, theology, poetry and music etc etc. And yet out of all this pretty learned and poetic milieu William was always considered the greatest poet and intellect a fact reflected for example in the fame awarded to his poem 'Diombaidh triall' which is sometimes even included in the Leaving Cert syllabus. 'Wit' was the Elizabethan word for intelligence and this is what Richard Stanihurst says of William in 'Hollinshed's Chronicles' (chapter 7):

"a proper gentleman and of singular good wit, he wrote in the English tongue divers sonnets".[98]

John Lynch, who is probably Ireland's most respected historian of the 17th century, says of him in 1667:

"He learned the more difficult niceties of the Italian language and carried his proficiency to that point that he could write Italian poetry with elegance. Before that however he had been very successful in writing poetry in Latin, English and Irish and would yield to none in the precision and excellence of his verses in each of these languages. His poems which speak for themselves are still extant."

Bonaventura O'Hussey the famous Irish poet says of him in 1602:

"...once the sun of my intellect...

Gaiety without insult to any...well of wisdom unfathomed...

Not a day would pass that I learned not some rare branch of knowledge by his side."[99]

As well as these influences from Ireland William must have imbued the atmosphere in England at the household of his guardian Thomas Radcliffe the third Earl of Sussex. This famous noblemen was fluent in Latin and Italian, a poet, and a "great patron of literature and drama". For our purposes it is particularly interesting to note that he founded a playing company to stage dramas for the court, known as the 'Lord Chamberlain's Men'.[100] He was the uncle of Sir Philip Sidney who is said to have started the sonnet craze in England, also the uncle of Henry Wriothesley 3rd Earl of Southampton (Shakespeare's patron) and finally an uncle of Robert Radcliffe 5th Earl of Sussex who is another well known patron of poets and dramatists like Robert Greene. (This Robert Radcliffe was entered as a Knight of the Garter in 1599 which maybe mentioned in Shakespeare's 'Merry Wives of Windsor'.)[101] Sussex seems to have been a good friend of William's father going by the letters he sent to Burghley imploring him to grant him the guardianship of William and Christopher on the grounds that his father had made this his dying request.[102] Furthermore Christopher is said to have been a "great friend"[103] of Sussex and in 1581 their uncle goes to England to see his friend Sussex.[104] It seems too that this connection between the two extended families survived the death of Sussex in 1583 because in 1602 Christopher was reported to be "very inward with Southampton".[105] It clearly isn't much of a stretch then to imagine William trying his hand at writing drama under the influence of his famous guardian.

CHAPTER 4

"I hope to obtain his head."

As well as these literary influences and experiences William had a very colourful political career which I think must have given him the type of insights into statecraft that adorn Shakespeare's works. I will try and illustrate this by giving a short chronology of his life, based mostly on Elizabeth Hickey's book:

1550 Born as the second son of the Baron of Delvin one of the old Norman lords of Westmeath.

1559 His father dies and his 14 year old brother Christopher becomes the next Baron of Delvin. Around these years William was fostered with the Maguires,[106] then after his father's death he was given in ward to the Earl of Sussex.

1563 His brother admitted to Clare Hall in Cambridge.

1565 Seems to have hosted a Gaelic scribe who writes on a brehon law tract that he was in the house of 'young William' in the Delvin area.

1566 Possibly called up with the army that defended the Pale from Shane O'Neill.

1571 Matriculated to Hart Hall Oxford, Edmund Campion was a tutor at St. John's college in Oxford at the time and Robert Persons was a fellow of Balliol at that time.[107]

1573 On the 12th December we get this colourful description of the courtship of his wife:

> "One Marward, late Baronet of Skyrne in the county of Meath, which held of the Queen 800 marks a year died leaving behind him only a daughter which was his heir and in the Queen's

ward. She was first granted to my Lord Deputy being then treasurer, and by him sold to [Nicholas, William's uncle] Nugent second Baron of the Exchequer, which married her mother daughter of Justice Plunkett.

And Nugent himself agreed, for some considerations of gain to himself, [to] marry her to the Baron of Delvin's brother which is his nephew; and afterwards by procurement of the mother, the maid being but eleven years old, was made to dislike of Nugent, and to like of the young Lord of Dunsany (being of the Plunketts) whereupon there fell great discord between both houses of Delvin and Dunsany.

And the maid, being by her mother and father-in-law (stepfather) brought into this city as the safest place to keep her, on Friday last at night (being the fourth of this month) the Baron of Delvin's brother being accompanied with a number of armed men, entered one of the postern gates of this city about twelve of the clock in the night (the watch being either negligent or corrupted) and with twenty naked swords entered by sleight into the house where the maid lay and forcibly carried her away, to the great terror of the mother and all the rest."[108]

1574 The Baron of Delvin and his cousin the Viscount Gormanston refused to sign the proclamation against the Earl of Desmond much to the displeasure of the Dublin and London governments.

1575 As part of this new frostiness the Earl of Kildare is arrested and "an easy restraint of liberty (yet a sure [one])[is placed] upon the Barons of Delvin and Louth and William Nugent."[109]

1577 William gets livery of his estate and was probably also at the convention of the poets at Turlough Luineach O'Neill's court in

Tyrone. There is a great dispute in the Pale over new taxes (the cess) and the Baron and his uncle Nicholas particularly try to organise meetings against it and even propose indicting the Lord Deputy in the courts for levying an illegal tax.

13 June – The ringleaders are thrown into jail in Dublin Castle,[110] these included the Baron, Sir Thomas Nugent [of Moyrath] and four of William's uncles Nicholas, Thomas, Lavallin and James.[111] For an account of the characters of some of these relatives we have this from c.Jan 1582:

> "Nicholas Nugent [the judge] ...well liked in the English Pale among his neighbours for he did always join with them in all their actions.
> James Nugent is uncle to William Nugent, he is a gentleman of great authority upon the borders where he dwelleth and can do great service there, if he be so disposed, and the only man that can keep those parts in quietness, where William Nugent's greatest haunts are.
> Lavallin Nugent is but a simple witted man and is of good living in lands; a good housekeeper and well beloved among his neighbours."[112]

1580 23rd December the Lord Deputy Grey, fresh from his bloody exploits at Smerwick, arrests the Baron of Delvin and the Earl of Kildare accusing them of involvement in the Baltinglass revolt. William is soon looked for by the government but he goes into hiding at first apparently just to avoid arrest and later this develops into a rebellion.[113]

1581 30 March Accused of going into rebellion at Robinstown in Co. Westmeath, leading many others like Brian McGeoghegan, his friend Richard Nugent of Donore, and his illegitimate brother Edmund.

April – Trying to get help from Turlough Luineach O'Neill in Ulster.

July 23 – Receives 400 Scots from Turlough to invade Westmeath with.[114]

August – Lord Deputy Grey and Sir Nicholas Bagenal invade Ulster to intimidate Turlough Luineach but he refuses to hand over William.
At this time John Cusack is traveling around the Pale (especially Meath) enlisting people to agree to go into rebellion.

September 1 – William sends his servant to Dublin to discuss peace terms. The government hangs the servant.

November – The government starts hanging some of those accused of involvement in the rebellion.

1582 January William flees to Scotland to try to get support for a rebellion. He goes from there to Paris, then to Rome via the lands of the Duke of Savoy, and finally he visited Duke Francesco in Florence before he eventually got to Rome.

Easter week – The trial of William's uncle, justice Nicholas Nugent, at Trim. He is found guilty of involvement in the rebellion.

April 6 – Nicholas is hung, drawn and quartered at Trim (or possibly Mullingar).

1583 In Rome he took service with the Pope and specifically the Cardinal de Como. Then in the summer of 1583 with his companion Brian McGeoghegan:

> "...The Cardinal sends for them and puts them in comfort that they shall have succour shortly. They talk with the Pope once a month or six weeks by means of the said Cardinal who telleth them that every turn of his head he remembereth them. Nugent resorts much to Signor Jacoma and sets down to him what friends he has in Ireland, O'Neill, Maguire, O'Rourke and O'Reilly, and how they are furnished to help him, and what commodities

of that country are in value in every way, and offers with 10,000 men to keep Ireland against the force of the Prince (Elizabeth)."[115]

Sometime in late 1583 or early 1584 he goes to Spain and possibly visits Ireland on a Spanish ship.

1584 23 January. His servant Nowland Tadee is held by the Irish government.

March 1 – The Bishop of Leon signs a safe conduct allowing him to go to Rome but it seems he uses it to go to Paris.

May 12 – Writes to Rome from Paris. His journey to Paris probably brought him through the lands of Navarre (half way between Madrid and Paris) between those two dates.

end of May – Having met the Duke of Guise they set out for Scotland.

June 12 – In Scotland where the English ambassador receives these instructions from Walsingham:
> "Her Majesty desires that you should carefully seek to discover the Irishmen's doings, as also upon promise of pardon to Nugent, who is attainted of treason, to see if you may recover him. But now this must proceed as a thing growing from yourself. His companion is one of mean judgement. The end of their repair into that realm is to head some new trouble in Ireland."[116]

The ambassador Davison replies inter alia:
> "It is confessed to him at court and not denied by the King, that Nugent made some overture to him for the troubling of the estate of Ireland, offering him a party there. But he denies having consented to anything to her Majesty's prejudice."[117]

As part of these European wide conspiracies William was trying to organise a Scottish army to invade Ireland from the north, in cooperation with Turlough Luineach O'Neill.

September 14 – The Lord Deputy John Perrot gets wind of this, invades Ulster and on this date writes of receiving hostages from Turlough. But William lands in Ireland anyway with some Scottish soldiers at Strabane and sets off to O'Rourke's country.

September 17 – Perrot reporting back to London:
> "William Nugent lurketh under Maguire and O'Rourke. He assures the Irish that the Spanish and Scottish Kings will confirm anything he shall conclude with them. He has shaven his head and otherwise disguised himself as a friar but he has laboured in vain. The whole realm is quiet. I hope to obtain his head. You may expect unprecedented success."

The Scottish invasion peters out with some skirmishing in Glenconkeine and Antrim with Walsingham continually pressing Perrot "that he wisheth William Nugent might be gotten".[118]

December 4 – Perrot couldn't catch William: "I have laid all the baits I could to catch William Nugent, but seeing myself dallied withal therein" he decided to offer him a protection if he would come in and reveal some of the European plotting. William submitted and apologised for his activities which had "proceeded not of malice but of an inconsiderate fear" of being arrested.[119]

1585 The Baron meanwhile had been all along in jail (or on bail) in England but he had charmed the Queen and Burghley with his works on language and politics and had been allowed back to Ireland to attend the parliament in this year.

It is clear now that William was receiving a lot of complaints that the Pale was secretly under the grip of a kind of corrupt clique which was headed by the Dillons, backed by the Lord Deputy and presumably supported by powerful figures in London. It meant that all jobs, and no doubt government contracts, only went to this clique, that the court system operated under their secret influence etc. It was kept secret because the state took great care to stop any of these stories about what the people of the Pale were going through from getting out. For example Edward Cusack, who had been tried along with Nicholas Nugent in 1582, tried to compile a book on his experiences of the justice system, but to no avail:

> "He wrote a book in which were contained divers misdemeanours of Sir Robert Dillon, especially of Sir Robert Dillon's hard usage of this deponent in his arraignment and likewise upon the arraignment of Justice Nugent attainted, and other matters of corruptions, that this book was taken out of his trunk by the sheriff of Meath, Christopher Plunkett, and he understands this book was in the possession of Sir Robert Dillon."[121]

In fact the whole populace seemed to be living in quiet fear of this corrupt group as John Nugent of Skurlockstown explains:

> "It is not unknown to such as know the English Pale in Ireland what stroake [sic] the Dillons have borne there these latter years clinging to credit with the Magistrates by following their humours though never so directly. To the spoiling of this poor country in so much as you shall not find man advanced or rejected to or from any office or charge in the country but by them preferred. Which hath won unto them such fear in the Commonality, and such duty with the jurors as you shall hardly see any matter in controversy pass against him they love, or with him they favor not. I speak not this, I promise you, for that I envy their credit but the better to intimate unto you what sway they carry in the country. In so much as a beck private half a word of one of them is enough to make a juror know his intent."[122]

William probably felt obliged to try to help out the people intimidated like this, especially since many of them were been blackmailed with allegations of involvement in his own rebel-

38

lion.[123] No doubt building on his great legal knowledge he decided then to launch a major court case against this judge and all his backers.

1591 August 4 The storm breaks as William launches the court case seeking to indict the leading judge Sir Robert Dillon with corruption. The case later involves indicting the Lord Deputy himself. This is William's own description of the start of the case:

> "On Wednesday, the 4th of August, I delivered to the Lords of Gormanston, Delvin and Howth an information, a copy is enclosed, requiring them to deliver the same to the Lord Deputy and Council. Two days afterwards I was called before the Lord Deputy, the Lord Chancellor, and Bishop Jones of Meath. After showing me the paper and asking if that were my hand, to which I confessed, then said the Lord Deputy to this effect,
>
> "Master William, you have entered into an action here wherein you have done as becomes a good subject, if the matters be true. If not and you cannot prove them, you have dealt in a dangerous and great matter against one of the Privy Council and a chief Judge in this realm. What proof can you bring us of these things?"
>
> I answered, "My Lord, I know your Lordship and my Lords here are both too faithful and too wise to admit exception of persons in the Queen's cause, and therefore, if that course be followed which I shall lay down, and which is ordinary in like cases, then will I bring forth my proofs; otherwise I may not with mine own safety, but especially for hindering her Majesty's service, show them."
>
> Herewith my Lord Deputy seemed to be somewhat altered, and asked, "Do you say then that except we commit Sir Robert Dillon you will not show us your proofs?"
>
> I answered, "Yea my Lord."
>
> Then said my Lord, "Mr. Solicitor, write what he

says," which Mr. Solicitor did. Then my Lord, something moved, uttered a few choleric words, imagining that I had suspected him of partiality and favour towards the party accused. Wherefore I besought his Lordship, like as he caused my former words to be written, so would he also do the reason which I would yield for the same, which I prayed that he would hear patiently. And then his lordship giving me hearing..."

Here are the initial nine charges against Sir Robert Dillon:

"1. Concealment of the treason of Robert Cusack, who threshed his corn by night in time of conspiracy, by which the said Sir R. Dillon extorted an easy purchase of land from his brother, Walter Cusack.

2. Receiving 12 kine from the late notorious traitor, Brian McFerrall Oge O'Reilly, when in open rebellion.

3. Procuring a false record to be made to entitle O'Connor Sligo to Sligo, upon the death of his predecessor, Donnell O'Connor Sligo, for 100 kine.

4. Inciting the Earl of Tyrone to hang Hugh Gavelagh, the son of Shane O'Neill, which the said Earl had been charged by the Lord Chancellor on his allegiance not to do.

5. Receiving a horse from Brian McHugh Oge McMahon when in open rebellion, and after his having burned the monastery of Clones.

6. Taking a bribe of £40 to secure that the seignory of O'Ferrall Boy should not be divided among the O'Ferralls.

7. Dismissed one Melaghlin Moyle McCongawney, a felon convicted by a jury.

8. Having conference in England with Parsons the Jesuit; and also,

9. Sir Robert Dillon said it were good for Ireland that there were never a nobleman in it, and no harm for England if there were not any there either.

Under the hand of William Nugent."[124]

October – The court case goes on for a long time, it was considered by commissioners and the Privy Councils in Dublin and London as part of which William probably had an audience with the Queen in London at this time.

1592 February to June – William is back in Ireland putting his case before Commissioners who are examining it at Christ Church Cathedral in Dublin. After this William returned to England but is back in Ireland in September.

November 20 – O'Rourke's former secretary leaks information from Dublin Castle, where he is imprisoned, that the Dillons et al had encouraged O'Rourke to rebel. The Barons of Delvin and Howth, alongwith William and Patrick Bermingham detail these allegations in a 'book' that they send to Burghley in London.

1593 19 March – William and his allies, Delvin, Howth and Patrick Bermingham, are disappointed at the progress the case is making in Ireland so they plan to bring charges against Sir Robert at each of the Circuit Court sessions as they are held in Meath, Westmeath and Longford.[125] This plan is superceded by the flight of Sir Robert and then William to London to plead their case before the Privy Council there.

By the Autumn of this year William had unearthed a whole new series of charges but the case had by now being sent to Sir Henry Wallop for decision. He was a noted ally of the Dillons and so Sir Robert was found not guilty in November and dies two years later and buried at Tara. In giving the case to Wallop the English council had clearly decided to acquit the Dillons et al, irrespective of the evidence, and it is interesting to speculate why Burghley, who was usually an ally of the Nugents in this, would allow that to happen. But still I'm sure he found ways of easing his discomfort, at one time for example Sir Henry Wallop had written to Burghley offering "acceptance of a small parcel of plate as a token of his good will" after Burghley had sided with him on a government matter![126]

The administration continued to keep a close eye on him:
> "What her Majesty's pleasure and your Lordship's to have done with William Nugent, who is quiet for anything I know at his house, and up and down the country, I humbly rest to know, but a most dangerous man if time and power would serve, he now by this manifestly appears to be."[120]

1594-1603 The nine years war, the great rebellion by Hugh O'Neill Earl of Tyrone.

1597 Sometime around this date Richard, William's son, joins O'Neill and becomes his chief lieutenant in Leinster alongwith Captain Tyrell.[127]

1600 August – This Richard goes to Spain via Scotland in company with Walter Stanihurst.

September 29 – William has time to launch a religious controversy in Dublin:
> "On the 29th of September, 1600, Mr. William Nugent, an honourable and learned esquire, maintained at the Rider's table that there was no diversity of belief between Catholics of the present day and those who lived at the time of the Apostles. Mr. Rider maintained that the difference was as great as betwixt Protestantcy and Papacy. Both agreed to abide a lawful resolution of the learned."[128]

1602 The Baron of Delvin was arrested for treason, accused of aiding O'Neill. He died on the 5th of September while on bail to see a doctor for the cancer that was visibly killing him during his incarceration. He was succeeded by his son Richard as the next Baron of Delvin.

1607 This Baron of Delvin was arrested and accused of being part of the Flight of the Earls conspiracy. He escaped from Dublin Castle two weeks later and raised a revolt around Clogh Oughter castle in Cavan.

1608 May – He submits and travels to London.

1621 November 22 This Baron of Delvin is created the first Earl of Westmeath.

1624 Friday of Easter week a great assembly at Fore is reported to have cried that the Earl of Westmeath should be declared the King of Ireland.

1625 William died on the last day of June this year.

1642 His nephew the Earl of Westmeath died sometime after deciding to support the Confederation of Kilkenny, although initially he did not join the 1641 rebellion. This rebellion of course marks the end of the power of those old Norman lords who were all swept away after it by Cromwellian planters.

Obviously this is quite a colourful history that Elizabeth Hickey found herself researching when she started to write her biography of William Nugent. As she researched this story she was struck by how much this career matches the character and experiences of Shakespeare, as is known from his works. Along with his poetic talents, that have already been mentioned, she saw that his European travel, legal knowledge, and political experiences matched the author of Shakespeare's works:

European knowledge
As you can see from the chronology he visited all the places that Shakespeare is reckoned to have been, particularly Italy, France and Scotland although there is no direct evidence of any travels to Denmark. Also not only did he know Italian, but he was an Italian poet, as narrated by Fr John Lynch. Furthermore he, and his companion Brian Geoghegan, wrote in Italian when they communicated with the Vatican.[129]

Legal learning

His legal knowledge and interest comes across from his court case of course and from other references in the state papers like this one from about 1584. Here his friends are writing to William from Paris explaining that he needs to grant proper powers of attorney, called a 'procuration', so that they can receive his pension for him from Rome, and they don't bother sending him draft letters for this because his skill in these matters is better than their own:

> "We need not to give you instructions for the manner of making the procuration, whereby it may be of vigour and force in law, because we know your own skill and practice therein to be better than ours."[130]

There is no doubt as well that William himself wrote the legal papers in use during the court case, as this summary of a complaint of his in the state papers shows: "Complains that not allowed to be present at the examination, though he pens the interrogatories."[131] Presumably he had studied law while he was at Oxford and he had also lived much of his life in the house of his uncle Nicholas, who was a leading Irish judge well known for his learning, as you can read in the 'Green Cockatrice'.[132]

Political Experience

Again it is clear I think from the chronology that William had an unrivaled knowledge of European politics, rebellions, warfare, corruption and political intrigue. Not only that but the Tudor wars in Ireland also provide that extra blood thirsty element that comes across in Shakespeare. What I mean is that Ireland was not a place where any kind of 'civilised' warfare was practiced at this time, it is almost unrelentingly gory with severed heads being a common backdrop to the viceroy's processions and even Dublin Castle.[133] This overt violence is really much much more so a feature of Ireland at the time than in England and therefore may explain the almost gratuitous violence of many of Shakespeare's plays.

CHAPTER 5

"This wonder of our Isle...his glorious muse... the treasure, that our Ireland hideth"

I guess the next step is to try and see specific traces of our William in the works of Shakespeare. But first I hope to show that there are indications in the sonnets that Shakespeare was using a pseudonym which shared the first name William with his real name. I suspect that sonnets 135 and 136 are written at the time that some of Shakespeare's sonnets were published under that name c.1600. Maybe if Shakespeare had sent out some of the sonnets in a manuscript form before that publication, under the name William Nugent, then the person who had the old sonnets might be wondering who is who, who is the real Shakespeare.

Possibly Shakespeare is explaining in these sonnets to that person that the pseudonym William Shakespeare is really just him and that there is no need for his correspondent to feel vexed or confused at the fact that the sonnets he is sending out under the name William Nugent are also published under the name William Shakespeare. I know this is a confusing argument :-) but its also possible that it works the other way around in that the correspondent could have just found out that the sonnets he was receiving under the name William Shakespeare were all along written by William Nugent and hence he feels angry at the duplicity. So that gives us two William's or Will's, a real one and a fake one, and maybe Shakespeare is trying to mollify him by saying look who cares its just me writing it anyways! There is only one 'Will' no matter what! Maybe when you read these two sonnets then you might be able to see how this logic seems to play out in the poetry:

no. 135
"Whoever hath her wish, thou hast thy 'Will,'
And 'Will' to boot, and 'Will' in overplus;
More than enough am I that vex thee still,
To thy sweet will making addition thus.
Wilt thou, whose will is large and spacious,

Not once vouchsafe to hide my will in thine?
Shall will in others seem right gracious,
And in my will no fair acceptance shine?
The sea all water, yet receives rain still
And in abundance addeth to his store;
So thou, being rich in 'Will,' add to thy 'Will'
One will of mine, to make thy large 'Will' more.
Let no unkind, no fair beseechers kill;
Think all but one, and me in that one 'Will.' "

Maybe the correspondent replies that there is no sincerity in all the talk of 'love' etc in the sonnets when he is using a false name, as if the correspondent's soul had been defrauded by being used like that, so again Shakespeare tries to get this person to just look upon him as one person and forget about the fact that he had used a pseudonym:

no.136

"If thy soul cheque thee that I come so near,
Swear to thy blind soul that I was thy 'Will,'
And will, thy soul knows, is admitted there;
Thus far for love my love-suit, sweet, fulfil.
'Will' will fulfil the treasure of thy love,
Ay, fill it full with wills, and my will one.
In things of great receipt with ease we prove
Among a number one is reckon'd none:
Then in the number let me pass untold,
Though in thy stores' account I one must be;
For nothing hold me, so it please thee hold
That nothing me, a something sweet to thee:
Make but my name thy love, and love that still,
And then thou lovest me, for my name is 'Will.'"

In any case it certainly seems to show that the poet's name was William, which rules out quite a few other candidates for Shakespeare. As regards Shakespeare's plays I thought this passage from Henry VI part 2 might be linked to William's legal struggles. Specifically, as pointed out in the chronology above, in the charges that William makes against Robert Dillon he accuses him of wanting to do away with all the nobility both in England and Ireland, and then in this play, written during the same years, he describes in detail a kind of leveller rebel figure who tries to destroy all hierarchy and respect for birth and privilege. So maybe he is sending a warning about the type of world that he feels would be created if the likes of Sir Robert Dillon have their way. Also there are a few other possible allusions to William in it that I note in the footnotes.

The first bit is said by York, (in Act III Scene I Henry VI part 2) who is the high up politician secretly manipulating the rebel leader Cade, much like William was saying about some Irish rebels during his court case. You can see how he hopes his manufactured 'black storm' in England will cause the ordinary people of England to cry out for him to return with his army from his Lord Deputyship in Ireland, and then make him King. It is followed by the famous account of Cade's rebellion:

> "Whiles I in Ireland nourish a mighty band,
> I will stir up in England some black storm
> Shall blow ten thousand souls to heaven or hell;
> And this fell tempest shall not cease to rage
> Until the golden circuit on my head,
> Like to the glorious sun's transparent beams,
> Do calm the fury of this mad-bred flaw.
> And, for a minister of my intent,
> I have seduced a headstrong Kentishman,
> John Cade of Ashford,[134]
> To make commotion, as full well he can,
> Under the title of John Mortimer.
> In Ireland have I seen this stubborn Cade
> Oppose himself against a troop of kerns,
> And fought so long, till that his thighs with darts
> Were almost like a sharp-quill'd porpentine;
> And, in the end being rescued, I have seen
> Him caper upright like a wild Morisco,
> Shaking the bloody darts as he his bells.
> Full often, like a shag-hair'd crafty kern,
> Hath he conversed with the enemy,
> And undiscover'd come to me again

And given me notice of their villanies.
This devil here shall be my substitute;
For that John Mortimer, which now is dead,
In face, in gait, in speech, he doth resemble:
By this I shall perceive the commons' mind,
How they affect the house and claim of York.
Say he be taken, rack'd and tortured,
I know no pain they can inflict upon him
Will make him say I moved him to those arms.
Say that he thrive, as 'tis great like he will,
Why, then from Ireland come I with my strength
And reap the harvest which that rascal sow'd;
For Humphrey being dead, as he shall be,
And Henry put apart, the next for me."

This is then the rebel Cade making his speech and being teased by his supporters in Act IV Scene II. I wonder too if this bit contains something of the Irish sense of humour, particularly the idea of friends slagging their colleagues who are getting too big headed and making grandiose speeches!:

"CADE: We John Cade, so termed of our supposed father,--

DICK:[Aside] Or rather, of stealing a cade of herrings.

CADE: For our enemies shall fall before us, inspired with the spirit of putting down kings and princes,
--Command silence.

DICK: Silence!

CADE: My father was a Mortimer,--

DICK:[Aside] He was an honest man, and a good bricklayer.

48

CADE: My mother a Plantagenet,--

DICK:[Aside] I knew her well; she was a midwife.

CADE: My wife descended of the Lacies,--[135]

DICK:[Aside] She was, indeed, a pedlar's daughter, and sold many laces.

SMITH:[Aside] But now of late, notable to travel with her furred pack, she washes bucks here at home.

CADE: Therefore am I of an honourable house.

DICK:[Aside] Ay, by my faith, the field is honourable;
and there was he borne, under a hedge, for his father had never a house but the cage.

CADE: Valiant I am.

SMITH:[Aside] A' must needs; for beggary is valiant.

CADE: I am able to endure much.

DICK:[Aside] No question of that; for I have seen him whipped three market-days together.

CADE: I fear neither sword nor fire.

SMITH:[Aside] He need not fear the sword; for his coat is of proof.

DICK:[Aside] But methinks he should stand in fear of fire, being burnt i' the hand for stealing of sheep.[136]

CADE: Be brave, then; for your captain is brave, and vows reformation. There shall be in England seven halfpenny loaves sold for a penny: the three-hooped pot; shall have ten hoops and I will make it felony to drink small beer: all the realm shall be in common; and in Cheapside shall my palfrey go to grass: and when I am king, as king I will be,--

ALL: God save your majesty!

CADE: I thank you, good people: there shall be no money;
all shall eat and drink on my score; and I will apparel them all in one livery, that they may agree like brothers and worship me their lord.

DICK: The first thing we do, let's kill all the lawyers.[137]

CADE: Nay, that I mean to do. Is not this a lamentable thing, that of the skin of an innocent lamb should be made parchment?[138] that parchment, being scribbled o'er, should undo a man? Some say the bee stings:
but I say, 'tis the bee's wax; for I did but seal once to a thing, and I was never mine own man since. How now! who's there?

Enter some, bringing forward the Clerk of Chatham

SMITH: The clerk of Chatham: he can write and read and cast accompt.

CADE: O monstrous!

SMITH: We took him setting of boys' copies.

CADE: Here's a villain!

SMITH: Has a book in his pocket with red letters in't.

CADE: Nay, then, he is a conjurer.

DICK: Nay, he can make obligations, and write court-hand.

CADE: I am sorry for't: the man is a proper man, of mine honour; unless I find him guilty, he shall not die.
Come hither, sirrah, I must examine thee: what is thy name?

CLERK: Emmanuel.

DICK: They use to write it on the top of letters: 'twill go hard with you.

CADE: Let me alone. Dost thou use to write thy name? Or hast thou a mark to thyself, like an honest plain-dealing man?

CLERK: Sir, I thank God, I have been so well brought up that I can write my name.

ALL: He hath confessed: away with him! he's a villain and a traitor.

CADE: Away with him, I say! hang him with his pen and ink-horn about his neck."

Remember this is written c.1592, exactly the same time that our William is pursuing his court case unearthing the kind of manipulated rebellions that are condemned, by ridicule, in the play.

And it gets better because I think I can also show that our William was also intimately acquainted with the literary milieu in London. What Elizabeth Hickey didn't realise when she wrote her book was that William Nugent seems to have compiled into book form the poems of his son Richard, and prepared them for publication in London in 1604.[139] Clearly it is fascinating to see William being so involved in the publishing scene in London at the height of Shakespeare's powers. Also some have remarked on the absence of any tribute work by Shakespeare commemorating the death of Queen Elizabeth, and yet this work is entitled simply 'Cynthia', which is the usual poetic name for that Queen, and is published in the year after her death. So possibly this was intended to be that missing commemorative work. Maybe too he felt more confident about revealing his identity, albeit only that of his son, in the early months of the new king's reign when many Irish Catholics hoped that he would be sympathetic to their plight. Here is another poem from it to give you a flavour of the work:

"Ay me, despair comes now to claim the scope,
Of my sad thoughts drowned in deep woes excess,
For I am reft(?), the object of my hope,
And my fierce faire, a stranger doth possess,
Yet Sydney's gentle shepherd could devise,
In such a case, to find a remedy,
who blear'd his jealous hosts mistrustful eyes,
By his kind hostess handsome industry,
Then why should I despair, of like success,
whose happy rival, is a harmless boy,
But ah, my Cynthia doth this hope suppress,
who chastely proud persists, and sweetly coy,
But Cynthia, why do I for this reprove thee,
Since for thou wast so chast, I first did love
thee."[140]

The 'Sydney's gentle shepherd' is apparently an allusion to various references in Sir Philip Sidney's and Edmund Spenser's works in the 1580s and 90s. I apologise that I cannot be clearer than that, the fact is that they frequently ramble on about some 'shepherd' type figure and its a nightmare trying to decipher who's who! In fact some people think that this 'gentle shepherd' is none other than Shakespeare himself.[141] If it is, then it could be that he hopes to get help from his father, and be as 'like success'-ful as his father in getting some kind of restoration of his estates after his rebellion. Either way you have to admit that he seems to know this 'gentle shepherd' personally, and that it is not just a throwaway literary reference. At the very least I think most people would agree with Andrew Carpenter that "Richard's work shows an intimate acquaintance with the kind of verse being written at that time in London."[142] So placing this Irish family at the heart of the literary scene in London in 1604, which is surely very interesting. Btw William did spend some time in England during those years going by this reference to the death, aged 101, of William Nicholls of Lench, Worcestershire, labourer:

> "He was descended from Richard Nugent, student
> of Magdalen college, Oxford, in the reign of King
> James I and one of the distinguished poets of that
> period."[143]

Although this refers to Richard probably William is meant here (obviously any descendant of William's is a close relative of Richard's) because there is no reference to Richard having ever been in England. Remember he died young and from 1598 he could hardly have ventured near England because of his rebellion.

Getting back to 'Cynthia' I think this poem in it raises the prospect that Ireland is harbouring some secret 'glorious muse' who's identity, if made known to the world, would shock all of Europe:

> "Oft have I wished, in my zeals excess,
> To make my Cynthia see proofs of my duty,
> That in these lines, I could as well express,
> As in my soul I do admire her beauty,
> Or that great Daniel, fit for such a task,
> This wonder of our Isle, had seen, and heeded,
> Then should his glorious muse, her worth unmask,
> And he himself, himself should have exceeded;
> Then England, France, Spain, Greece, and Italy,
> And all that th'Ocean from our shores divideth,
> Would over-run their bounds, and hither fly,

To find the treasure, that our Ireland hideth,
But best is, that we never do disclose it,
Since known but of our selves, we shall not lose
it."[144]

This person whoever he is is much better at writing poetry than Richard and maybe when Richard says 'her worth unmask' he is poetically calling for her, Queen Elizabeth, to unmask his (Shakespeare's?) worth. In a way if you did 'unmask' Shakespeare then William Nugent, who is already known to be a learned person, would suddenly exceed his own reputation: "And he himself, himself should have exceeded." If it isn't Shakespeare he is talking about then he certainly seems to exaggerate a lot! The sense possibly is the same as the other poem in that he wants his father to petition Elizabeth to try and get him pardoned, since he would be much better at writing lines that prove Richard's fundamental loyalty to the queen. Incidentally if it seems that many of these sonnets are addressed to his father then possibly they correspond with Shakespeare's sonnets which some would say are addressed to his son. They could have been writing sonnets over and back to one another disguising the political content behind these literary allusions, for obvious reasons of security. This is not that much of a stretch because Richard was certainly in exile for a while so they had to communicate by letter and some kind of code would be essential, and we know they are two poets so why not incorporate it into poetry? And finally don't forget that both of them are pretty obsessed by politics and were usually much hated by the powers that be. In fact we know that William and his brother Christopher used to do something like this as you can see from the statement of John Nugent of Skurlockstown:

"He confesseth that William Nugent told him that a little before Michaelmas last, the Baron Delvin wrote a letter to the said William of this tenor viz. "Let the poor man enjoy his sheep, or else you do him great wrong." This letter William answered in this sort viz. 'if it had been a sheep that had been scabbed, it had been better he should have perished, than the whole flock.' "[145]

So it is clearly the case that this Catholic family used codewords in their letters, to get around government surveillance, and this fits in rather neatly with the new thinking about Shakespeare that he was a Catholic using secret codewords in his works. This new perspective on Shakespeare is reflected, for example, in the highly regarded book by Claire Asquith.[146] She also feels that Shakespeare was probably educated in Oxford, where William Nugent was also educated incidentally.[147]

CHAPTER 6

Conclusion

Finally at the end of all that I guess you are waiting for some detailed explanation about how this William and William Shakespeare, the actor from Stratford, interact. Sorry, I'm damned if I know! As I see it there just isn't enough evidence available to figure out what really happened between these two people, and the circumstances under which the works originated, and I don't really want to speculate without corresponding evidence. At a guess I think what happens is similar to what Elizabeth Hickey speculates and which you can see in the character of Roberto in 'Groat's Worth of Wit'.[148] Our William is back in Ireland in early 1585 totally broke and unable to take up most employment because of his attainder, which he had received when he had rebelled and which was never rescinded. Again this is kind of a legal black mark which is held over a person who has rebelled, he cannot bear arms, inherit titles etc because of it. In fact on his grave his coat of arms are left blank because of the attainder.[149] So penniless he might have had the idea of making some money using his great literary talents.[150] It may be that he was encouraged by his cousin from Gray's Inn to try his hand at writing some works for the stage, in order to make ends meet.[151] Then at some point it was decided that he would use the name of William Shakespeare, maybe because he thought the name kind of suited an Irish rebel, and was also alike enough to the name of an actor called William Shaksper that he could pawn off his work as the latter's, if he ever needed to. There is no doubt at all that in his circumstances in 1585 he couldn't possibly use his own name with his very recent treasonable activities on everybody's lips in Ireland and I guess England. Picture Danny Morrison writing episodes for Eastenders and you get the general idea! Not a great surprise then that he would not want to use his own name.

Incidentally one other famous author of the period has perplexed scholars over the centuries with his apparent anonymity in the surviving literature. This is Thomas Shelton who is credited with being the translator of one of the books of Don Quixote, but seemingly anonymous in the other translated volumes. He was also considered to have a great command of English:

"Lord of the golden Elizabethan speech, an exquisite in the noble style.

...

Cervantes was indeed fortunate in having such a brilliant translator. If his identity were known, he would have his rightful place as one more distinguished figure in that golden age of English literature."

Only recently, in the latest edition of the DNB, has the family background and history of this author being established. It transpires that he was Irish, and in fact kept his identity quiet because he had been in trouble with the British government. His fault was that he had rebelled alongside Richard Nugent, William's son, and that was the reason he was anonymous in most of his works! In practice I think British scholars sometimes forget about Ireland, and forget that Irish people had a great command of English even then, which is probably why this writer's identity had remained a secret for so long.

Returning to William Nugent, his circumstances don't get a lot better for the period 1590-94 either because then he is taking on the state in his great court case, so no need to scare the public with using his own name for those poetic works that I think he hoped the Earl of Southampton would reward with some money. There must though have been some connection to William Shaksper the actor, who was probably paid some money to allow our William to use his name. An obsession with money after all emerges from the surviving papers relating to this actor. Maybe Sir George Carew, Shaksper's neighbour in Stratford and a leading figure in the Irish scene, could be a potential go between.[152]

The point is that there is such heavy use of pseudonyms in the works of the time that I think the idea that 'Shakespeare', as written on some of the title pages of his books, is not the writer's real name is really not at all unlikely. At least until you get to the First Folio, the fact is that whatever name is written there is no great proof of authorship. After all some works attributed to Shakespeare on the title page are now accepted as not being by him e.g. *London Prodigal* in 1605 and *A Yorkshire Tragedy* in 1608.

This is true of all the authors of the time. For example Robert Greene's most famous work *Groat's Worth of Wit* (1592) is now thought by many mainstream scholars to have been written by Henry Chettle.[153] Samuel Daniel's first published works were in fact just stuck in at the end of Sir Philip Sydney's *Atrophel and Stella* of 1591, and this without the author's consent.[154] Indeed the first publication of Shakespeare's sonnets came in a 1599 book called *A Passionate Pilgrim* which is attributed on the title page to William Shakespeare. Yet in fact only 5 of the 20 poems in it are attributed now to Shakespeare.[155] And the printer of this work is none other than William Jaggard, the same guy who prints the First Folio. Hence you can see the chaos, and maybe corruption, that really underlines the publishing scene in London at this time, so much so that the attribution of any work's authorship should be treated with care, and maybe even some suspicion, and Jaggard's First Folio of Shakespeare's works should be no exception?

There is no doubt though that if Shakespeare is not from Stratford then the title pages of that Folio, and the soon to follow subsequent Folios, are a very deliberate and calculated fraud. But as pointed out that is true, in a way, of Jaggard's earlier works, he is just going the extra mile here in burying the facts. I respectfully submit that frauds and forgeries etc do happen, and publishers do sometimes have their reasons. Therefore if pretty much all the evidence of 400 years of research into the Stratford author have yielded so little fruit, then the idea that these title pages, which represent the only real evidence linking Shaksper with the works, are deliberately falsified should be seen as the most likely explanation. But the next question is why? Well it seems that there was some problem with publishing Shakespeare's works, an otherwise very lucrative undertaking for these printers, in the years prior to the Folio coming out in 1623. It appears that when William Jaggard tried to print his collected works in 1619 they were stopped half way by the Lord Chamberlain who had written to the Stationary's Company forbidding the publication of any more of these plays without the consent of the 'King's Men' actors.[156] Maybe if the publisher can make this story about William of Stratford-upon-Avon stick, then he won't have any more problems with the state. Presumably if it is seen to be by a dead person, with the permission of his estate, then it might get around whatever was holding back publication. I am only guessing but I think as well that William Nugent might have been at heart a modest kind of person who actually wanted to remain anonymous in 1623, and would have agreed to this fraud.[157] Also he might have been embarrassed by the pornographic nature of some of the poetry which was attributed to Shakespeare, and maybe he wanted to distance himself from that, for religious reasons. So I think this older and more religious William helped the publisher and edited the First Folio, leaving out those poems and some pornographic references in the plays.[158] Finally you have the question of the monument in Stratford. I think that George Carew, who was a powerful figure in Stratford, might have helped there and created it as part of this coverup as it were. I admit this is just speculation, but I trust plausible enough and a more likely explanation of events, I think, than the increasingly unsatisfactory Stratford tale.

To sum up then the case for William Nugent, including some of the points made above and which are to follow in the Appendices and footnotes:

1. All the great scholars of Hiberno-English, from the mid 19th century to the present day, have found Shakespeare to be a great exponent of obscure Irish words and phrases. Probably one of the first scholars to attempt an Hiberno-English dictionary was Rev Abraham Hume, a clergyman and native of Hillsborough who had studied most of the dialects of Britain and Ireland. He was educated in TCD, Belfast, Glasgow and later taught in Liverpool so I guess was uniquely qualified to give an opinion on the various dialects in these islands and how they relate to the old English writers, which he describes thus:

> "In the works of Addison or Swift, there is little that would not be understood by a modern Englishman. Milton is more difficult; and there are many passages even in his prose works that would be greatly simplified by a note or a glossary; while a glossary of more than 2,000 words is required to enable the modern Englishman to read his

favourite Shakespeare. Chaucer cannot be read at all by the uninitiated; while the few works which were written antecedent to his time, are almost all sealed books, even to the majority of scholars. Yet the curious fact is, that probably not 200 words, or one in ten, would be required to enable an intelligent Irish peasant to understand Shakespeare. One is amazed at the ponderous waste of criticism on such terms as "dry", meaning thirsty, or "bell book and candle". And the expression of Othello, "let housewives make a skillet of my helm," would be understood by every cottager from Carrickfergus to Cape Clear."[159]

This work was followed later in the century by two writers in the Irish Ecclesiastical Record who attempted also to navigate the then uncharted waters of Hiberno-English, including 'G.M.' who wrote:

"If it were really a part of the Irish idiom [the use of 'shall' and 'will' which is common in Ireland and in Shakespeare], it would only be another example of what we so often find, that what are considered Irish peculiarities are, in fact, pure Shakespearean English."

This article was followed by William Burke who quotes so much Shakespeare in describing Hiberno-English that he includes thirteen specific Shakespearean references in the eleven pages of his article, including these:

"Sir Henry Irving's rendering of Macbeth would be barely intelligible to Shakespeare, while (as far as we can be certain in matters phonetic), Mike O'Brien would be readily understood. Take, for example, two of the most marked Hibernicisms – the substitution of *a* for *e* in such words as fear, speak, tea, eating, and of *oo* for *o*, and *u* in Rome, done, love, etc. In Hamlet iii 2, 146, we have:-

"Where love is great, the littlest doubts are fear;
Where little fears grow great, great love grows there."

The rhyming 'fear', with 'there', and the double assonance with "great," prove that Shakespeare would say "fare", not "feer". Again a few lines lower:-

"I do believe you think what now you speak;
But what we do determine oft we break."

...

In our accentuation also very many relics of the past may be detected by the careful observer, Shakespeare's putting the accent on the penult of "contrary"

"You may contrary me! marry,
'tis time" (Romeo and Juliet i 5)
is only what is done in Ireland ever day."

All the later Hiberno-English scholars have said much the same thing, from Sir John Byers (the Professor of Midwifery at Queen's College Belfast who wrote a book on *Shakespeare and the Ulster Dialect* in 1916 concluding that:

"These illustrations, which are only samples from a large collection, indicate in some degree what we owe in the North of Ireland to the same language which Shakespeare used as no other writer has ever done either before or since his days."[160])

to Professor James J Hogan of UCD, who wrote a book on Hiberno-English which no doubt helped him to notice those Shakespeare references already met with in Chapter 2, to James J Walsh writing in 1926:

"There is no easier way to get an adequate idea of just how Shakespeare and his contemporaries spoke the English tongue of ours than to listen to two reasonably educated Irishmen, who come from the same country place in Ireland, talk English. The sounds they utter are almost exactly those which Shakespeare was accustomed to hear in his day, and which he was accustomed to utter when he took his part upon the stage as he often did in his plays.

...

If Shakespeare were to come back to us talking as
he did in his own time, his speech, not only in pronunciation, but in many more essential characters,
would be better represented by what we know as
the Irish brogue than in any other way."

to Diarmaid Ó Muirithe,[161] the well known Irish Times columnist,
all the way up to a recent book by Daniel Cassidy,[162] who has outlined the Gaelic roots of some words that are used both in Irish
slang and in Shakespeare. Also other actors have noted what
Pauline McLynn has, that somehow the flow of Shakespeare's
words seem suited to an Irish accent. Anew McMaster, for example, was an actor that owned a playing company in England in the
1920s which nearly went bankrupt trying to put on Shakespeare
plays in the provincial towns in that country. He found that they
didn't seem to understand Shakespeare whereas when he brought
the company to Ireland in 1927 he found everybody understood
the plays, as reported by the Irish Times:

"Many readers will learn with surprise that Shakespeare is being played almost continuously in Irish
country towns, steadily drawing large audiences.
Mr Anew McMaster, an Armagh man and the leader of the company, told our correspondent that recently houses of 600 persons a night attended his
performances for a week in a western country town
with a population of only 5,000 persons. He finds
that a very different class in Ireland attends Shakespearean plays from that which attends them in
England. Instead of audiences made up of strictly
intellectual ranks of society and school and college
students, it is the Irish "man-in-the-street" who
throngs to "Hamlet" and "Othello"."[163]

Its not just words and phrases either, Shakespeare clearly had
a real knowledge of Ireland. He knows about obscure Irish folklore, like the legend of rhyming rats and the association of Lough
Derg with Purgatory,[164] and, as pointed out, knew the exact title of
an ancient Irish harp melody. I respectfully submit that the list of
Irish references given in Chapter 2 is quite long, long enough for
people to start asking some serious questions about how he knew

so much about Ireland? After all Ireland has always been a fruitful source of poets and playwrights, think of Sheridan, Wilde and Shaw, probably the next greatest playwrights in the English language after Shakespeare, all born and reared in Ireland.

2. It seems pretty clear that the Irish character Captain Macmorris, in Henry V, is, at one level, a clever allusion to Captain James Fitzmaurice Fitzgerald. (Fitzmaurice is translated as MacMorris in Irish, as Captain Fitzmaurice himself writes in one of his Irish letters, and he was always known as Captain.) This then is very significant, I suspect that only an Irish nationalist and Catholic writer would include such an infamous Irish rebel in his works, which matches nicely with the thinking and experiences of our William. Its also significant of course that the only Irish character talks so much about nationality and leaves question marks as to who is talking about Irish nationality:

> "Of my nation? What ish my nation? Ish a villaine,
> and a bastard, and a knave, and a rascal. What ish
> my nation? Who talks of my nation?" (Henry V
> Act II Scene II)

But on top of this its now clear that the reference originally comes from a petition debated by the Irish Council in 1614 where Fleming, the Baron of Slane, is debating his precedence (meaning which of the Baronies is the oldest, and hence entitled to walk in front of the other on State occasions) with McMoris the Baron of Kerry. As part of this row it was claimed at one point that McMoris was not Lord of Kerry at all but only: "capitanus suae nationis", which translated means "captain of his nation". This is obviously way too much of a coincidence and shows that Shakespeare either was present when the Irish Council heard this petition, or maybe had access to the same papers where we get this reference, the papers of Sir George Carew who was a neighbour of Shakespeare's in Stratford upon Avon. Carew is very famous in Irish history, where he must have spent at least half his life, and his papers also seem to have been read by Shakespeare before he wrote about Cade in Henry VI pt 2 (as pointed out in footnote 134 below). Whoever was Shakespeare must have had access to a large collection of historical documents, and it seems that Carew's papers would fit that bill nicely?

In any case if it wasn't from these papers then as I say Shakespeare would have had to be present in Dublin when they were debating this, no problem for William Nugent of course who's nephew was in the thick of it anyway:

> "At that time the Lord of Slane seemed partly con-
> tented with this order, but that the Lord of Delvin
> and others the Pale Barons, incited him to persist
> in challenging place, and that they would also con-
> test against the Lord of Kerry; and in especial the
> Lord of Delvin, to which the Lord of Slane yiel-
> ded, and so prepared for the second day."

Remember again that nobody has ever proved that Shakespeare, the actor from Stratford, ever came to Ireland and anyway no mere traveller could be present when the nobility debated issues such as this.[165]

3. Unlike so many candidates for Shakespeare, the chronology of the works coincides nicely with the dates of William's life, even more so than it does for Shakespeare of Stratford. In particular a lot of scholars feel that Shakespeare was mentioned in works dating from about 1585, when William had just returned from exile and was now in a position to start a literary career while the Stratford actor was possibly too young, and (as you can read in Appendix B) it seems that the real author was alive in 1623, as William Nugent was while the Stratford actor was dead by 1616.

4. William Nugent uses the word 'either' where others would use 'each' or 'both', for example in his statement of 1584:

> "The Duke of Guise hath correspondence with the
> Pope, Spain and Scotland whereby it may be
> gathered that though there be no immediate nor
> direct dealing betwixt the King of Scots and the
> Pope or the King of Spain, yet he practiseth with
> either indirectly by the intermediation of Guise."

And in his letter of 1591 where he talks about the two brothers, Walter and Robert Cusack, who had accused each other of treason:

"The very same day that those two brethren had
accused either other to Sir Robert of treason."

This reads much easier if you substitute 'each other' for 'either other'. Shakespeare has the same quirk, for example in Romeo and Juliet (Act II Scene 6 line 29): "unfold the imagined happiness that both receive in either by this dear encounter," which is glossed in a modern edition as: "in either: in each other". A few more examples:

PROTEUS: Inconstancy falls off ere it begins
What is in Silvia's face, but I may spy
More fresh in Julia's with a constant eye?
VALENTINE: Come, come, a hand from either:...
'Twere pity two such friends should be long foes.
(The Two Gentlemen of Verona Act IV Scene V 121)

PROSPERO: "they are both in either's powers"
(Tempest Act I Scene II 450).[166]

5. Elizabeth Hickey pointed out that in William Nugent's handwriting a capital 'N' looks very like a 'H'.[167] This would neatly explain why the Sonnets were first published on the instructions of a mysterious 'Mr W. H.'.

6. Note as well that our William is tied into the literary and publishing scene in London via the 'Cynthia' book that he guided through the press there in 1604, a book (printed by a firm that also did some of Shakespeare's works) which makes reference to some mysterious secret Irish 'muse'. Its not just that book either, if you look at the pictures of Christopher's (William's brother) phrase book of 1583, shown on the back cover of this book, you can see a little image on one of the pages that looks exactly like a woodcut for a printed book. Therefore it seems likely that those pages are actually proofs for a book that he intended to publish (or actually did publish but is now lost), with that image being intended for the woodcut in the book? Also at one point during the court case William and his allies wrote to London saying that: "The particulars of our proceedings we have laid down in a

book." They go on to say that a copy of this 'book' is available from Edward Nugent at Gray's Inn, which is the phraseology that was printed on the covers of most contemporary books (e.g. on the cover of the 'Cynthia' book is written: "to be sold at his shop by Gray's Inn new gate in Holborne"). For what its worth my guess is that they intended to publish this as a printed book, which would also account for the exceptionally colourful nature of the depositions written in the 'book' (which you can read in Appendix E under 1593). They just seem so much more gossipy and exciting than normal legal documents, as if William is hoping to entertain an audience with a non-fiction book?

Also on the subject of connections between William Nugent and the London printing scene it should be pointed out that he was a first cousin of Fr William Bathe SJ (Bathe's mother Eleanor Preston was a sister of our William's mother Elizabeth). He was also closely associated with him, too closely in the eyes of the state as this reference from the State Papers of 1591 shows:

> "One William Bathe, a gentleman of the Pale,
> dwelling near Dublin, one known to your Lordship
> for his skill in music, and for his late device of the
> new harp which he presented to her Majesty, who
> has lately gone to Spain, did at his departure leave
> a cipher with William Nugent, whereby to carry on
> a correspondence on matters of State."

Anyway Bathe was a musical and languages genius who published two books on music in London during those years (*A Brief Introduction to the Art of Music* (London, 1584) printed by Abel Jeffes and *A Brief Introduction to the Skill of Song* (London, c.1596) printed by Thomas East), and then later wrote *Janua Linguarum* in Spain which was a publishing sensation going through 30 editions in 11 languages from 1611-c.1634 including an English edition published in London in 1617 by Richard Field (of Stratford-upon-Avon, the publisher of Shakespeare's poems) and printed by Matthew Lownes.[168]

Hence we can say that our candidate has jumped through all the hoops that we know the real author must have, as pointed out earlier he was a legal expert, brilliant poet, diplomat, soldier, linguist and traveller, and now also clearly clued into the writing and printing scene in London exactly at the time when Shakespeare was flourishing.

7. Listed in the footnotes and Appendices A and C are quite a few scattered references that seem to echo the life of William Nugent, I think enough to show that it is hardly all coincidental? You have elaborate references to a 'Pale', a 'Jenet' – seemingly the great love of the author – mentioned in Venus and Adonis, contemporary authors who use words like 'pure gentle blood' (meaning 'new gent', and 'blood' for 'surname'?) to describe Shakespeare, and references in his court case to a person burned in the hand for stealing sheep which is exactly what he wrote in a play he was writing in the same year.[169]

8. Maybe the secret ingredient in Shakespeare's work is that the author has lived the type of life that he is describing in his plays, that this gives his work an unrivalled immediacy and insight. Look at the runaway marriages in Shakespeare (e.g. beginning of Othello, Romeo and Juliet etc) and compare that to the account of William Nugent's marriage, think of all this talk of hermits and friars and ancient burial grounds which abound in Shakespeare (e.g. Romeo and Juliet) and compare that to the world of the Nugents with the hermit at Fore and the friars at Multyfarnham (as described in Appendices D and E), feel the atmosphere of betrayal and ambition caught in the final scenes of King Lear and match that to the account of William's illegitimate brother Edmund (given in Appendix E under 1583), and finally there is remarkable insights into spying given in Act II Scene II of Hamlet, something that our William would have known a lot about. The whole story of Measure for Measure would remind you of his legal exploits, for example compare the account of Isabella and her brother Claudio in that play to this reference from the court case:
> "The sheriff dismissed the prisoner for certain money, and (as it was informed to the Lord Deputy) for the use, or rather the abuse, of his sister."
> (See under 1593 VIII no.5.)

Also the Duke disguised as a friar in that play is easy for

Shakespeare to imagine because he did that himself in 1584. Consider Shakespeare talking about religion and rebellions in Henry IV pt 1:

> "For that same word, rebellion, did divide
> The action of their bodies from their souls;
> And they did fight with queasiness, constrain'd,
> As men drink potions, that their weapons only
> Seem'd on our side; but, for their spirits and souls,
> This word, rebellion, it had froze them up,
> As fish are in a pond. But now the bishop
> Turns insurrection to religion:"
> (Henry IV pt 2 Act I Scene I 248-260)

Is he not giving here more than just a plain account of a rebellion, its as if he lived it, as if he knew from instinct the effect that religion would have on a rebellion? Of course William Nugent lived through exactly that type of episode, which is why he can give here a deeper insight than can be found in any book?

9. An Act of Attainder was passed against William Nugent in the Irish parliament after his rebellion, this meant that he couldn't inherit, or pass on to his children, titles or bear arms etc. It was considered a great shame and 'blot' (or blood stain) on the honour of an aristocratic family, as Shakespeare himself describes it in Henry VI:

> "Was not thy father, Richard Earl of Cambridge,
> For treason executed in our late king's days?
> And, by his treason, stand'st not thou attainted,
> Corrupted, and exempt from ancient gentry?
> His trespass yet lives guilty in thy blood;
> And, till thou be restored, thou art a yeoman.
> ...
> This blot, that they object against your house,
> Shall be wiped out in the next parliament."
> (Henry VI pt 1 Act II Scene IV 90-95, 116-117.)

As you can read in Appendix A there are many explicit references in the Sonnets (e.g. "I am attainted") that seem to show that the author had been attainted. Imho this is the clearest fact that we know about the author of the Sonnets and matches beautifully

William Nugent's troubles and even some curious references by Ben Jonson. Since I am pretty certain that no other candidate for Shakespeare was attainted, and certainly not Shakespeare from Stratford, I think that this question of the Attainder is actually the best clue we have that William Nugent was the author of the Sonnets.

10. Remember the lines from the Shakespeare monument in Stratford-upon-Avon, usually dated to c.1616, which begin: "Stay, passenger, why goest thou by so fast?" and talk about a tomb and "living art"? Well I will invite the reader now to peruse two c.1617 inscriptions in Donadea church in Co. Kildare in Ireland:

"Stay, passenger! thy hasty foot;
This stone delivers thee
A message from a famous 'twin,'
That here entombed be."
"Live, for virtue passeth wealth
As we do find it now,
Beauty, riches and worldly state
Must all to virtue bow."

Isn't there a genuine comparison between these two texts dated approximately to the same date? And at least it shows how Shakespearean sounding Irish writers of the period were? Who wrote it is unknown but I should point out that the monument is to Julia Aylmer née Nugent, a niece of our William Nugent.[170]

11. If you look at the top of the backcover of this book you can see a picture of William Nugent's gravestone, and beside it an illustration of the first version of Shakespeare's monument in Stratford-upon-Avon. If you look carefully you can see a helmet, a little bird on top of it, etc, a similar design on both pictures. Could they be by the same sculptor? At least its very coincidental?

While this subject remains something of a mystery I just hope that this Irish candidate for Shakespeare will be considered alongside the many others that have emerged in recent years.

Footnotes

Note that where just a date is listed (e.g. 'see under 1667') that refers to an entry under that date in Appendix E.

1. wikipedia article on 'Yes Minister'.

2. wikipedia on John le Carre.

3. http://www.timesonline.co.uk/article/0,,2087-2220566,00.html .

4. Charles Ogburn, *The Mysterious William Shakespeare: The Myth and the Reality* (1964), quoted by L. James Hammond 1996 at http://home.swipnet.se/nordling/shakespeare/4.html.

5. http://www.sourcetext.com/sourcebook/essays/polonius/corambis2.html .

6. Edmund Campion and Robert Persons alluded to in Act IV Scene II of Twelfth Night: http://www.everreader.com/allusio3.htm.

7. A short reference that maybe Spurio in "All's Well that End's Well" was intended to be the Duke of Guise: W. Ron. Hess, *The Dark Side of Shakespeare: An Iron-fisted Romantic in England's most perilous Times.* (2002), p.163.

8. W. Ron. Hess, *The Dark Side of Shakespeare: An Iron-fisted Romantic in England's most perilous Times* (2002), passim mentions the international, mainly French and Italian, allusions in Shakespeare. That work is highly detailed and draws on some interesting, and neglected, French writers. As an example of these allusions he, and many other scholars, reckon that the Claude Tonart trial in Paris in 1582 is alluded to in Measure for Measure (W. Ron. Hess, *The Dark Side of Shakespeare: An Iron-fisted Romantic in England's most perilous Times.* (2002), Vol I p.169 and p.372.) The latter writer also, drawing on the works of some important French scholars, specifically draws attention to Florence as a locale that comes across in Shakespeare's plays (ibid passim). Note that the Irish poet mentioned later as a candidate for Shakespeare was in Paris in 1582 and a short time later met the Duke of Florence in Florence.

9. For his extensive legal knowledge see for example http://www.sourcetext.-com/lawlibrary/ , Daniel Kornstein, *Kill all the lawyers?: Shakespeare's Legal Appeal* (Lincoln, 2005) and http://www.shakespearefellowship.org/virtualclass-room/Law/index.htm .

10. For example he used the Italian original of Cinthio's (Giovanni Battista Giraldi.1504-73) *Epitia* (1583) as a source for Measure for Measure (not just through George Whetstone's, *Promois and Cassandra* (1578)) for which see Stanley Wells ed. *Shakespeare Survey* (Cambridge, 2002), p.167. From the

same book in an article called *Shakespeare's Knowledge of Italian* by Naseeb Shaheen:

"The best evidence that Shakespeare could read Italian, however, comes from the close adherence of his plays to his Italian sources. For some plays, those Italian sources had not been translated into any other language, and the only logical conclusion is that Shakespeare must have read the source in Italian. In other instances, although the Italian source had been translated into French or English, Shakespeare's play is often closer to the Italian original than to the translations or adaptions of the original. At times, there is also a verbal similarity which adds to the evidence that Shakespeare had read the original Italian.
...
Several verbal parallels exist between Othello and Shakespeare's Italian sources which reinforce the conclusion that Shakespeare could read Italian... [describes in detail these similarities, and explains clearly that they come from the Italian text, not from the French translation by Chappuys nor from the English one by Sir John Harrington]...
Nonetheless, even without any of the above verbal similarities, the evidence from Othello that Shakespeare had read [Mateo] Bandello's account [of an Albanian captain in 'Novelle'(1554), for the murder scene in Othello] in Italian is substantial.
Another play for which there is strong evidence that Shakespeare read an Italian source is 'The Merchant of Venice'...Of the extant sources, the most important for Shakespeare was 'Il Pecorone', a collection of prose stories by Ser Giovanni Fiorentino (Ser Giovanni of Florence), published in Italian in 1558 and not translated into any other language when Shakespeare wrote his play."
(p.163-7)

11. Edmond Malone *The Plays and Poems Of William Shakespeare* (London, 1790) Prolegomena II, p.107-9.

12. All the surviving documentation on William Shakespeare the actor is outlined here: http://fly.hiwaay.net/~paul/shakspere/evidence1.html.

13. Diane Price, *Shakespeare's Unorthodox Biography* (Westport CT, 2001), summarised by Feste at
http://www.shakespearefellowship.org/ubbthreads/showflat.php?Cat=0&Number=33053&page=&fpart=1&vc=1 . Her website is at http://www.shakespeare-authorship.com/ .

14. Edward Ravenscroft, *Titus Andronicus, or the Rape of Lavinia* (London, 1687), p.1.

15. "It was once thought that the first scene of Titus Andronicus was written by George Peele, but scholars now regard the play as wholly by Shakespeare." (http://www.bl.uk/treasures/shakespeare/titus.html)

16. Robert Greene, *Farewell to Folly* (London, registered 1597 printed 1591). As regards this being an allusion to Shakespeare see Robert Simpson, *The School of Shakespeare* (London, 1878), Vol.II p.378.

17. See Appendix C on the allusions to Shakespeare.

18. "Many there be that are out of love with the obscurity wherein they live, that, to win credit to their name....these upstart reformers of arts..." (Thomas Nash, *Anatomy of Absurdity* (London,1589)).

19. Where they were mainly involved in farming, like Mullidor in Robert Greene, *Francesco's Fortunes* [Also known as the second part of *Never too late*] (London, 1590): "...and yet he was a proper scholar and well seen in ditties. This ruffling shepherd amongst the rest, and more than any of the rest, was enamoured of Mirimida, so that he would often leave his sheep at random to pass by the fields where she sat, only to feed his eye with her favour. Well, as fools have eyes, so they have hearts, and those oft harbour fond desires; love sometimes looks low, and will stumble on a cottage as well as on a palace; fools are in extremities not easily to be persuaded from their bauble, and when they begin to love, folly whets them on to restless thoughts...The crow thinks her fowls the fairest,...Well, the cloth was laid and the brown loaf set on the board; Mullidor, full of passions, sat down to his pottage and eat off his bowlful;"
[Quoting Mullidor:]"Mistress Mirimida, here is weather that makes grass plenty & sheep fat; by my troth, there never came a more plenteous year, and yet I have one sheep in my fold that's quite out of liking; if you knew the cause, you would marvel."
Mullidor is noted as an allusion to Shakespeare in Richard Simpson, *The School of Shakespeare* (London,1878), pt.2 p.370. That chapter of Simpson's book describes all these early references to Shakespeare. Simpson was a highly regarded scholar, and an adviser to William Gladstone on church policy (see wikipedia article on Simpson), the interesting thing being that he is unselfconsciously relaying on these references because he in fact assumed that they were referring to Shakespeare of Stratford upon Avon. Doron in Greene's Menaphon is a similar country bumpkin type character that Simpson talks about (p.362).

20. Thomas Nash in a letter attached to Robert Greene, *Menaphon* (London,1589): their "mother-tongue, that feedeth on naught but the crumbs that fall from the translator's trenches." Note how it seems to say then that the person(s) is not English. Simpson just assumes that Nash is giving out about players (actors) in general. I wonder would 'King of the Fairies' be an Irish type illusion? Nash again: "they may have anticked it until this time up and down the country with the King of the Fairies and dined everyday at the pease porridge ordinary with Delfrigus."(from Simpson op.cit. p.359) As regards the dancing this is from Simpson same page: "The 'jig' of 'plain Doron, as plain as a packstaffe'."

21. Ibid available here: http://drk.sd23.bc.ca/DeVere/new_files_nov_29/Preface_to_Greenes_Mena_2C.pdf .

22. Cockatrice op.cit. p.99 referring to Simpson op.cit. p.22. Hickey also points out that the Phoenix was again an emblem of Ireland at that time.

23. Sir D. Plunket Barton, *Links between Ireland and Shakespeare* (Dublin,1919), p.53. Barton was an Irish High Court judge who dug up a lot of these references which he assumed showed how Ireland preserved 16th century speech longer than England did:
"More than 50 Shakespearean phrases which were obsolete in England, lingered among the descendants of the English settlers and had passed into common usage among their Irish neighbours." (From an article in the Irish Book Lover.)
But this seems to underestimate the age at which 'Hiberno-English' became a distinct dialect from standard English. After all when Ben Jonson wrote his Irish Masque in 1613 he clearly shows that the Irish accent, and Hiberno-English diction, at that time was very distinctive to an English ear.

24. The Pauline McLynn quote is from *Village Magazine* 23 Feb 2006, and as regards the "God bless the mark!" phrase there is this from John Carey writing in *The Gentleman's Magazine*:
"Among the less enlightened portion of the Irish population, if a person, describing a wound or hurt, should, with the view of illustrating his verbal description, happen to touch the corresponding part of his own or another person's body, that touch is fearfully noticed, as ominous of ill, a sure precursor of similar mischief to the person and the part so touched, unless the narrator, or some other individual present, be careful immediately to subjoin, "God bless the mark!" or "God save the mark!" which prayer avails as a charm, to avert the dreaded disaster.
...
Let me add, with respect to the Irish superstition, that the touch in those cases, is deemed to possess equally malign influence, whether applied to the naked body itself, or to the garment covering the area." (v.88 pt.2 Oct 1818 p.328.)
'Bless the mark' is from Gaelic phrase 'slán an comhartha' (Diarmaid Ó Muirithe, *Words We Use* (Dublin, 2006), p.123).
The 'shall' reference is from Barton op.cit. p.217 and P.W. Joyce, *English as we speak it in Ireland* (1910), p.74 et seq available at www.chapters.eiretek.org/Joycenglish/ . As pointed out above both Barton and Joyce assume that this just proves that Ireland retains the language of Shakespeare's time better than in England but Joyce here shows that these Irish style 'shall' references are not followed by all English writers of the period.

25. Barton op. cit. p.217, raisin and Macbeth references respectively p.216 and p.215.

26. George Sigerson, *Bards of the Gael and Gall: an example of the poetic literature of Eiren...*(New York, 1907), p.224.

27. Sigerson himself, ibid p.7-9 referred to by Barton op.cit p.243: "if not [if Shakespeare didn't know the Irish poem] then the coincidence in thought between Shakespeare and an archaic Irish poem is marvellous." As regards his knowledge of Celtic mythology in general, W.H. Gratton Flood in his *History of Irish Music* (p.169) points out: "And does not Mr Alfred Nutt admit that Shakespeare's fairy mythology is taken from Celtic fairy tales?"

28. Barton op.cit. p.16 who refers to Sigerson op.cit. The translation is by W. M. Hennesey.

29. Luke Wadding for example refers to this 'dump' as an old Irish dance form: http://www.ibiblio.org/fiddlers/DT_DUMPE.htm .

30. Gratton Flood's chapter on Irish Music and Shakespeare is online here: http://www.waterfordcountylibrary.ie/library/categories/onlineresources/article96/Shakespeare%20and%20Irish%20Music%20-%20Chap %20XVII.pdf;jsessionid=DAD24A79075D1C93810AB4D91E9A6F7Ch .

31. See for example Willy Maley's article *The Irish Text and Subtext of Shakespeare's English Histories* in Jean E.Howard and Richard Dutton ed., *A Companion to Shakespeare's Works: The Histories.* (Oxford, 2003), p.94, where he quotes Norton's Shakespeare on the subject.

32. From a search of Cailín Og a Stuair Me at www.ceolas.org . As noted previously Gratton Flood mentions it as well and Barton op.cit.p.110. See also Michael Cronin *Shakespeare Translation and the Irish Language* in Mark Burnett ed *Shakespeare and Ireland* (1997), p.202. In 'Alls Well That Ends Well' Act IV Scene I one of the characters says:"Throca movousus, cargo, cargo, cargo" and I wonder could that be gaelic? Maybe it could be translated as something like: 'thirty in my hand...', just guessing.

33. Sigerson op.cit p.73. As pointed out in the paragraph above, Gratton Flood interprets this slightly differently.

34. Barton op.cit. p.113 from Merry Wives of Windsor Act II Scene II 316.

35. In his *The Irish Masque at Court* (1613).

36. W.H. Gratton, *A History of Irish Music* (Dublin, 1905), in the Shakespeare chapter under 'Peg a Ramsay'.

37. Richard Simpson, *The School of Shakespeare* (London, 1878), pt.1 before

p.143. Michael Neill, in *Broken English and Irish: Nation language,* Shakespeare Quarterly (Washington, Spring 1994), admits that the playwright of Stukely shows an accurate knowledge of gaelic. Note as well that the political story of Stukely is similar to that of Fitzmaurice and also similar to the experiences of the Irish poet that I mention as a candidate for Shakespeare. On the subject of apocryphal plays, here is this from the play Sir John Oldcastle Act V Scene IX:

"What intricate confusion have we here?
Not two hours since we apprehended one,
In habit Irish, but in speech not so:
And now you bring another, that in speech
Is altogether Irish, but in habit
Seems to be English: yea and more so,
The servant of that heretic Lord Cobham.

Irishman
Fait, me be no servant of the Lord Cobham,
Me be Mack Chane of Uister"

There is a later reference to this Irishman being hanged after 'the Irish fashion' and I think this could be an allusion to the hanging of Hugh Gavelagh O'Neill who was known as one of the McShane's of Tyrone and Ulster, 'Mack Chane' being McShane presumably. It just shows again that maybe there is some unknown Irish playwright at large in London at the time, and possibly the play alludes to such a person disguised as English? Here are a few curious phrases from another of these anonymous plays, and a play that many think was actually by Shakespeare, called Richard II pt 1:

"[Act III Scene III]
nay, sweet mr Schoolmaster, let us hear it again, I
beseech ye.

Schoolmaster
patientia. you are a servingman, I am a scholar. I
have shown art and learning in these verses, I assure
ye,
...
this paper shall wipe their noses, and they shall
not boo to a goose for it;
...
come, come, all is safe I warrant ye.
...
well, sir, if we be: we will speak more ere we be
hanged, in spite of ye.
...
the truth is, sir. I had lost two calves out of my
pasture, and being in search for them, from the top of

the hill I might spy you two in the bottom here, and
took ye for my calves sir; and that made me come
whistling down for joy, in hope I had found them.
...
...I will spoil
your whistle, I warrant ye!
...
[Act IV Scene I]
there is no question on it; King Richard will betake
himself to a yearly stipend, and we four by lease must
rent the Kingdom.
...
Green
I will ask no favour at your hands, sir.
ye shall have your money at your day, and then do your
worst, sir!
...
[Scene II]
good troth, my lord I have no mind to ride.
...
[Scene III]
he will have the devil and all shortly.
...
much good may it do ye, my lord.
...
all in prison, my lord. mr ignorance, the Bailey of
dunstable, and I, have taken great pains about them.
besides, here is a note of seven hundred whisperers,
most on them sleepy knaves.
...
[Act V Scene I]
what, is he dead?

2nd Murderer
as a door-nail, my lord.
...
[Scene III]
stay, my dear lord; and once more hear me,
princes.
the King was minded, ere this brawl began,
to come to terms of composition."
(Richard II pt 1 http://www.hampshireshakespeare.org/notes/TOWact3.html)

38. David Comyn, *Irish Illustrations to Shakespeare* (Dublin, 1894), p.7. The
epitaph was published in Roger Cotton, *Armor of Proofe* in 1596 but that was
after this play was written (pre 1595). See the Cambridge edition of this play

p.160.

39. This passage has perplexed many commentators (see e.g. Andrew Murphy p.52 in Ton Hoenselaars edit *Shakespeare's History Plays: Performance, Translation and Adaptation in Britain and Abroad* (2004)) but I wonder could it be a few choice words from an Irish guy fed up with the goings on in his own country! The phrases: "What ish my nation? Who talks of my nation?" could be read as a reference to the author speaking through the actor. 'Mac' in Irish is obviously the same as 'Fitz' in French giving you Fitzmaurice for Macmorris. In fact the whole episode surrounding Macmorris sounds very like someone involved in a religious war or religious dispute e.g. the references to him start off with "an Irishman, a very valiant gentleman, i' faith", meaning "valiant in [the defence of the] faith"? Note the numerous references to Rome, Christ, and the trumpets sounding at the walls like Jericho which you can read in that scene online at:
http://www.shakespeare-online.com/plays/henryv_3_2.html .
Surely this is an obvious attempt to start a religious dispute with the Captain:
"Captain Macmorris, I beseech you now, will you voutsafe me, look you, a few disputations with you, or partly touching or concerning the disciplines of the war, the Roman wars, in the way of argument, look you..."
James Fitzmaurice was the most famous Catholic rebel in Ireland until his death which was just at the time when William himself rebelled, who then, in a sense, took over that role. Fitzmaurice had been appointed the 'Captain' of the Desmond territories in Munster during which time he successfully besieged Kilmallock.

40. Michael Neill, *Broken English and Irish: Nation language ...*(Washington, Spring 1994), Shakespeare Quarterly he refers the reader to Gary Taylor ed., *Henry V* (Oxford, 1984), where these references are listed.

41. Wiley Miley, *The Irish Text and Subtext of Shakespeare's Histories* in Richard Dutton and Jean E. Howard edit., *A Companion to Shakespeare's Work: The Histories* (Oxford, 2003).

42. Andrew Hadfield, *Hitherto she ne're could fancy him* in *Shakespeare's British Plays and the Exclusion of Ireland*, in Mark Thornton Burnett and Ramona Wray eds, *Shakespeare and Ireland: History, Politics, Culture* (Basingstoke, 1997).

43. T.F. Healey, *Shakespeare Was An Irishman* (The American Mercury, September, 1940), pp. 24-32
(available at http://www.angelfire.com/poetry/irish_shakes/Shakes.htm).

44. Charles Bullard Fairbanks [1827-1859], *My Unknown Chum Aguecheek* (New York, 1912), p.321. This is a fuller quotation from it:
"There is a tradition common in the north of Ireland that Hamlet's father was a

native of that country, named Howndale, and that he followed the trade of a tailor; that he was captured by the Danes, in one of their expeditions against that fair island, and was carried to Jutland; that he married and set up in business again in that cold region, but that he afterwards forsook the sartorial for the regal line, by usurping the throne of Denmark. The tradition represents him to have been a man of violent character, a hard drinker, and altogether a most unprincipled and unamiable person, though an excellent tailor."

45. Lisa Hopkins, *Writing Renaissance Queens: Texts by and about Elizabeth I and Mary, Queen of Scots* (2002), p.136. and http://www.hull.ac.uk/renforum/v4no2/hopkins.htm by Lisa Hopkins from Sheffield Hallam University.

46. See F.M.O'Flanagan, *Glimpses of Old Dalkey,* Dublin Historical Record Vol.IV no.2 Dec.1941-Feb.1942 p.41-57.

47. THE DALKEY SOUND Nov 1966 *Coliemore* by Michael Fanning http://www.dalkeyhomepage.ie/poembymichaelfanning.html.

48. http://www.ireland.com/newspaper/property/2004/0916/4052686532ELSI-NORE_C.html . Also Sorrento park in Dalkey has a plague to John Dowland which mentions his link to Shakespeare: http://www.dlrcoco.ie/parks/sorrento.htm. Grattan Flood convincingly shows that Dowland came from Dalkey in his article: W. H. Grattan Flood, *Irish ancestry of Garland, Campion and Purcell*, Music and Letters Vol III, No. 1 (Jan 1922) p.61.

49. "My mam asked me the other day if I knew Shakespeare was an Irishman, I said no I didn't. She said well it's right here in the Savannah paper; and sure enough some gent from the University of Chicago had made a speech somewhere saying Shakespeare was an Irishman." (Flannery O'Connor *The Habit of Being.*)

"There lived here [Drogheda] about sixty years ago, one Guy Harrison, who boasted of his descent from Shakespeare: he said he was his grand nephew, and delighted in speaking of his uncle. This anecdote is mentioned by a gentleman who often conversed with him, but who was then too young to take much interest in anything that related to our immortal bard. Harrison kept a small shop, in which he sold thread, lace, and other small haberdashery..."
(Seanchas Ardmhacha Vol III No.2 (1959) p.388 quoting John Gamble, *Sketches of History, Politics, and Manners in Dublin and the North of Ireland* in 1810.)

"...Shakespeare was an Irishman and he knew it. The name has long been a puzzle to Englishmen who saw nothing more in it than the cave man sobriquet "Shake a spear", but an American writer (Mr. Smith author of *The Wild Rose of Lough Gill*) has shown beyond all doubt, that the name is Seabhach is bior, (a hawk and a spear), and that as it happens is the armorial bearing of the family of Shakespeare." (*Meath Chronicle* 6 Oct 1928 p.8) You might be inclined to dismiss this reference as of little consequence but I should point out that the writer, Mr. Smith, was a particularly knowledgeable historian, going by his book 'The Wild Rose'. That book is a remarkably accurate account of the famous Myles the Slasher otherwise known as Myles McEdmond O'Reilly, one time sheriff of Co. Cavan.

50. Basil Iske [Elizabeth Hickey], *The Green Cockatrice* (Tara, Meath Archaeological and Historical Society, 1978).

51. New DNB under Richard Nugent.

52. Cockatrice op. cit. p.179 incorporating Fr. Thomas Brady, *The O'Coffey Poets.*

53. ibid p172 et seq.

54. See ibid p.186. Part of it is printed in J T Gilbert's *Facsimiles National Manuscripts of Ireland* (London,1882), IV p.xxxiv and plate xxii. The date is taken from PRONI D/3835/A/4/274 and is I think a more likely date than the one usually given.

55. Cockatrice op. cit. p.21 .

56. 'Articles for reformation of certain abuses in Ireland' by the Baron of Delvin 26 May 1584 PRONI D/3835/A/3/14 (see John Gilbert *Account of Facsimiles of the National Manuscripts of Ireland* (London, 1882), Vol IV c. p.xxxiv).

57 Cockatrice op.cit.p.37 based I think on the references to Christopher in Holinshed's Chronicles.

58. John Lynch, *Supplementum Alithinologiae* (St Omer, 1667), translated at PRONI D/3835/A/1/82.

59. "I can offer nothing, at this distance of time, but vain regret, for not having felt the necessity in my younger years of committing to paper this melancholy air, which I have often heard played by Arthur O'Donnell and Arthur O'Neill, the best harpers in Ireland. Such exquisite touches of nature, ought not to be abandoned to the faithless uncertainty of tradition. The poetical vein seems to have been hereditary in the Nugent family." (Charles O'Conor, *Historical Address,* Part 1 p.148 et seq. PRONI D/3835/A/6/190.)

60. Joe Ainsworth, *Nugent Papers,* Analecta Hibernica no.20 p.166. He died in 1602 wishing his son Gilbert to be "well maintained to learning (as the rest)

until he is of age."

61. For theology see his negotiations with O'Neill in 1599, history: "my great grandfather what service he did in the troublesome time wherein he lived, your lordship may learn by the records of Dublin and the ancient people of the same." (Cockatrice op. cit. p.12), architecture, law and books:
"Every term I am in Dublin, following the law to recover certain lands taken from me during my late unfortunate troubles. The term ended I attend the judges at the assizes so often as they come into these parts where I dwell. The rest of my time I spend in books and building." (Cockatrice p.98).

62. Cockatrice op. cit. p.97.

63. Cockatrice op. cit. p.133. He is usually listed alongside Captain Tyrell as one of O'Neill's two most important lieutenants in Leinster e.g. in a document dated prob. 1597 PRONI D/3835/A/5/105, in a letter of 11 Aug 1600 he is reputed to have fled to Scotland on the way to Spain. PRONI D/3835/A/4/435 .
Elizabeth Hickey in her book, relying on an inaccurate reference in the DNB, presumed that Richard Nugent of Kilkarne, son of the judge, wrote it but I don't think that is the case. It has also been claimed that Richard Nugent of Donore wrote Cynthia but this couldn't be the case because this Richard is explicitly stated in the book as being the author of a poem addressed to the main author of the book. This book is registered at the stationers office 4th June 1604 and has an author Richard Nugent, publisher Henry Tomes and printer Thomas Purfoot. Purfoot also printed a few works by Shakespeare (Henry IV pt 1 (1622), Richard II (1615) and Richard III (1622)) but that could be just coincidental. Incidentally Henry Tomes published a book for Francis Bacon in 1621. It is fairly easy to establish William's son Richard Nugent as the real author based on the following facts revealed about the writer in the book:
a) He is dead by the time Cynthia is written in 1604 and presumably died not long before that. As pointed out William's son died c.1603. (This fact also rules out Richard of Donore and the first Earl of Westmeath who die much later, but not Richard of Kilkarne who died in 1602. I think the other two reasons point towards the other Richard.)
b) He went into exile some time before his death which again matches what we know about our Richard's movements in the years before his death.
c) The author of the poem has a great interest in astronomy which matches a State Papers reference to William's son.
d) Whoever compiled the work before publication (some person is clearly doing this after the death of the main writer) remains anonymous but contributes an Italian poem at the end of the work. There cannot be that many Italian poets floating around so we can safely say that it is William himself who compiled this work after the death of his son.
The compiler writes for example: "His leave taking Cynthia, wherein his own death is presaged." And at the end "A sonnet in Italian, made in commendation of the author, and persuading Cynthia to leave her sorrow." This is then the

Italian poem by our William:
"Cynthia quel cigno che di re canoro
Fe risnomar al mondo 'l chiaro nome,
Lasciando in terra le terrene some.
Salit' al ciel canra nel' also choro.
Ilor choronate di celest' alloro
L'amato vise e quell' aurare chiome
Chi le sue fiere voglie bancangia dome,
Innita al premio del mortal lanoro.
Il er sente tuoi sospir' e'l piant' e dice,
Non ti lagnar non ti guastar il viso
Che tosto finir ann' itnoi lamenti,
Saroi tu come moi anchor felice,
Alma gentil tra le beate menti
Ebella pinche mai in Paradiso."
(Note though that the writing is faded badly and mistakes are inevitable in the transcription.)
Although it is not absolutely clear it is nonetheless likely that this English sonnet was added to the end by William Nugent:
"Sweet is the life, that clad in base estate,
Far from the reach, of envy's hateful sting,
Devoid of malice, rancour, and debate,
The chief attendants, on the court, and King,
Doth yet enjoy, a quiet calm content,
Estranged from the pomp of Prince's train,
Unto whose bow, there may be found no bent.
No bounds their high aspiring to contain:
Such was the blissful life those shepherds led,
Those harmless shepherds, that for love so mourned,
Piping unto their flock, while that they fed
On the green banks, by Flora Queen adorned;
So, happy live they, though they live obscurely,
who live contented, quiet, and securely."
Obviously he is promising here that he will live quietly and hopes that this means that the State will not harass him, as you can see from the title of the poem:
"A Sonnet preferring the quiet life of the mean estate, to wealth and honours which procure envy, and for the more part accompanied with danger."
As well as Richard Nugent of Donore there are poems contributed by a Master William Talbot and a Master Thomas Sheldon. This Thomas Shelton, the translator of Don Quixote, was a close friend of Richard's. (Edwin B. Knowles, *Thomas Shelton, Translator of Don Quixote*, Studies in the Renaissance, (1958), Vol. 5, pp. 160-175. Also see the new DNB article under Thomas Shelton.)
In a recent description of the 'Cynthia' book Anne Fogarty also picks up on this idea that its really a political account of Richard's troubles with the state

rather than just a romance (available at Margaret Kelleher and Philip O'Leary eds., *The Cambridge History of Irish Literature* (Cambridge, 2006), Vol I p.156, the article being *Literature in English 1550-1690*).

So to add to the Italian poem I might as well include here William's famous Gaelic poem 'Ⴃiombáiⴅ ⴐⴎⴀll ó ċulcⴀiⴆ Ⴕáiⴠ:

"Ⴃiombáiⴅ ⴐⴎⴀll ó ċulcⴀiⴆ Ⴕáil,
ⴃiombáiⴅ iⴀċ Éiⴐeⴀnn ⴅ'Ⴕáⴃⴆáil,
iⴀċ miliⴐ nⴀ mbeⴀnn mbeⴀċⴀċ,
iⴐiⴐ nⴀ n-eⴀnⴈ n-óiⴈeⴀċⴀċ.

Cé ⴅá mo ċⴐⴎⴀll ⴅⴀⴐ Ⴕáⴠ ⴐoiⴐ,
ⴀⴐ ⴅⴀⴆⴀiⴐⴅ cúil ⴅ'iⴀċ Ⴇionⴅⴀin,
ⴅo ⴐⴝⴀⴐ ċⴐoiⴅe Ⴕⴀn ⴐóⴅ linn-
níoⴐ chⴀⴐ Ⴕóⴅ oile ⴀċⴅ Éiⴐⴎnn.

Ⴕóⴅ iⴐ ⴐⴎiⴐe ⴅoⴐⴀⴅ ⴐⴀnn,
Ⴕóⴅ iⴐ Ⴕéⴀⴐⴎⴀine Ⴕeⴀⴐⴀnn;
ⴐeⴀnċláⴐ íⴐ bⴐⴀonⴀċ beⴀⴐⴅⴀċ,
ⴀn ⴅíⴐ ċⴐⴀoⴆⴀċ ċⴐⴎiċneⴀċⴅⴀċ.

Ⴅíⴐ nⴀ ⴈcⴎⴐⴀⴅ iⴐ nⴀ ⴈcliⴀⴐ,
ⴆⴀnⴆⴀ nⴀ n-ⴀinneⴀⴐ n-óiⴐċiⴀⴆ;
ⴅíⴐ nⴀ ⴐⴐeⴀⴆ nⴈoiⴐmeⴀlⴅⴀċ nⴈlⴀn
'ⴈ nⴀ bhⴕeⴀⴐ n-oiⴐⴆeⴀⴐⴅⴀċ n-áⴈⴉⴀⴐ.

Ⴃá ⴆⴕⴀoⴉⴀⴅh Ⴃiⴀ ⴅⴀⴉ ⴅⴀⴐ m'ⴀiⴐ
ⴐoċⴅⴀin ⴅom ⴅoⴉⴀn ⴅúⴅċⴀiⴐ,
ó Ⴈⴀllⴀiⴆ ní ⴈéⴀⴆⴀinn ⴅol
ⴈo clⴀnnⴀiⴆ Ⴕéⴀⴈⴀinn Sⴀcⴐⴀn.

Ⴃá mbeiⴅ náⴐ ⴆⴀoⴈⴀl muiⴐe
Ⴕáⴈⴆáil leⴀⴐⴀ Lⴀoⴈⴀiⴐe,
mo ⴉeⴀnmⴀ ⴐiⴀⴐ ní Ⴕéⴀnⴅⴀ-
ⴐⴎⴀll ó Ⴃeⴀlⴆnⴀ iⴐ ⴅoⴅⴉéⴀnⴅⴀ.

Slán ⴅon Ⴕeⴀⴅⴀin ⴐin ⴅⴀⴐ m'éiⴐ,
ⴅo ⴉⴀcⴐⴀiⴅ ⴅíⴐe Ⴅⴎiⴐⴈéiⴐ,
ⴅⴐeⴀm iⴐ cⴀoine i ⴈcláⴐ ⴉiⴅe
ⴅáⴉ iⴐ ⴐⴀoiⴐe ⴐoċⴐⴎⴅe."

This is a translation of the poem by Gerard Murphy given in *Cockatrice* op.c-it.p.30:
"It is pitiful to go from the hills of Fál,
pitiful to leave the land of bee-filled mountains,
island of fields where young steeds race.

Though I journey eastwards across the sea,
setting my back to Fiontan's land,
my heart has left me as I go;
it loves no other realm but Ireland.

Realm where the fruit of every tree is heaviest,
realm where fish are more plentiful in every river,
Íor's ancient plain well-watered and rich in sheaves,
this land of branches and of wheat.

Land of warriors and of poets,
Banba of the gold-tressed women,
land of blue bird-haunted clear streams,
and of bold deedful men.

Were God to grant me return to my native country,
I should accept from the Goill no offer of visiting the families of England's nobles.

Were I in no peril from the sea as I leave Laoghaire's Steading,
it may not be denied that my spirit looks westwards:
it is not easy to go from Delvin.

Farewell to those I leave behind,
the youths of Turgesius' land,
the fairest folk in all Meath,
men who excel in nobility of heart."

64. Cockatrice p.134. The text is from Bergin *Irish Bardic Poetry* no.36.

66. Cockatrice p.151 and p.97.

67. Honourable Gerald Nugent to the Earl of Salisbury Jan 1607 PRONI D/3835/A/4/566. There are two poems here which are very alike and the subject of some controversy as to their authorship over the years. You have 'Diombáidh triall ó thulcaibh Fáil' and this poem which are sometimes attributed to Gerald Nugent and sometimes to William himself. Modern thinking usually attributes both poems to William but I think that is probably wrong. Firstly it doesn't make sense to write Gerald out of the history books like this. He is not known to have written any other poems and yet even has a praise poem written on his death (RIA MS no.1 p.67) so it seems quite a deliberate step for any scribe to attribute him as the author of these poems. In other words if he was famous for something else, or for other poems, you could understand scribes getting him mixed up with someone else but since he is such an obscure figure it must be that he was famous only for writing one or other of these poems. Also some of the reasons given for ascribing the poems to William alone are I

think unsafe, in particular it was felt that there was unlikely to be two Nugent poets and they knew that William was definitely a poet and also it was claimed that Gerald had only been in exile in France. As you can see there are plenty of Nugent poets and Gerald certainly had been in England. But then you are left with these two poems which are sometimes attributed to Gerald and sometimes to William. I think a clue to the mystery is provided by Patrick Fagan who feels that this poem 'Fada in éagmais..' is on a similar theme but not as well written as the second one (he thinks that 'fada' is a first draft of the other poem, see *Éigse na Íarmhí* op. cit. p.64). So my guess is that these two poems follow the same pattern that you can see in Cynthia and between Thomas Dease and Seamus Dubh Nugent (ibid p.40) where you have a lot of people sending poems to one another on much the same theme and vying with each other to produce the best poem. Hence I think Gerald wrote one and William the other. I take it that William wrote the better of the two poems ('Diombáidh triall') since he is widely considered to be a great poet.

68. Cockatrice op. cit. p.31 and p.176 .

69. Charles O'Conor, *An Historical Address on the calamities occasioned by foreign influences in the nomination of bishops to Irish sees.* (Buckingham and Dublin, 1812), pt.1 p.51, 148 et seq, and 239 (transcribed at PRONI D/3835/A/6/190). It is said that one of his poems "extolled the pure generosity of" the Earl of Ormond which is somewhat surprising because Robert was a strong supporter of the 1641 rebellion which he called "a just cause and a holy war" (24 March 1642, IJA Ms A 76 referred to in Fergus M O'Donoghue SJ – whom I'd like to thank –, *The Jesuit Mission in Ireland 1598-1651,* a dissertation at the Catholic University of America Washington DC 1981, p.270).

70. John Lynch (St.Omer, 1662) Chapter IV, translated by Matthew Kelly, *Cambrensis Eversus* (Dublin, 1848-52), p.319. Kelly in his notes is somewhat surprised at all these references and remarks that "Musical talent appears to have been hereditary in the Nugent family."

71. *Irish Book Lover* (1936) p.103.

72. George Oliver, *Collections towards illustrating the biography of the Scotch, English and Irish members of the Society of Jesus.* (Exeter,1845).

73. W. Gratton Flood, *A history of Irish Music* (Dublin,1906), p.190.

74. Pádraig Ó Fágáin, *Éigse na hIarmhí* (Baile Átha Cliath, 1985), p.64 identifies him as being of Kiltomb and later Dungimmon Co.Cavan which when matched with Skey's genealogy NLI M/F Pos.6849 p.38 establishes his family history.

75. Pádraig Ó Fágáin, *Éigse na hIarmhí* (Baile Átha Cliath, 1985), p.73,79.

76. Éigse op. cit. p.64.

77. In ibid p.36 his mother is described as Eleanor Nugent of Carlinstown. The only possible Eleanor this could be is the daughter of Sir Thomas Nugent of Carlinstown (Co.Westmeath) and his wife Elizabeth Fleming (John Lodge, *Peerage of Ireland* (London, 1789), second edition updated by Mervyn Archdall Vol.III p.321) which makes the bishop William's second cousin.

78. Jesuit Mission op. cit. p.273.

79. Patrick Fagan, *Thomas Dease Bishop of Meath 1622-1651,* Riocht na Mídhe Vol XVII 2006 p.90.

80. Eigse op. cit. p.36. The letter mentioned could be the one quoted in Appendix E under 1618.

81. Fagan on Dease op.cit. p.77.

82. Fagan in Eisge gives three of his poems 'Gabh mo threagasg, A inghean óg', 'Sochair na Haimsire' and 'Tiomna Thomáis Déis'.

83. Flood Irish Music op.cit. p.196.

84. Patrick Fagan, *Eigse na hIarmhi* (Dublin, 1985), p.50,57.

85. J. T. Gilbert, *Contemporary History of Affairs in Ireland, 1641-1652* (Dublin, 1879-80), Vol I p.278.

86. This was mentioned in his biography (see index under Earl of Westmeath) F.X. Martin, *Friar Nugent* (London, 1962).

87. Fr O'Connell, *History of the Irish Capuchin Mission to Ireland* (1653) liber 1 p.5 NLI M/F Pos 803 Bibliotheque Municipale Troyes Ms1103.

87. Described as being an expert in Hebrew and Greek in his entry in the public domain copy of the Catholic Encyclopedia.

89. Friar Nugent op. cit. p.16.

90. From ibid passim as well as his entry in the New DNB.

91. ibid p.209.

92. ibid p.13. Lavallin was a fourth cousin of William's. Curiously Lavallin approached some English actors as they were travelling through Cologne

c.1610/11 and converted the leader of them called Spencer to Catholicism (ibid see index under Spencer).

93. Inquisition Post Mortem held at Navan 9 Jan 1626 no.18 Meath. James Hardiman edit, *Inquisitionum in Officio Rotulorum Cancellariae Hiberniae ..* (Dublin,1826), Vol I.

94. Cockatrice op. cit. notes that William must have an inside track to the prisoners and on 22nd Dec 1591 we find Richard Nugent of Donore petitioning the English privy council to at least get the Irish Council to charge him with something which they neglected to do despite holding him in Dublin Castle for the previous 2 years (PRONI D/3835/A/6/422).

95. Cockatrice op.cit. p.37 and p.134.

96. Ibid p.104 mentions that Delvin and Howth are first cousins. Hall's Chronicle must be the source for the famous Jerusalem room reference in Shakespeare which is also in the Book of Howth (J.S. Brewer and William Bullen ed., *Calendar of Carew Manuscripts* (London, 1876), Miscellaneous Volume p.xii.)

97. The Earl of Sussex says of him c.1556 that: "His wit and ability to serve is right good." Cockatrice op.cit.p17.

98. Actually it says 'diverse' sonnets but I feel confident that this is a misspelling for 'divers' – meaning many – which is a very common tudor word. In case you are wondering no example of these 'divers' sonnets in English have ever come to light, unless it is in the works of Shakespeare.

99. Cockatrice op.cit. p.94 "An Exile's Yearning". The Lynch quote is from the chronology appendix under 1667.

100. Encyclopedia Britannica 1911 is where I got the patron quote, Cockatrice p.28 where it states he was a poet and the new DNB mentions the playing company.

101. New DNB.

102. 13 March 1562/3 PRONI D/3835/A/4/107.

103. Old DNB.

104. Interrogatory 11.

105. Cockatrice p.125 from *Calendar of State Papers* 1602 p.405.

106. Confession of Nowland Tadee PRONI D/3835/A/5/37.

107. Cockatrice op.cit.p.33. Other references can be traced by looking at the index of Mrs. Hickey's book.

108. ibid p.39 from *Acts of the Privy Council in Ireland* p.167.

109. ibid p.46.

110. ibid p.47.

111. PRONI D/3835/A/5/676-678.

112. PRONI D/3835/A/5/11.

113. ibid p.55. For the rebellion see the papers in Appendix E for 1580-4.

114. Edward Waterhouse from Dublin to Walsingham PRONI D/3835/A/6/353.

115. ibid p.69 from the confession of Nowland Tadee CSPI 1584 p.492.

116. ibid p.74 from *Calendar of Scottish Papers* 1854,-5,p.230.

117. ibid p.76 from *Calendar of Scottish Papers* 1854 op.cit.p.289 24th August 1584.

118. The shaven head quote is from ibid p.80 (quoting *Calendar of Carew Papers* 1584 p.531), the Walsingham quote is from ibid p.81.

119. see under 1584 in the Appendix E.

120. p.96 from CSP 1588-92 p.361.

121. Examination of Edward Cusack of Lismullen 22 April 1592 PRONI D/3835/A/5/61.

122. See under 1582 in the Calendar appendix.

123. See under John's account ibid.

124. Cockatrice op.cit.p.104 from CSPI 1591 p.414.

125. PRONI D/3835/A/4/309/328.

126. PRONI D/3835/A/4/255.

127. PRONI D/3835/A/5/105-6.

128. Cockatrice op.cit.p.136 from Hogan *Distinguished Irishmen* p.240.

129. *Archivium Hibernicum* Vol VII 1918-1922 p.323 et seq.

130. Henry Sedgrave and John Fox in Paris to William Nugent, called the Baron of Screen, and Brian Geoghegan in Edinburgh PRONI D/3835/A/5/35.

131. C.S.P.I.p.416 28 Aug 1591.

132. Basil Iske [Elizabeth Hickey], *The Green Cockatrice* (Tara, Meath Archaeological and Historical Society, 1978), Chapter V. He was described by Nicholas White, the Master of the Rolls, writing across to Burghley in London on the 22nd April 1581 (PRONI D/3835/A/5/5): "I assure your honour [Nicholas] is (to my knowledge) a dutiful man to her Majesty and well known here to be both learned, sober and wise." The DNB, in a strange echo of the this, states that Sir William Gerard referred to him as "sober, learned, and of good ability", and that he conducted his own defence at his trial "with great learning, courage and temperancy to his own commendation and satisfaction of most of his audience."

133. You can see just how much severed heads were a feature of the Irish wars from a book published in London in 1581 referring to wars of c.1578. This is obviously exactly contemporaneous with William's military exploits. (http://www.lib.ed.ac.uk/about/bgallery/Gallery/researchcoll/pages/bg0057_jpg .htmsee).

134. From the famous collection of state papers on Irish history compiled by Sir George Carew, the one time President of Munster, we get this reference which might be relevant here:
"...He [York] went into that country [Ireland], where he couched himself out of the eyes of the world, and bare a low sail in all his actions, the better to avoid the suspicion of his ill willers, who nevertheless gave out that the commotion of Jack Cade, the Irishman naming himself Mortimer, was his doing, thereby to bring the King in mislike of the Commons."[i]

I wonder could this Sir George Carew, Earl of Totness, (1555-1629) be the missing Irish link between Shakespeare the actor and this Irish poet? A member of the Council of Virginia 1609, which could make him a source for the letter that the Tempest is based on,[ii] his father was the Dean of Windsor giving him the local knowledge for the "Merry Wives of Windsor", he was a good friend of Robert Cecil [iii] and accompanied him to France at the time he must have received his famous letter from his father alluded to as Polonius' precepts, he was the treasurer for Essex's campaign in Ireland (directly referred to by Shakespeare), and he was the next door neighbour of Shakespeare's in life and in death, his grave is beside Shakespeare's in Stratford upon Avon, a town that he was the High Steward of.[iv] It is amazing, as well, how similar Carew's portrait is to the figure portrayed on the original monument to Shakespeare at Stratford.[v]

So he seems to interact a lot with Shakespeare's research while at the same time he is actually better known in Ireland and patronised Irish poets like Tadhg O'Daly.[vi] Furthermore we can see there is some connection between Carew and our William because:

(a) Carew was a leading figure in the Irish government – a member of the Irish Council – and army at the time when William had many dealings with the government especially in 1590 when both were friends of Perrot;

(b) Carew must have bought the Book of Howth from William's first cousin and;

(c) they were at Oxford together at the same time as well.[vii]

Also it might be interesting to relate this story about Carew's old residence, Clopton House in Stratford upon Avon, which apparently housed Shakespearean Manuscripts as late as the 18th century:

"Soon after my father went into the country, it being long vocation, I obtained permission of the gentleman with whom I was articled, to accompany him. The last place we visited before our return to town, was Stratford upon Avon, where we remained about ten days; during which time, my father made eager enquiries concerning Shakspear, but acquired little more knowledge than those who went before him.

We visited Clopton House, about a mile from Stratford, the gentleman who occupied it, behaved with much civility. On my father saying, he wished to know any thing relative to our Bard? the gentleman replied, that had he been there a few weeks sooner, he could have given him a great quantity of his, and his family's letters. My father, much astonished, begged to known what was become of them? The gentleman's answer was, that having some young partridges which he wished to bring up, he had, for the purpose, cleared out a small apartment wherein these papers lay, and burnt a large basket-full of them, he said they were all rotten as tinder, but to many of them, he could plainly perceive the signature of William Shakspear; and turning to his wife, said to her, "Don't you remember it my Dear?" Her answer was, "Yes, perfectly well, and you know at the time, I blamed you for destroying them." My father exclaimed, "Good God, Sir!" you do not know what an injury the world has sustained by the loss of them." He then begged permission to see the Room, which the gentleman acquiesced in, adding, "If there are any left Sir, you may have them, for they are but rubbish, and litter up the place." Accordingly, we proceeded into the chamber, but found no trace of any papers; and in every other part of the house our search proved equally ineffectual."[viii]

Finally there is even traditions about Clopton House being alluded to in the Taming of the Shrew":

"For centuries the inhabitants of Warwickshire have repeated the story that some characters found in The Taming of the Shrew are based on Cloptons, most notably, the "local Lord," who is mentioned first in the Induction, Scene 1"[ix]

And that Lord is said to be Sir George Carew who had married into the Cloptons:

"From Thomas the property [Clopton Manor House] passed to his son William, and from him to his daughter, the wife of George Carew, from 1605 Lord Carew of Clopton, and afterwards Earl of Totness. Clopton House was, as Mr. Lee says [in Sidney Lee, *Stratford-on-Avon from the Earliest Times to the Death of Shakespeare* (new edition, 1890)], without doubt one of the houses near Stratford where Shakespeare frequently visited schoolfellows in the retinues of the owners. On the other hand, there are many reasons against, and none directly in favour of, the assumption that the scene of the Induction in The Taming of the Shrew (which abounds in Warwickshire allusions) is Clopton, and the lord its ennobled owner, formerly President of Munster, on whose papers Pacata Hibernia was founded."[x] The links between Carew and Shakespeare, and then from Carew to Ireland, do seem very strong.

Footnotes to the above.
i. J.S. Brewer and William Bullen ed., *Calendar of Carew Manuscripts* (London, 1876), Miscellaneous Volume p.xii.
ii. http://www.danbyrnes.com.au/business/business5.html .
iii. DNB.
iv. http://www.shu.ac.uk/emls/08-2/abrapete.html , Steward reference is from GEC under Totness.
v. Portrait at
   http://www.shakespeare.org.uk/museums/index.php?record&id=75079 and original monument at http://www.hollowaypages.com/Shakespearemonument.htm , 1911 encyclopedia on: http://www.everything2.com/index.pl?node_id=1739500 . Some think as well that the Carew monument, at Stratford, and Shakespeare's are by the same person:"Robert Bell Wheler [A correspondent of Malone's] thinks Ws & Carew monument may be by same sculptor and likeness of Carew v close to extant portraits." (http://shakespeare.folger.edu/other/html/dfostrat.html)
vi. Eigse 15 (1971) p.27-28.
vii. Carew at Broadgates Hall 1564-1573
(http://en.wikipedia.org/wiki/George_Carew_(Ireland)) and William at Hart Hall 1571-73 (Cockatrice op.cit.p.33).
viii. William Henry Ireland, *An Authentic Account of the Shakespearean Manuscripts, &c.* (London, 1796), http://newark.rutgers.edu/~jlynch/Texts//ireland.html .
ix. http://homepages.rootsweb.com/~clopton/warwick.htm .
x. http://www.lang.nagoya-u.ac.jp/~matsuoka/EG-Clopton.html .

135. The Nugents are also were known to be descended from the de Lacy's in the female line. Btw the Nugents are a branch of the ancient Counts of Perche

in France from whence they came to Hastings etc. Notice for example the crest of those counts is similar to the Nugent one. Incidentally there is a new detailed study of these counts recently written by: Kathleen Thompson, *Power and Border Lordship in Medieval France, The County of Perche, 1000-1226* (Woodbridge/Rochester, 2002).

136. About the same time that this play is written a relative of William's, Christopher Nugent of Laragh, came forward as part of William's court case and swore that he knew of a person burnt in the hand for allegedly stealing sheep at a court case in Cavan: "...the said Cahill was condemned about 4 years past at Cavan before Sir Robert Dillon, Justice there, for stealing sheep and saw the said Cahill have his book to read, as a clerk, and whether he read or not he cannot tell because he was not within hearing; but the deponent saw him burned in the hand and heard him cry with the pain of burning..." (PRONI D/3835/A/6/407). His evidence was given on 6 June 1592 but probably William was acquainted with the testimony for a while before that. The meaning is that if a person could read then he was allowed the 'benefit of clergy' which meant that he would be branded instead of hanged. Nonetheless it seems an unusual coincidence that it came up in William Nugent's life and at the exact same time in Shakespeare's plays.)

137. Of course 10 years before that William's beloved uncle, a judge famous for his legal knowledge, was hung drawn and quartered at the instigation of the same people that he accuses of wanting to see all the noblemen banished.

138. William was well acquainted with parchment as he was the owner of a vellum poem book (NLI G992
http://www.isos.dias.ie/libraries/NLI/NLI_MS_G_992/english/index.html), vellum being a similar type of 'paper' made from animal hide.

139. See footnote 63 above.

140. Richard Nugent, *Cynthia* (London, 1604), 2nd pt. Sonnet VI.

141. 'In Spenser's *Colin Clout's Come Home Again* published in 1595, occur four lines that are commonly supposed to refer to Shakespeare--
"And there though last not least is Aetion
A gentler shepherd may nowhere be found: Whose muse, full of high thought's invention,
Doth like himself heroically sound."'(http://www.sonnets.org/minto6.htm)
Notice too how you could play around with the last two lines to see puns on the word NewGent which is how you pronounce Nugent.

142. Andrew Carpenter in Raymond Gillespie and Andrew Hadfield eds, *The Irish Book in English, 1550-1800* (Oxford, 2006), p.304. He also says that "Nugent was a poet of considerable skill and it is worth quoting here a fine

sonnet..."

143. James Easton, *Human Longevity: recording the name, age, place of residence, and year, of the decease of 1712 persons...*" (Salisbury, 1799), p.256.

144. Richard Nugent, *Cynthia* (London, 1604), 1st pt. Sonnet IX.

145. See under 1582, near the end.

146. It is called 'Shadowplay' and is reviewed here: http://observer.guardian.-co.uk/uk_news/story/0,6903,1557964,00.html .

147. See the earlier chronology. Btw his brother Christopher was educated at Clare Hall Cambridge, (DNB) and his cousin Edward Nugent, who served as his agent in London during the court case, was educated as a lawyer at Gray's Inn (Cockatrice op.cit.p.110 quoting CSPI 1593 p.195). This could be a source of the information that Shakespeare seems to possess about those places. (For Cambridge there is Dr. Caius in the "Merry Wives of Windsor" and other references you can see at http://www.sirbacon.org/eaglecambridge.htm, and there are numerous accounts out there speculating about why his early plays seemed to be performed first at Gray's Inn.)

148. Some people say that this character is Robert Greene himself, but I don't think that is a good fit because AFAIK he didn't come from that aristocratic background which is essential to Roberto's story.

149. See Cockatrice op.cit.p.143-144 where you can see a drawing of the arms. Btw I think that Mrs. Hickey is wrong about the Orwen and Sabina story that she relates on that page. This story relates to the 'Black Baron' which is a nickname of the second Earl of Westmeath's, and is set in the Cromwellian wars which of course post date Shakespeare.

150. I don't see where he could have got money after he had rebelled, and before that his wife referred to:
"her goods (which her husband had sold before to a merchant for payment of debt.)" (Jane Nugent to the lords of the Privy Council Prob. June 1583 PRONI D/3835/A/5/29).

151. See footnote no.147 above for references to his cousin.

152. See footnote no.134 above for references to Carew.
For more speculation on why he might have liked the name 'Shakespeare' see the end of Appendix A. The quote on Thomas Shelton comes from http://www.shakespearefellowship.org/ubbthreads/showthreaded.php?Cat=0&Number=31504&page=&vc=1 and for his story see the new DNB under Thomas Shelton.

153. http://www.sourcetext.com/sourcebook/essays/greene/malim.html .

154. http://en.wikipedia.org/wiki/Samuel_Daniel .

155. http://en.wikipedia.org/wiki/The_Passionate_Pilgrim .

156. http://www.bl.uk/treasures/shakespeare/henry5.html and http://www.sirba-con.org/merrywiveswindsor.htm . Maybe the death of Shakespeare the actor threw the normal arrangements (i.e. paying the actor to allow his name to be used as the author) into confusion? Until they use the idea of praising him as a dead person in the First Folio?:

"During Shakespeare's lifetime, there was a thriving industry devoted to reprinting his plays: Richard II, Richard III, and Henry IV Part 1, for instance, were each reprinted five times in quarto between the years 1597 and 1615. Remarkably, there was not a single Shakespearean play published in the three years following the dramatist's death in 1616. When reprints began to appear once again in the years immediately prior to the publication of the First Folio, the dates on the title-pages are often bizarre."
He goes on to point out that in 1619 Thomas Pavier published King Lear and Henry V and dated that edition as 1608 alongwith The Merchant of Venice and A Midsummer's Night Dream both dated as 1600. While in 1622 John Smethwick publishes Romeo and Juliet and Hamlet and takes the unusual step of omitting the date (http://www.uv.es/~fores/RasmussenEric.uk.html).

157. I think modesty was considered a great virtue among this family. William's uncle Nicholas, for example, was described as "of modest disposition", although that didn't mean that he wouldn't take on the state forcibly during the cess episode.(see under 1576) His first cousin Robert was described thus: "his modesty, his learning and his virtue are above all praise" (Charles O'Conor, *An Historical Address on the calamities occasioned by foreign influences in the nomination of bishops to Irish sees* (Buckingham and Dublin, 1812), pt.1 p.51,148 et seq, and 239 (transcribed at PRONI D/3835/A/6/190)). Fr Lavallin Nugent is described here by his biographer and friend Archbold: "was so sparing, and, so to say, tongueless in uttering any word that relished in any wise his own proper honour or glory that herein he displeased us all, for hereby we are ignorant of many worthy things which both he knew and did" (F.X. Martin, *Friar Nugent* (London, 1962), p.60). Andrew Nugent of Donore described by Fr John Lynch: "He also bound himself by a religious promise that he would never do anything for the sake of ostentation" (See end of Appendix E).

158. See Appendix B.

159. Rev Abraham Hume, *Remarks on the Irish Dialect of the English Lan-*

guage (Liverpool, 1878), p.15.

160. Sir John Byers, *Shakespeare and the Ulster Dialect*, published in Northern Whig 22 April 1916, p.11. A few more examples from his book:
Dun – a dull brown or dull grey brown colour, like the hair of the ass or mouse. "Tut...ears! Dun's the mouse and his colour." (Romeo and Juliet I iv 40).
Hold – to wager (Taming of the Shrew III ii 79).
Kibe – a sore or chapped heel (Tempest II i 276).
Puke – to vomit, "Shakespeare was the first writer to use the word in 1600." (As You Like It II vii 140).
Scantling – a small portion or sample (Troilus and Cressida I iii 348).
Skillet – cooking utensil (Othello I iii 271).
Trencherman – one with a good healthy appetite (Much Ado About Nothing I i 51).
"'Savin' yer presence' is an apologetic statement made by someone when something disagreeable has to be said, as when a doctor is told an unpleasant fact about a patient this introductory statement was made. It means 'with all respect to you' or 'except in your presence'...'Your reverence' is a respectful form of address used in Ulster in speaking to a clergyman as Shakespeare Henry V I II 20."
The first IER quote is from: G.M., *Shall and Will-iana*, Irish Eccelesiastical Record Jan 1896 Vol XVII no 1 p.48, and the second from: William Burke, *The Anglo-Irish Dialect*, Irish Eccelesiastical Record Dec 1896 Vol XVII no 12, p.699 et seq.

161. James J Walsh, *Shakespeare's pronunciation of the Irish brogue*, in *The World's Debt to the Irish* (Boston, 1926), p.299, 327.
Diarmaid Ó Muirithe, *Words We Use* (Dublin, 2006):
"*Motions* is a Cork word...Motion in this sense of carnal impulse was known to a rather better poet than our Cork balladeer. He has it in Othello where Iago says: 'We have reason to cool our raging motions, our carnal stings, our unbitted lusts.' "(p.58)
"Macbeth: There's not a one of them but in his house I keep a servant fee'd."(p.74)
"A few weeks ago near the estuary of the lordly Barrow I saw a man mending lobster pots by plaiting sally rods. He was pleaching them, he told me; he pronounced the word playchin...I had heard the word only once previously, used by the chanteuse of Neamstown, Co.Wexford, the late Liz Jeffries...'Shaksper, the Stratford clown', as somebody was pleased to call him, knew pleach...Antony says to his page, Eros...'Thy master with pleach'd arms.'" (p.174)
"Three oldish men were sitting in the snug of a bar in the city of Waterford the other night when I made my entrance with a friend. They were talking about the recent bank robbery in Belfast, and to my great surprise one of them used a word that, I have found out since, is considered obsolete in the Waterford man's sense. That word is *competitor*, a confederate, an associate, one who

94

seeks the same object, not against, but in alliance with another...Shakespeare had this meaning. In 1591, in Two Gentlemen of Verona we find 'Myself in counsaile his competitor.' In 1594 he wrote this in Richard III: 'In Kent, my liege, the Guildfords are in arms, and every hour more competitors.' He also has this particular meaning of competitor in Twelfth Night and in Antony and Cleopatra." (p.206)

"Mr O'Kane's book [an account of Ulster diction: William O'Kane, *You Don't Say* (Dungannon, 1991)] contains many forgotten Tudor words. Colly is a small soot particle in coal dust. In Shakespeare's time *to colly* meant to blacken. We find 'brief as the lightening in the collied night' in A Midsummer Night's Dream." (p.290)

"Americans still use *mad* in the sense of *angry*, as Shakespeare did, and as we Irish do..." (p.272)

"*Abide*: In Ringsend to say 'I can't abide that fellow' means 'I can't tolerate him'...In the sense of tolerate, Shakespeare has 'I cannot abide swaggerers' in Henry IV pt 2." (p.283)

162. Daniel Cassidy, *How the Irish Invented Slang* (Oakland, 2007):
'Helter-skelter' (Henry IV Act V Scene III) from the Gaelic 'Ailteoir Scaoilte' (p.175)
'Sneaking' (Henry IV Act IV Scene III) from the Irish 'Snaigaim' meaning 'I creep'. (p.271)
'Square' meaning 'fair' or 'just' (Anthony and Cleopatra Act II Scene II) from the Irish "'s cóir é" meaning fair play. (p.282)

Incidentally a recent book by Raymond Hickey covers Hiberno-English is considerable detail and also mentions some comparisons to Shakespeare's English – although without entertaining any doubts as to Shakespeare's birth in the English West Country:
"The use of paratactic construction introduced by 'and' were already noted by early scholars working on Irish English e.g. P. W. Joyce who cites as an example
"He interrupted me and I writing my letter"
...[this then is also found in Shakespeare e.g.:]
"Suffer us to famish, and their storehouses cramm'd with grain" (Coriolanus Act I Scence ii).
...
Shakespeare's language also shows structures which have been regarded as exclusively Irish in provenance...This use can be assumed to have been present in the input to Ireland at the beginning of the early modern period...Many non-standard features of Irish English can be attributed to this English input. For instance, Irish speakers frequently confuse complimentary verb pairs distinguished by direction such as bring, take; rent, let; learn, teach. With the latter pair the first is used in the sense of the second. This is also found with Shakespeare, e.g. in the words of Caliban:
"the red plague, rid you for learning me your language" (The Tempest, Act I,

Scene ii).
(Raymond Hickey, *Irish English: History and present day forms* (Cambridge, 2007), p.261, 298.)

163. *Irish Times* 28 Nov 1927, for his experiences in England and Ireland see also *Irish Times* 27 Sept 1968.

164. For the latter two references see Sir D. Plunket Barton, *Links between Ireland and Shakespeare* (Dublin,1919).

165. James Fitzmaurice's Irish letters are printed in John Thomas Gilbert, '*Facsimiles of National Manuscripts of Ireland*' (London, 1882) Vol IV and see footnote 39 infra. The McMoris legal dispute is given in J.S. Brewer and William Bullen ed., *Calendar of Carew Manuscripts* (London, 1876) Miscellaneous Volume, p.318 and 320, referring to Irish Council Orders given on the 11th and 18th November 1614.

166. The modern edition of Romeo and Juliet mentioned is: Roma Gill ed., Oxford School Shakespeare: Romeo an Juliet (Oxford, 2001), p.57. That Shakespeare has this peculiar use of 'either' is confirmed by Alexander Schmidt in his '*Shakespeare Lexicon*' (Berlin, 1902), who puts this into his explanation for 'either' in Shakespeare:
"each of two, both...= each, used of more than two."

167. Basil Iske [Elizabeth Hickey], *The Green Cockatrice* (Tara, 1978), p. 150.

168. The quote that refers to a 'book' is from CSPI 20 Nov 1592. The Bathe quote is from Basil Iske [Elizabeth Hickey], *The Green Cockatrice* (Tara, 1978), p.96 quoting CSP 1591 p.440. For other references to Bathe see: William H Gratton Flood, *History of Irish Music* (Dublin, 1905), Chapters XV and XVI available at http://www.libraryireland.com/IrishMusic/XVI.php#161 et seq.; Rev T Corcoran SJ, *Studies in History of Classical Teaching, Irish and Continental, 1500-1700* (London, 1911), passim; Rev John Kingston, *William Bathe, SJ*, Irish Ecclesiastical Studies Sept 1954 Vol.82 p.179-182; and http://www.henrysweet.org/rizza_nov97.pdf .

169. Footnote 136 infra. Note also footnotes 134 and 135 for echoes of William Nugent's life in that play.

170. For details on Donadea see: http://shaksper.net/archive/2010/291-september/27702-shakespeare-allusion-on-irish-monument .

APPENDIX A

Further interesting references in Shakespeare's Works

Hamlet
Clearly there are various sources used for Hamlet, which gives you the basic story, but is it elaborated on in a way that mimics the current political landscape of the time? Certainly in those years all citizens of the Pale were watching events in Ulster, and the growth of Hugh O'Neill in particular. So my guess is that Denmark is Tyrone/Ulster and the King of Denmark is Turlough Luineach O'Neill.

Fortinbras
I think its Red Hugh O'Donnell who started the rebellion that destabilises Turlough and Ulster in general. In the early 1590s the crown of Tyrconnell (Norway) was contested between his father, his granduncle, and him and Donegal is obviously north west of Tyrone. Furthermore you might need to cross Tyrone to get to Fermanagh (Poland), which is where those wars began when Red Hugh marched there in aid of the Maguires. Also of course the O'Donnells contested the overlordship of Ulster with the O'Neills. This quote in the last scene could be said to imply that Fortinbras was going to fight the English:

> "Young Fortinbras, with conquest come from Po-
> land,
> To the ambassadors of England gives
> This warlike volley."

Claudius King of Denmark
Turlough Luineach O'Neill is effectively the king of Ulster in the very early 1590's but was continually being undermined by Hugh O'Neill then Baron of Dungannon (Hamlet). He had earlier murdered Hugh's brother who was the former Baron of Dungannon, and some references like this might be to the Red Hand of Ulster the famous insignia of the O'Neill's:

> "What if this cursed hand

Were thicker than itself with brother's blood"
(Act III Scene 2)

Similarly the King talks about Hamlet taking the hand from him before the duel in the last scene. Incidentally William knew Turlough Luineach quite well, he was protected by him in 1581 and probably had been at the meeting of the poets in Tyrone in 1577. Finally in Act IV Scene 7 the King is explaining the reasons why he doesn't move openly against Hamlet, which amount to being nervous of his popularity but more so being unable to challenge the power of the Queen who was backing Hamlet. This could be read I think as showing the reasons why Turlough Luineach most of the time didn't overtly attack Hugh O'Neill, the main reason being that Hugh was strongly supported by the Queen and the Dublin government. Notice too that Turlough is Hugh's cousin, not his uncle, and in the play its amazing how often he seems to call him his cousin even though according to the story he is supposed to be his uncle.

Hamlet
Hugh O'Neill, Baron of Dungannon who later succeeded Turlough Luineach as lord of Tyrone and Ulster. Coming at it from the perspective of a Pale lord like William the point about Hugh is how duplicitous he was in supposedly being the Queen's ally but doing so much to undermine and rebel against her. Also William might blame Hugh for all the tragedy and loss of life that the Pale and the rest of Ireland suffered in the 1590s and if you look at scenes like the graveyard one you could easily get that impression from Shakespeare's portrayal of Hamlet. You can see it too possibly in this from Act IV Scene 4:
"   ...while to my shame I see
The imminent death of twenty thousand men"

William and his brother were of course very Catholic figures and they may have resented how Hugh O'Neill claimed to be a great Catholic champion although he was actually a Protestant, and a particularly loyal one, when these two brothers were going through the mill in the early 1580s. Consequently William might have added in a bit about this in his portrayal of Hamlet's duplicity. For example in the advise that is given to Ophelia to beware

of :
> "that with devotion's visage
> And pious action we do sugar o'er
> The devil himself."
> (Act III Scene 1)

He also travelled to England at this time and Turlough might have thought they would clip his wings out there somewhat but he had no such luck.

Queen

So possibly the scene where the Queen and Hamlet argue in Act IV Scene 4 represents the episode when he met Queen Elizabeth and the English Council in London. The Queen at that time, advised by Burghley, wanted him to at least curtail his undermining of Turlough Luineach. As the 1590s go on though her troubles with Hugh only increase, especially after she loses the advice of Burghley, who died in 1598. Possibly then, in the opinion of William, that left the Queen and Ireland isolated without his wisdom and care which may be seen in the symbolic death of Polonius in the latter scene.

Polonius

He is usually taken as representing Burghley (who until his death in 1598 is practically the Prime Minister of England and Ireland) and William and his brother were certainly close to Burghley with frequent correspondence going over and back between them e.g. in 1592 Burghley was briefing William on what informers were saying about him (Cockatrice p.14). But I also think that earlier on in the play he is meant to represent the third Earl of Sussex who was, like Polonius, the Lord Chamberlain until he died in 1583. He also ran a company of actors called the Chamberlain's Men and he seems to take that role in the play too. The thing is that Sussex was William's guardian as well as being a senior English politician. So imagine the scene in 1582/3 when William has fled Ireland and gone to Paris while his legal father was sitting at the English Council table reading the spy reports on the Irish in Paris as they reported back on William and his friends and note the similarities with Act II Scene1 with William as Laertes. Admittedly Sussex would be dead before William saw him again but not Burghley who must have swapped some stories with William when they were getting on well in the 1590s. Incidentally the players that are mentioned might have offended Hamlet (as in O'Neill) with some of their work in the past which might be a reference to Shakespeare's other works that were critical of O'Neil (Act II Scene 2).

(http://www.sourcetext.com/sourcebook/essays/polonius/corambis 2.html has a discussion of Polonius as Burghley.)

Ophelia
Ireland, drowning with sorrows and with all these people fighting over her grave.

Laertes
I think its meant as William initially and then his brother the Baron. They of course are of Norman/French ancestry which they were very proud of as you can see in the way they used the word 'Fitz' like the Gaelic Irish used 'Mac' e.g. the famous Jesuit Fr Robert Nugent was described in spy reports as Robert fitz Oliver Nugent because he was the son of Oliver of Ballina. Anyway Laertes seems to be associated with France and Normandy in the last scene and Act IV Scene 7. The Baron of Delvin was a very active opponent of Hugh O'Neill throughout the 9 years war, in fact at one point O'Neill is said to have declared that Delvin was "the only block that hindered him over-running the whole kingdom" (PRONI D/3835/A/4/403 24 Nov1599). It could be said then that the duel scene represents the 9 years war and the earlier fight over Ophelia's grave could show how pointless was this fight over a nation destroyed. In 1602 the Baron was arrested and charged with treason, accused of doing a deal with Tyrone, but he died before the charges were proven. This might be referred to in the last scene where Laertes is said to have justly died because of his treachery. The Queen also dies just at the end of the 9 years war too and that might have been obvious when the play was written which was some time before being registered in 1602.

Rosencrantz and Guildenstern

They were spies working for Claudius who employed them to spy on Hamlet and try and trap him into going over to England. What is interesting is that in c.1592 Turlough O'Neill employed two English captains, Willis and Fullart, to assist him against Hugh O'Neill. (See the Annals of the Four Masters under 1592 http://www.ucc.ie/celt/published/T100005F/index.html)
Of course as English soldiers you would expect them also to spy on the Queen's behalf.

Sonnets
Some thoughts on allusions and correspondents referred to in the sonnets.

1- et seq
Possibly many of the sonnets, including the first few, are to his son where he his hoping that he will get married and have children so keeping up William's line which was always the obsession of the nobility. That it is to his son seems to be implied when he mentions how he feels old when his son seems old in no.22 and 126:

> "O thou, my lovely boy...who hast by waning
> grown, and thein show'st thy lovers [his parents]
> withering, as thy sweet self grow'st."

Of course this is all supposed to be homosexual but a sonnet to his son seems a simpler explanation! In 20 it says that if he does get married and have kids then dreaded Nature (time) will be defeated "by addition me of thee" meaning maybe that he having an heir will protect the poet from time which figures if he is to get a grandchild.

25
These lines clearly match with William labouring under an attainder:

> "Let those who are in favour with their stars
> Of public honour and proud titles boast,
> Whilst I, whom fortune of such triumph bars,"

and in 26:

> "When, in disgrace with fortune and men's eyes,

I all alone beweep my outcast state...
Yet in these thoughts myself almost despising,"
So to clarify William was attainted because of his rebellion in 1581 and the attainder was never reversed (Cockatrice p.142). The attainder was an Act passed in the Irish Parliament branding him as a traitor. It was basically a disgrace on a person and family representing the fact that he had rebelled and preventing a person from holding titles and bearing arms etc. It was considered a kind of spot on a person's blood (because the children of an attainted person could not inherit titles through the one attainted) and you can see how seriously it was taken by this statement by William's brother just before William was attainted:

> "I protest unto your Lordship there is nothing in
> this world wherof I make more accompt than that
> mine ancestors were never spotted in blood, and
> have always from the conquest been servitors to
> the Crown of England." (Cockatrice p.12.)

Therefore it naturally hit William hard when it happened to him, in his submission he says that he hoped at some point: "the stain now abiding in my name which makes me ever loathsome unto myself may be wiped away" and he concludes: "The most unfortunate and hateful to himself William Nugent" (PRONI D/3835/A/5/40 prob. Dec 1584.)

30
Could this refer to a court case 'sessions' involving Fore which maybe mentioned?

36
Some of these last few might have been to his brother the Baron who was closely identified with him even though it must have cost him some political capital. Here William is maybe saying that he should bear the ignominy of the attainder (the blot) alone, William will be happy just to see the Baron do a good job and fight the good fight!:

> "Let me confess that we two must be twain,
> Although our undivided loves are one:
> So shall those blots that do with me remain

Without thy help by me be borne alone.
In our two loves there is but one respect,
Though in our lives a separable spite,
Which though it alter not love's sole effect,
Yet doth it steal sweet hours from love's delight.
I may not evermore acknowledge thee,
Lest my bewailed guilt should do thee shame,
Nor thou with public kindness honour me,
Unless thou take that honour from thy name:
But do not so; I love thee in such sort
As, thou being mine, mine is thy good report."

A blot is often used to describe an attainder for example in Richard II Act IV Scene 1 where the word blot is used among many allusions to an attainder. (See also http://www.answers.com/topic/attaint where it quotes as an idiom of attainder: "a blot on one's escutcheon.")

Incidentally on the subject of blots here is a few lines by Ben Jonson (*Timber*, 1640) on Shakespeare:

"I remember, the Players have often mentioned it as an honour to Shake-speare, that in his writing, (whatsoever he penn'd) hee never blotted out line. My answer hath beene, would he had blotted a thousand. Which they thought a malevolent speech. I had not told posterity this, but for their ignorance, who choose that circumstance to commend their friend by, wherein he most faulted."

I wonder does the ending of that poem also indicate a person who has fallen out with the state and who has lost the power to control what he wants to say:

"His wit was in his owne power; would the rule of it had beene so too. Many times hee fell into those things, could not escape laughter: As when hee said in the person of Cæsar, one speaking to him; Cæsar thou dost me wrong. Hee replyed: Cæsar did never wrong, but with just cause: and such like; which were ridiculous. But hee redeemed his vices, with his vertues. There was ever more in him to be praysed, then to be pardoned."

Some people think too that "Person Guilty" in Jonson's poems is another reference to Shakespeare and I wonder could it mean that Jonson will name him if the attainder is lifted:

"Believe it, GUILTY, if you lose your shame,
I'll lose my modesty, and tell your name."
(*The works of Ben Jonson*, 1616)

38

This could be to the Baron's son Richard in commemoration of his taking over as the 10th Baron of Delvin in 1602 on the death of his father:

"Be thou the tenth Muse, ten times more in worth
Than those old nine which rhymers invocate; "

The last bit meaning the praise poems that were read out on the death of the previous Barons. (The numbering of the Barons of Delvin is not always consistent but this numbering that is mentioned here follows that of John Lodge's *Peerage of Ireland* (as updated by Archdall) which is certainly the definitive account of this family.)

39 et seq

Maybe at this stage he is writing to his son again who c1602 is probably now living in exile:

"O, how thy worth with manners may I sing,
When thou art all the better part of me?"

40

Bear in mind too that his son Richard had gone over to Hugh O'Neill's side during the 9 years war much to the chagrin no doubt of his father:

"Kill me with spites; yet we must not be foes. "

46

I think this refers to the two parents of his son, William (mine eye) and Jenet (my heart) and they start off arguing about which of them their son takes after. Note too that the son should inherit the title of Baron of Skyrne from his mother and also lands from his mother rather than his father. (PRONI D/3835/A/4/435

11Aug1600). Maybe a lot depends on the goodwill of his wife's tenants to see how the inheritance actually devolves.

"Mine eye and heart are at a mortal war
How to divide the conquest of thy sight;
Mine eye my heart thy picture's sight would bar,
My heart mine eye the freedom of that right.
My heart doth plead that thou in him dost lie--
A closet never pierced with crystal eyes--
But the defendant doth that plea deny
And says in him thy fair appearance lies.
To 'cide this title is impanneled
A quest of thoughts, all tenants to the heart,
And by their verdict is determined
The clear eye's moiety and the dear heart's part:
As thus; mine eye's due is thy outward part,
And my heart's right thy inward love of heart."

47

William to his son again saying how he and herself are getting on well etc.

48

To the same outlining how William has made a settlement of his estates and Richard is not to be included in it as such. William had set up a sort of trust in 1603 (a trust at that time is known as a 'use') settling his estates. (See the printed calendars of Inquisitions post mortem Meath no.57 held at Trim 25 April 1625).

49 and 52

My guess is that William might have entered Holy Orders before he died which was common enough at the time. Eoghan Roe O'Neill for example was reported to have died in the habit of a Dominican monk. I think this might be implied from the friar on William's headstone, anyway there are some references in these two sonnets that seem to point that way such as referring to a tabernacle?: "as the wardrobe which the robe doth hide".

53

On the death of his son Richard who will live on in those verses and specifically in Cynthia which he gets published.

56 -et seq
I think this is to his wife while he is in exile in the early 1580s. In 58 "the imprison'd absence of your liberty" could refer to her being jailed while he was away.

59
To his wife again, here he could be referring to the birth of a second son of his called Richard. (Cockatrice op.cit.p.185) It was common to do that when as in this case an earlier son called Richard had died: "The second burden of a former child". Then he is looking up old history books and bragging that there was an earlier Richard Nugent who was famous 500 years ago.

60 -et seq
To his son again this time giving out about Hugh O'Neill who is 'time' the great enemy of the sonnets. In 63 he refers to him "whereof now he's king".

61
The Irish Council had managed to turn his brother-in-law into an informer as Burghley told him once when he was in England. (Cockatrice op.cit.p.13) The amazing thing about it is that this man was named Thomas Wakely and you can obviously wonder about some of the references to being awake in this sonnet? It could be addressed to the Queen herself? Chiding her on recruiting an informer who was 'all too near' him in Navan, (also maybe referring to Burghley as allied to him and close to the Queen) but still protesting that his real love is trying to protect his lawful monarch:

> "Is it thy will thy image should keep open
> My heavy eyelids to the weary night?
> Dost thou desire my slumbers should be broken,
> While shadows like to thee do mock my sight?
> Is it thy spirit that thou send'st from thee
> So far from home into my deeds to pry,

To find out shames and idle hours in me,
The scope and tenor of thy jealousy?
O, no! thy love, though much, is not so great:
It is my love that keeps mine eye awake;
Mine own true love that doth my rest defeat,
To play the watchman ever for thy sake:
For thee watch I whilst thou dost wake elsewhere,
From me far off, with others all too near."

64

Possibly writing to his great friend Bonaventure O'Hussey who lived for a time in Holland (Cockatrice p.134).

66

Giving out about the state of Ireland etc:

"And needy nothing trimm'd in jollity" – I think nothing is O'Neill which I derive from the Latin for nothing 'nihil' and the 'O' being zero which is nothing obviously! The idea of using a mathematical pun is not as strange as it sounds because Shakespeare does that in no.136 where he mentions the fact that the first number in mathematics is actually zero: "Among a number one is reckoned none". The line might be a reference to O'Neill getting a great deal at Mellifont from Mountjoy (jollity).

"Purest faith unhappily forsworn"– Catholic religion in trouble of course;

"maiden virtue rudely strumpeted" – Queen's virtue being superceded by corrupt local officials;

"art made tongue-tied by authority" – some crackdown on the poets in Ireland?

The 'desert' mentioned could be the Irish placename Dysert where a branch of this clan lived? Is it also referred to in the 'Rape of Lucrece' Part II c.line1142 "Some dark-deep desert, seated from the way, That knows not parching heat nor freezing cold,"

69-71

Writing to his brother or nephew the 9th and 10th Barons possibly warning of the dangers of rebellion. To recap Christopher was accused of treason in 1602 and his son Richard rebelled in 1607. Then in sonnet 71 he is again saying don't acknowledge me because I will only bring you down:

> "Nay, if you read this line, remember not
> The hand that writ it; for I love you so
> That I in your sweet thoughts would be forgot
> If thinking on me then should make you woe
> ...
> And mock you with me after I am gone."

Maybe he doesn't want his career as a playwright to impinge on Richard's difficult political life.

72

Well worth reading for speculation as to whether he devised some kind of 'virtuous lie' to bury knowledge that he had written the sonnets, a secret that was to remain even after he died:

> "O, lest the world should task you to recite
> What merit lived in me, that you should love
> After my death, dear love, forget me quite,
> For you in me can nothing worthy prove;
> Unless you would devise some virtuous lie,
> To do more for me than mine own desert,
> And hang more praise upon deceased I
> Than niggard truth would willingly impart:
> O, lest your true love may seem false in this,
> That you for love speak well of me untrue,
> My name be buried where my body is,
> And live no more to shame nor me nor you.
> For I am shamed by that which I bring forth,
> And so should you, to love things nothing worth."

82

To his wife who is complaining that she is Mrs Nugent not Mrs Shakespeare and complaining that he uses a pseudonym, he writes back saying that its ok for her talking like that she is not under an attainder:

> "I grant thou wert not married to my Muse
> And therefore mayst without attaint o'erlook

The dedicated words which writers use
Of their fair subject, blessing every book"
Other than that he is saying she uses too much makeup!

83 and 83
He is answering her now when she said that he didn't praise her
enough in his poetry and he complains that she needs praise too
much!

88
"I am attainted". I think a lot of these sonnets are arguments with
his wife and in 95 maybe she is seeing someone else?

109
Saying he never deserved the attainder even though some would
say that his flight abroad proved his guilt:
> "O, never say that I was false of heart,
> Though absence seem'd my flame to qualify.
> As easy might I from myself depart
> As from my soul, which in thy breast doth lie:
> That is my home of love: if I have ranged,
> Like him that travels I return again,
> Just to the time, not with the time exchanged,
> So that myself bring water for my stain.
> Never believe, though in my nature reign'd
> All frailties that besiege all kinds of blood,
> That it could so preposterously be stain'd,"

You can see clearly the references to the attainder?

111
The attainder again the result of his deeds:
> "The guilty goddess of my harmful deeds,
> ...
> Thence comes it that my name receives a brand, "

Rape of Lucrece
My guess basically is that Lucrece is Queen Elizabeth (there are
so many references that point that way that it seems beyond

doubt), Collatinus is Ireland, and Lucius Tarquinus is Hugh O'Neill. Yes I know I go on about him the whole time but if you lived in the Pale as the storm clouds gathered over Ulster in the early 1590s you might be moved to warn about the huge army and double dealings of the Great O'Neill! Maybe it is intended to refer to the time when O'Neill went to London in 1590 and to the surprise of a lot of people came back more powerful than ever despite all the talk of Spanish and Scottish plots that Burghley for one was warning about (See the DNB under Hugh O'Neill. In fact the Baron of Delvin stated in a letter back to London that Hugh O'Neill had murdered Hugh Gavelagh because he was going to accuse the Earl of treason. This is as early as a letter of the 17th May 1590 (PRONI D/3835/A/4/294)).

He seems to accuse Hugh of nearly everything including murder (maybe a reference to Hugh Gavelagh) and incest (Hugh O'Neill had his marriage annulled on the grounds of consanguinity) in lines 967-971. There was a lot of talk in the 1590s of the local officials not heeding the Queen's instructions to arrest O'Neill, which admittedly would be more of a phenomenon later in the 1590s than 1594 when this poem is registered but still the pattern had been established I think even then and this might be alluded to in parts like line 1332. William in the poem might also be saying, when he refers to the Romans in line 1855, that maybe the Catholics should not dwell too long on issues like the death of Mary Queen of Scots and use those old issues as an excuse to rebel. It appears that William himself features in the poem, as Philomel complaining again about his attainder which is preventing him from helping the Queen. His honour can only live now in his writings:

> "Is to let forth my foul-defiled blood.
> 'Poor hand, why quiver'st thou at this decree?
> Honour thyself to rid me of this shame:
> For if I die, my honour lives in thee;
> But if I live, thou livest in my defame:
> Since thou couldst not defend thy loyal dame,"
> (1079-1084)

Its interesting that when the Queen then addresses Philomel she says "As shaming any eye should thee behold" which seems like a reference to the cockatrice. The cockatrice is a mythical bird which was the insignia of the Nugents, it could turn you to salt just by looking at you.

Venus and Adonis

Unsurprisingly perhaps I make Adonis Nugent and Venus his wife Jenet Marward. Adonis refers to the two Nugent's, William and his uncle Nicholas who was also Jenet's beloved stepfather, Nicholas being the learned popular guy who is dead at the end and William the lover going off to battle at the beginning. The events described being the rebellion of William in 1580/81 and then the subsequent execution of Nicholas which occurred while William was in exile.

So in the beginning William and Jenet are meeting maybe on Tara which is associated with St.Patrick: "Here come and sit, where never serpent hisses". They talk about a beautiful "ivory pale" (249) full of hillocks and rivers etc. They get on well indeed and at one point she turns into a horse which is actually called Jennet (279) which is supposed to be a corruption of the Spanish horse gennet. He goes straight to her which if you follow the pun means he goes 'mare ward'! He seems after this to explain the reasons why he has to go away (and rebel) talking about things like Cynthia (749, a common reference to Queen Elizabeth) letting her administration go corrupt: "obscures her silver shine" and for framing religion which is the proper preserve of the Pope: "For stealing moulds from heaven that were divine". So he has to go and she misses him as lovers do but then things get violent as they did in 1581 more than anybody could have predicted. She finds herself in great trouble while her Adonis was away and was petitioning politicians etc to get some relief for her plight when she was arrested etc, maybe this refers to these petitions:

> "Full of respects, yet nought at all respecting;
> In hand with all things, nought at all effecting."(932)

She also must have been worried about her baby son that the state wanted to snatch which could be mentioned in "there lives a son that suck'd an earthly mother" (a wet nurse rather than the real mother?) and "Hasting to feed her fawn hid in some brake."

But what happened was that Nicholas was caught up in this and he was killed rather than William and maybe there are references at the end to this death of her (step)father who is of the same family as her lover. The exalted praise of this Adonis would I think refer to Nicholas. Nicholas specifically was given the impossible task by the state of bringing in William's son and it was a perceived lack of will to do this that caused him to be accused of treason and executed. So somewhat mixed up possibly this refers to it:

"Thy mark is feeble age, but thy false dart
Mistakes that aim and cleaves an infant's heart."

In the dedication to this poem, in 1593, Shakespeare talks about a 'graver labour' that he also hopes to bring to fruition and this could be a reference to the big court case that he was pursuing at the time and which was well known and no doubt much talked about in political circles in England.

A Lover's Complaint

My best guess is that it describes his son Richard talking about his woes to Bonaventure O'Hussey when the two might have been in Holland c.1603. The first line "concave womb reworded" could mean hollow Holland? Richard had gone over to Hugh O'Neill probably when Hugh's forces had besieged Ross castle, so possibly this is Richard explaining how faithless Hugh O'Neill was etc. He was in exile because of the rebellion of course and maybe he hoped he could come back with the incoming James I but was possibly cheated of this hope: "Of monarch's hands that lets not bounties fall". William might be complaining again of O'Neill's use of religion:

"Thus merely with the garment of a Grace
the naked and concealed fiend he lover'd"

Btw Hugh O'Neill was well acquainted with Shakespeare's work and had identified himself with the character Kildare, presumably from Henry VIII (*Irish Book Lover* Vol. XIII Feb-March 1922 p.142).

The Passionate Pilgrim

This might be on the same topic, in this case the anger and bewilderment that William must have felt when his son "an untutor'd youth unskillfull in the world's false forgeries" joined the rebellion in 1598. He talks maybe about conflict between fathers and sons in general in verse 12. In verse 6 et seq he could be referring to some incident that caused his son (Adonis) to stray from the law in the person of the queen (Cytherea).

King Richard II

'Pale' is surely a reference to Ireland that would be recognised by all contemporaries and I wonder if in Shakespeare's reply to this question he is saying that it is worthwhile chasing up the corrupt people in his court cases even though it seems pointless because all Ireland is full of rebels anyway:

"Why should we, in the compass of a pale,
Keep law and form and due proportion,
Showing, as in a model, our firm estate,
When our sea-walled garden, the whole land,
Is full of weeds; her fairest flowers choked up,
Her fruit-trees all unpruned, her hedges ruin'd,
Her knots disorder'd, and her wholesome herbs
Swarming with caterpillars?"
(Act II Scene IV 40-47)

Cockatrice and Basilisk References

The cockatrice, which is a mythical bird like a phoenix, was the famous insignia of the Nugents. This emblem sometimes resembled a basilisk which was also a mythical creature which could kill someone just by looking at them. The two insignias are very alike and sometimes used interchangeably which is why when Elizabeth Hickey wrote her book, which again is called 'the Green Cockatrice', she used the pseudonym 'Basil Iske' meaning 'basilisk'. Shakespeare mentions the cockatrice and basilisk quite a lot and seems to put those references in the context of a person's surname. Note for example these references which start with a basilisk on a ring (obviously the Nugents had the insignia on their rings as a seal for letters):

"O, no, no, no! 'tis true. Here, take this too;
Gives the ring

113

It is a basilisk unto mine eye,
Kills me to look on't."
(*Cymbeline* Act II Scene IV 136-139)

"For marks descried in men's nativity
Are nature's faults, not their own infamy.'
Here with a cockatrice' dead-killing eye
He rouseth up himself and makes a pause;"
(*The Rape of Lucrece* 540-543)

"Make me not sighted like the basilisk:
I have look'd on thousands, who have sped the bet-
ter
By my regard, but kill'd none so. Camillo,--
As you are certainly a gentleman, thereto
Clerk-like experienced, which no less adorns
Our gentry than our parents' noble names,
In whose success we are gentle,"
(*A Winter's Tale* Act I Scene II 453-459)

Could 'I' be a reference to the playwright?:
"...say thou but 'I,'
And that bare vowel 'I' shall poison more
Than the death-darting eye of cockatrice:
I am not I, if there be such an I;
Or those eyes shut, that make thee answer 'I.'
If he be slain, say 'I'; or if not, no:"
(*Romeo and Juliet* Act III Scene II 48-53)

King Henry IV pt 2
Act III Scene 2 the part where he brings in two old judges Shallow and Silence.

Shallow
I think Shallow is the wealthy Sir Thomas Cusack one time Lord
Chancellor of Ireland who died c1571. 'Cuasach' in Irish means
hollow or concave which is obviously similar to shallow. He had
once being master of revels at the Inner Temple in London and

this would have been almost exactly 55 years ago from when William would have known the two judges in 1570 (http://www.chapters.eiretek.org/books/chancellors/Chancellors15.htm). His son John was a famous stone carver (Cockatrice p.37) which is interesting in the light of Falstaff saying about him that his head was "carved on him with a knife". He lived at Lismullen which is near where the Pale musters were held at Tara. His widow, Jenet Sarsfield, remarried the guy that I think was Justice Silence:

Silence
Sir John Plunkett Chief Justice of the Queen's bench. He was the father of William's mother-in-law Ellen and another old respected lawyer in the East Meath/ North Dublin area. Notice how he repeats the words 'Sir John' in the scene and is the mother of an Ellen. 'Plúcadh' in Irish means to smother or stifle like 'fuaim a phlúcadh' to smother sound. But it gets even more coincidental when you consider that Ellen then married an Aylmer (Inquisition Post mortem op. cit.) and the insignia of the Aylmer family is the blackbird (http://archiver.rootsweb.com/th/read/ELMORE/1998-07/0900044363). Its certainly possible that Ellen was Cusack's God daughter because the two families would have known each other quite well with for example Ellen's first husband being raised in Cusack's house (Cockatrice ibid). This is the bit I am referring to:

> Shallow: And how doth my cousin, your bedfellow? and your fairest daughter and mine, my god-daughter Ellen?
> Silence: Alas, a black ousel [an old word for a bird], cousin Shallow!
> Shallow: By yea and nay, sir, I dare say my cousin William is become a good scholar: he is at Oxford still, is he not?
> Silence: Indeed, sir, to my cost.
> Shallow: A' must, then, to the inns o' court shortly."

Notice too that William studied at Oxford presumably as preparation for a legal career considering how skilled he was on legal matters later. It seems to this observer anyway that the odds of all

these references being purely coincidental is quite long and if they are these two judges then the next point is very interesting. This Sir John is from a place in North Dublin called Donsoghly and in the scene there is a reference to where he is from:
"Shallow:....How a good
of bullocks at Stamford fair?

Silence: By my troth, I was not there.

Shallow: Death is certain. Is old Double of your town living

Silence: Dead, sir.

Shallow: Jesu, Jesu, dead! drew a good bow; and dead! 'A shot a fine shoot. John a Gaunt loved him well, and betted much his head. Dead! 'A would have clapp'd i' th' clout at twelve score, and carried you a forehand shaft a fourteen and a half, that it would have done a man's heart good to. How a score of ewes now?

Silence: Thereafter as they be—a score of good ewes may be ten pounds.

Shallow: And is old Double dead?"

The whole reference to Double is clearly interesting if the writer could be alluding to his stage 'double' Shakespeare who comes from a business background and I wonder is 'Stamford' too much of a stretch to 'Stratford'? As you can see this 'Double' comes then from Sir John's home town of Donsoghly which so far as I know is not a very big place and the only reference I ever came across of anybody living there, apart from these Plunketts, is an account in the Book of Howth of an old man who died aged 107. He was called Walter Hussey, actually from Dobbore beside Donsoghly, who wrote a book detailing events such as the battle of Knockdoe, including this story of debates in the Fitzgerald camp before the battle:

> "And so O'Connor asked the Earl what he would do with the judges and men of law in his company. 'We have no matters of pleadings, no matters of argument, no matters to debate, nor to be discussed by pen and ink, but by the bow, spear and sword and the valiant hearts of gentlemen and men of war by their fierce and lusty doings and not by the simple, sorry, and weak and doubtful stomachs of learned men; for I never saw those that was learned ever give good counsel in matters of war, for they were always doubting, staying and persuading more in frivolous and uncertain words, more than [H]Ector or Launcelott's doings. Away with them! They are overbold to press amongst this company: for our matter is to be discussed by valiant and stout stomachs of prudent and wise men of war practised in this same faculty, and not matters of war nor matters of religion'... Lord Delvin [William's gt. grandfather] declared: "His learning was not such, that with a glorious tale he could utter his stomach; but I promise to God and to the Prince I shall be the first that shall throw the first spear among the Irish in this battle: let him speak now that will for I have done...Accordingly, a little before the joining of the battle (in which he commanded and led the horse) he spurred his horse and threw a small spear among the Irish, with which he chanced to kill one of the Burkes and retired. Whereupon the Lord Deputy told him, he kept promise well, and well did and valiantly seeing that after his threw he retired back." (J.S. Brewer and William Bullen edit, *Calendar of Carew Manuscripts* (London, 1876), p.182, and p.195.)

APPENDIX B

Dating Problem FAQ

Basically my argument is that the person who compiled the 1623 Folio was Shakespeare (meaning the true author whoever he is) and yet he is supposed to have died in 1616. This of course supports the claim of William Nugent since he doesn't die until 1625. The Folio by the way is a sort of complete works of Shakespeare, as opposed to various plays that had been published earlier which are known as Quartos. To clarify the problem here is a mini FAQ list.

1) How do we know that the Folio was genuinely published in 1623 and not maybe earlier like during Shakespeare's lifetime?

There is no dispute about this and as you will read the Folio text incorporates material from works printed as late as 1622 and therefore couldn't have been published earlier. They have dated some of these earlier works (the Quartos) by elaborate means including watermarks so again there is no dispute about the dating of these works.

2) So why do you think the Folio was written by Shakespeare, and not revised and compiled by somebody else?

Its always been a truism in Shakespearean scholarship that the Folio text is quite an improvement over the earlier texts and includes many deletions, new speeches and scenes that improve greatly the plays as they were written in the Quartos. It also includes many plays previously unpublished. Everybody has always known that and I think its fair to say that most scholars in the past were always at least vaguely of the opinion that Shakespeare must have worked on this Folio text before he died.

3) So what has changed?

What is new now as far as I can see is the fact that mainstream scholarship now accepts that whoever compiled the Folio was using Quartos published after the death of Shakespeare, like the 1622 publications of Othello and Richard III, 1619 copy of The Midsummer Night's Dream etc.

4) Well surely you mean that the compiler was using the same manuscript that the printer used when printing those works in 1622 etc, it doesn't have to be the actual printed volume?

No I mean the actual printed volume. This is because people can trace by complicated means printing errors used by the printer when publishing those works and those errors reappear in the Folio. There is no debate as to this because of the huge amount of work put into it. The Folio compiler is definitely using those printed Quartos, and as pointed out there is no debate about the publication date of the Quartos in the sense that they are definitely published after the date of Shakespeare's death.

5) Ok so it was compiled by somebody else using the earlier Quartos, big deal it doesn't have to be Shakespeare?

Yes but don't forget the other unquestionable phenomenon which is that the Folio adds in many new clearly Shakespearean speeches and scenes and similarly deletes at will from the Quarto texts in a way that enhances the plays. Again nobody disputes that the Folio text does this and that the changes are unquestionably by Shakespeare.

6) So how do mainstream scholars explain this?

They talk about various manuscripts that Shakespeare or the acting company must have left behind them and that the compiler of the Folio was able to use these along with the Quartos to arrive at the finished Folio text. For me anyway that all seems to be castles in the air. They don't have copies of any of these manuscripts, nor do they have any record of any such manuscripts, where they were held, why they emerge in 1623 and disappear again or any example of manuscripts being used before in that way. You see bear in mind there are extensive changes and improvements being made to plays that were written some 30 years before and the survival of 'golden' manuscripts that have kept a pure and coherent version of all these plays intact all those years (and not used for the publication of the Quartos) is clearly remarkable in the chaotic world of the playing companies. They are basically just assuming all this because of course they are also assuming that Shakespeare is dead then and the simpler explanation is therefore unthinkable. The simple explanation of course is that Shakespeare was alive then and sat down to revise his canon and probably scribbled his changes on a copy of the Quarto as no doubt a Joyce or any author would do.

Of course what you might say is that Shakespeare had kept a good set of these manuscripts which became available after his death, but there is no record to support this. He mentions no manuscripts in his will despite it being very elaborate detailing famously his 'second best bed'. His eventual heir was his daughter and son-in-law Dr John Hall. Hall has left a diary and papers that include a detailed inventory of his library but there is no mention anywhere of books or manuscripts from his father in law or that connect to the stage and the plays. In 1642 an army surgeon called James Cook called on the family and spoke to Shakespeare's daughter and was told that there weren't manuscripts or books there in any way connected with her father (http://www.elizabethanauthors.com/problem.htm). As regards the playing companies that seems a very erratic and confusing scene with various companies travelling all over the place without any set headquarters and unlikely to be the great preservers of these manuscripts. Also the censorship of profane language in the Folio text (e.g. From Othello (http://www.shakespeare-literature.com/l_biography.html no.28) and Troilus and Cressida (http://www.shu.ac.uk/emls/01-2/godsshak.html Section C no.18)) and the dropping of Pericles from the Folio (which is very explicit about incest and prostitution) is also compatible with an older and maybe more religious Shakespeare leaving out those references as he revised his text. There are even additions to the plot and body of plays that post date 1616 and the question must be asked would any normal publisher of a famous authors works add in parts like that? So you have to arrive at the conclusion that the idea that Shakespeare was alive in 1623 is a lot more likely than other explanations.

Source Notes

For a list of examples of how the First Folio greatly changes and improves the works of Shakespeare: http://home.att.net/~tleary/gitche.htm .

For plot and deliberate post 1616 textual additions see: International Shakespeare Association, *Shakespeare and the Mediterranean: The Selected Proceedings of the International Shakespeare...*(Delaware, 2004), p.249 where it is pointed out that 'Measure for Measure' contains one stanza of a two stanza song that appeared in Fletcher's play 'Rollo Duke of Normandy' which was written in 1617-1620. Also a source for Lucio's remarks about the Duke and the King of Hungary seems to come from a printed English newsletter of 6 Oct 1621. The same page notes that there is much added 'posthumous' material in Macbeth.

What follows is a list of references that show how the 1623 Folio incorporates text from the later Quartos that postdate his death in 1616:

Othello

http://www.sirbacon.org/othello.htm

Shows some of the passages added into the Folio but missing from the 1622 Quarto of Othello, hence showing how much the Folio compiler confidently re-engineered the text.

The editor of the Arden edition of Shakespeare, E. Honigmann, in *Texts of Othello* (1996), p.1, admits that the 1623 Folio includes material from the printed 1622 Quarto of Shakespeare although he has an elaborate theory to explain this away!:

> "F[olio] shows signs of contamination directly from Q[uarto,
> the only Quarto of Othello is 1622]."

King Lear

http://www.bl.uk/treasures/shakespeare/kinglear.html

> "It is now agreed that the second Quarto [1619] was used in
> the printing of the text. It has been suggested that the printers
> used a transcription of an annotated copy of the second
> Quarto, rather than the printed text...with the Quarto text de-
> liberately revised (possibly by Shakespeare himself) to pro-
> duce the Folio text."

So it is a copy ultimately from the second Quarto of 1619. Notice how much of a stretch it is to say that Shakespeare worked on this text when it is admitted that the compiler is using the 1619 text.

Romeo and Juliet

http://www.bl.uk/treasures/shakespeare/romeo.html
> "First Folio, 1623. Printed from the third Quarto [1609], although a number of passages follow the fourth Quarto. [1622]"

Midsummer Night's Dream
http://www.bl.uk/treasures/shakespeare/midsummer.html
> "First Folio, 1623. Printed from the second Quarto [1619], apparently annotated from a promptbook."

Richard III and The Merry Wives of Windsor
http://www.schulers.com/books/an/s/Shakespeare__Bacon_and_the_Great_Unknown/Shakespeare__Bacon_and_the_Great_Unknown1.htm
> "The editing of the Folio is so exquisitely careless that twelve printer's errors in a Quarto of 1622, of Richard III, appear in the Folio of 1623. Again, the Merry Wives of the Folio, is nearly twice as long as the Quarto of 1619, yet keeps old errors."

Richard III and Othello.
Shakespeare Survey: Volume 7 Style and Language (Cambridge), p.153: Research by Miss Walker agrees that the 1622 Quarto was used for the Folio with changes. The same for Othello (she is Alice Walker who wrote *Textual problems of the First Folio* (Cambridge,1953)).

Henry VI pt 2
The Oxford shakespeare (p.99) referred to the research of William Montgomery which shows that the Folio used the 1619 Quarto.

Richard III
See British museum *Guide to the Manuscript and Printed Books of the First Folio of Shakespeare* (London, 2005), p.45 and http://www.sirbacon.org/btheobaldenterchxiv.htm for this by Bertram Theobald:
> "Cambridge editors say:"...the passages which in the Quarto are complete and consecutive, are amplified in the Folio, the expanded text being quite in the manner of Shakespeare. The Folio, too, contains passages not in the Quarto, which though not necessary to the sense, yet harmonize so well, in the sense and tone, with the context, that we can have no hesitation in attributing them to the author himself."
> Not only so, but for some unexplained reason twelve printer's errors are identified, as having been taken over bodily from the Quarto into the Folio! Thus it is virtually demonstrated that in preparing the Folio edition, the author worked from this 1622 Quarto and no other."

Henry V
http://www.gradesaver.com/classicnotes/titles/henryv/about.html
The 1619 Quarto was used for the Folio.

APPENDIX C

Allusions to Shakespeare

These allusions are contemporary literary references to Shakespeare, and speculation on how they could refer to William Nugent.

Robert Greene, *Groat's Worth of Wit* (London,1592)
To begin with you have the most famous allusion:

> "Yes, trust them not: for there is an upstart Crow, beautified with our feathers, that with his Tygers heart wrapt in a Players hyde, supposes he is as well able to bombast out a blanke verse as the best of you: and being an absolute Iohannes factotum, is in his owne conceit the onely Shake-scene in a countrey."

Note how its 'a' country and 'our' feathers which leaves you with the impression that it is a foreigner that he is referring to. The 'upstart crow' thing would remind you a lot of the Cockatrice, which is the insignia of the Nugents, while 'upstart' itself makes a great pun of New Gent ('Nugent' is pronounced, and in the 16th cent frequently spelt, 'Newgent'). Furthermore our William (if it is he) must have come across as a kind of Jack of all trades figure to an English audience considering how he would have been known there for his political and later legal exploits before he became famous for his poetry. Finally the 'tigers heart' phrase (which mimics the later Davies reference to courage) also fits the image of the Irish rebel quite neatly.

John Davies of Hereford *Microcosmos* (1603)
One of the clearest references to Shakespeare:

> "Players, I love yee, and your Qualitie,
> As ye are Men, that pass time not abus'd:
> And some I love for painting, poesie
> And say fell Fortune cannot be excus'd
> That hath for better uses you refus'd:

Wit, Courage, good shape, good partes, and all
good,
As long as al these goods are no worse us'd,

And though the stage doth staine pure gentle
bloud,
Yet generous yee are in minde and moode."[1]

While the "fell Fortune" and the blood stain seem to be quite
good matches for the attainder the real interest in this quote lies in
those three words: "pure gentle bloud". If you take 'pure' for
'new' it seems a dead ringer for the surname (a persons family
name being his 'blood' of course) NewGent. Also that line: "Wit,
Courage, good shape, good partes, and all good," seems a close
match to this description of the Nugents by the Lord Deputy in
1590: "And being of great credit through the Pale for their kinred,
affinities, possessions, wits, and courage, specially the Baron and
his brother [William], of whom we may forbear to speak."[2]

John Davies of Hereford again *Scourge of Folly* (1610):
"To our English Terence, Mr Will Shake-speare

Some say (good Will) which I, in sport, do sing,
Had'st thou not plaid some Kingly parts in sport,
Thou hadst bin a companion for a King;
And, beene a King among the meaner sort.
Some others raile; but, raile as they thinke fit,
Thou hast no railing, but a raigning Wit:
And honesty thou sow'st, which they do reape;
So, to increase their Stocke which they do keepe."

Terence was a Roman poet that was rumoured to be only a front-
man for an upper class poet known as Scipio.[3] Clearly Davies is
saying that Shakespeare had consorted with real kings and in that
context it should be noted that William knew and met personally
the Kings of Scotland,[4] France (the English ambassador saw him
in the "King's great chamber"[5]) possibly Spain (he had visited the
Spanish court,[6] and Perrot says of him in 1584 "He assures the Irish that the Spanish and Scottish Kings will confirm anything that
he shall conclude with them"[7]) the Queen of England [8] and the

Pope.[9] Also his rebellion could be interpreted as playing the role of King "among the meaner sort".

Edmund Spenser, *The Tears of the Muses* (included in a volume called 'Complaints' 1591):
>"But that same gentle spirit from whose pen
>Large streams of honnie and sweete Nectar flowe,
>Scorning the boldnes of such base-borne men,
>Which dare their follies forth so rashlie throwe,
>Doth rather choose to sit in idle Cell,
>Than so himself to mockerie to sell."

As you can see it seems to show that the real author of the plays shunned publicity. Also I would hold forth that "Scorning the boldnes of such base-borne men" could be another pun on William's surname.[10]

Joseph Hall, *Virgidemiarum* [Satires] (1597) in Book IV Satire 1
The poem is satirising a poet known as Labeo who has been identified as Shakespeare:
>"Labeo is whip't and laughs me in the face
>Why? for I smite and hide the galled place,
>Gird but the Cynicks Helmet on his head
>Cares he for Talus or his flayle of lead?
>Long as the craftie Cuttle lieth sure
>In the black cloud of his thick vomiture
>Who list complaine of wronged faith or fame
>When he may shift it on to another name?"[11]

As you can see the last line highlights the idea of Shakespeare as a pseudonym while the previous line is compatible with William Nugent disguising his name because of the attainder ('wronged...fame') and his unflinching Catholicism ('wronged faith'), which you can see in Sept 1592 for example when it was said of William that "he could not go over to England for fear of making a breach in his conscience, lest he should be forced to swear the Oath of Supremacy."[12]

Ben Jonson, *The Irish Masque at Court* (1613) [13]
First you have four Irish ambassadors at court who speak with a

very pronounced accent and dance jigs and stuff, then along comes a very well spoken Irish gentleman who speaks almost a Shakespearean passage and he introduces an "immortal bard". This bard seems to praise some step of King James' which "breaks the Sun earths rugged chains, Wherein rude winter bound her veins". Because of this step the Irish guests were able to take off their mantles and show the players garb that they wore underneath. This could be read as an allusion to William's petition to get his attainder reversed which was being discussed at court in the same year of 1613.[14] If he had got that it might have allowed him to be revealed as a player or playwright. Also this phrase could I guess be a pun on his name:

> "Tis done by this; your slough let fall, And come
> forth new-born creatures all."

Robert Greene, *Groats worth of wit* (London, 1592)[15]
It is often said that the story of Roberto in this work is an allusion to Shakespeare, hence it might be worth pointing out the many comparisons to William's life that you can see in this story. Roberto's father is described "as an old new made Gentleman" which is a bizarre way of phrasing a sentence if it isn't an allusion to his surname! William's father was both a member of the Irish Council and of the Irish House of Lords so the reference to Roberto's father as "wise he was, for he boare office in his parish and sate as formally in his foxfurd gowne" follows the analogy quite well. He is even said to be a patron of the poets as well. Of course William was one half of a famous double act in that his only legitimate brother Christopher was also well known in England. After all Christopher had been in jail and on bail in London for many years in the early 1580s so the reference to the two brothers with Roberto being the younger and the scholar is also neatly analogous. In any case the story ends with Roberto being seduced into working for the players to make ends meet and that is what Elizabeth Hickey says happened to William.

Thomas Nash, *Anatomy of Absurdity* (London, 1589), p11.
This is another one of those works where Greene and Nash are giving out about some new 'upstart' playwright that is taking over

the London stage and which is usually taken to mean Shakespeare (e.g. by Simpson in his book op. cit.) Here is some of the criticism which could be read as a reference to an attainder? Also note the basilisk (which is like the cockatrice) and the Irish lack of serpents thing:

> "Very requisite were it that such blockheads had some Albadanensis Appolonius to send them to some other mechanical art, that they might not thus be the stain of art. Such kind of poets were they that Plato excluded from his commonwealth, and Augustine banished ex ciuitate Dei, which the Romans derided, and the Lacedaemonians scorned, who would not suffer one of Archilochus' books to remain in their country, and amiss it were not if these which meddle with the art they know not were bequeathed to Bridewell, there to learn a new occupation, for as the basilisk with his hiss driveth all other serpents from the place of his abode, so these rude rimers with their jarring verse alienate all men's minds from delighting in numbers' excellence, which they have so defaced that we may well exclaim with the poet, Quantum mutatus ab illo."

Robert Greene, *Francesco's Fortunes* (London,1590), [also known as the 2nd pt. of *Never too late*] p.1.
Francesco has to live with the consequences of his affair and this is described thus at the beginning of the second part (again could it be the attainder if the affair is an allusion to the rebellion?):

> "The Athenians counted such men unworthy their commonwealth as were ingrateful, and Plato, seeing an unthankful man prosper, said: See, men of Greece, the gods are proved unjust, for they have laden a thistle with fruit. When (right worshipful) these reasons entered into my reach, and that I saw how odious in elder time ingrateful men were to all estates and degrees, lest I might be stained with such a hateful blemish.."[16]

Robert Greene, *Never too Late* (London,1590)
It continues some of these allusions to Shakespeare according to
Simpson and maybe again it alludes to an attainder p6:

"Yet for all he was so quaint
Sorrow did his visage taint,
Midst the riches of his face
Grief deciphered high disgrace,"
...p13 [interesting in context of skull on
Shakespeare's grave]:
"If that the world presents illusions,
Or Satan seeks to puff me up with pomp,
As man is frail and apt to follow pride,
Then see, my son, where I have in my cell
A dead man's skull, which calls this straight to
mind,
That as this is, so must my ending be;
When then I see that earth to earth must pass,
I sigh and say all flesh is like to grass."
...p.31[the cockatrice's eye?:]
"Sweet Adon dar'st not glance thine eye,
N'oserez vous, mon bel ami,
Upon thy Venus that must die"

(It should be pointed out that the pretty widely accepted references to Shakespeare in the last three works are to some 'upstart'
characters that are not explicitly the subject of the above quota-
tions. But still they seem to be referring to some person who
suffered an attainder and who that is is I think worthy of some
speculation.)

Furthermore its amazing how often the word 'gentle' is used
to describe Shakespeare and this again could be an insiders way
of identifying him with William New 'gent'. e.g. Ben Jonson describes him as gentle twice in the Folio – 'my gentle Shakespeare'
and 'for gentle Shakespeare cut'; and Spenser, as noted above,
calls him 'that same gentle spirit'.

Overall I think its quite impressive the coincidences that you
can find between William and these quotes, but then I would say
that wouldn't I!

Footnotes

1. http://www.rahul.net/raithel/Derby/allusions.html where its origin as a Shakespeare allusion is discussed.

2. PRONI D/3835/A/4/301.

3. http://www.fictionpress.com/read.php?storyid=1269395 .

4. Cockatrice p.74-76.

5. 1 Nov 1582 PRONI D/3835/A/6/321.

6. Cockatrice p72.

7. ibid p80.

8. ibid p.106.

9. ibid p.69.

10. For a discussion of this poem's link to Shakespeare see the Earl of Derby site http://www.rahul.net/raithel/Derby/allusions.html . There is another allusion in Spenser's poetry mentioned in footnote 141 in the main text infra.

11. Mentioned in the Shakespeare allusion books, see: http://www.shaksper.net/archives/1994/0408.html .

12. Cockatrice op.cit. p.13.

13. For a performance held at court in December 1613 http://www.holloways.com/jonson1692irish.htm .

14. Cockatrice p.142 from Standish O'Grady, *Catalogue of Irish Manuscripts in the British Museum* (London, 1926), Vol 1 p.406.

15. http://darkwing.uoregon.edu%7Erbear/greene1.html .

16. Works by Robert Greene are available online here: http://www.oxford-shakespeare.com/groatsworth .

APPENDIX D

The Policy of the Barons of Delvin 1575-1642

While anybody can read a narrative of the history of this family in the DNB and 'The Green Cockatrice' I thought it might be useful to try to analyse in more detail the relationship between the two successive Barons of Delvin, Christopher and his son Richard the first Earl of Westmeath, and the state for the period roughly 1575-1642. Specifically I try to explain why people like William's brother Christopher were so enthusiastic supporters of the Queen, and enemies of the Queen's rebels, while at the same time they were being persecuted by that government. Christopher's whole political career seems to consist on the one hand of periods of warfare against Irish rebels, especially the Nine Years War, and the rest of the time he was in jail or on bail answering spurious charges thrown up at him by the same state that he was so enthusiastically defending. This enigma really comes across when you read the history of the period. Hence John Lynch refers to Christopher becoming "melancholy through his long abode in prison"[1] and yet when he is out of jail in the 1590s we find him listing a long and impressive list of – frequently gory – actions that he undertook on the state's behalf during the Nine Years War.[2]

One simple explanation for this enigma is that in the latter instance we rely on a letter in the State Papers sent by Christopher where he is bound to play down his Irish nationalist and Catholic sympathies, while John Lynch on the other hand, as an exiled Catholic historian, is free to extol those qualities saying at one point that "the Nugents were at all times noted for their Patriotism and Catholicity".[3] You can see this again where Delvin at one time in writing to Burghley claims that no suspected rebel had ever been admitted to his house – in answer to false charges of that type – which might have a curious echo in the fact that when one of the Cusacks, who was facing possible treason charges, met Delvin its specifically stated that he did so in his garden. Which might be a clue to the sort of details that Delvin is glossing over in his letters![4] Another instance of this can be seen in the two documents written by John Nugent of Skurlockstown. The first was a confession written while a prisoner in Dublin Castle and the second was an account of the judge's trial that he wrote anonymously to the Judge's widow shortly after his death and by comparing the two we can see how the story was influenced by the necessity of not offending the government in his first document.[5] In the confession he talks about John Cusack – the government's star witness in the trial – knowing a lot about the conspiracy without going into any details while in the second he lets rip at his agent provocateur activities at that time. So any history based on the family's letters to the government in the state papers has to be underestimating the degree of antipathy they must have felt towards that government, although at the same time I don't think it can explain away the genuinely loyal actions of this family through most of this period.

I think a further understanding of the nature of that loyalty might be in order to explain this, but first we should look at the two models of this loyalty current at this time. While it might seem speculative I respectfully submit that there is in a sense two models of state and monarchial loyalty current in this period, a French and an English model. Both France and England, it seems to this observer, often strike you as being very centralised countries always loyal to the King or Queen in Paris or London but at the same time with subtle differences between them. In England, I think it could be said, the subject is maybe loyal to the monarch as a kind of bargain where the citizen expects to get reward and favour in return for giving that to the Crown. In France its possibly a more passionate and almost religious thing where some of the nobles will give a fierce allegiance to an almost God like monarch simply because that King is their lawfully anointed prince. It doesn't really matter to them how they are treated by the government or its officials, they are loyal and true to their King no matter what. You can see some of that atmosphere captured maybe in fiction in the Three Musketeers or in the elaborate courtly rituals of Louis XIV while in England at the time there is a much more carefree and dispassionate allegiance shown to their monarch in my opinion. In England its more a question of favour guaranteeing loyalty. So basically my contention is that this family followed a French – the home of their ancestors – rather than an English model of loyalty. It might be subtle but it does have a bearing on understanding their actions in my opinion. Consider Christopher's statement of loyalty to Burghley in c.1580:

"There is passed since mine ancestors coming hither, four hundred and odd years, since which time if any man by chronicle or record is able to show that ever any of them held arms against the crown of England I am content to lose my head, beside that they have always been servitors to the Crown, which I am able to show by the liveries they sued and other writings.

My great grandfather what service he did in the troublesome time wherein he lived, your Lordship may learn from the records of Dublin, and the ancient people of the same. My father also how he served during the reign of King Edward, Queen Mary, and in the beginning of our Sovereign's reign that now is, many that yet live can testify. As for myself, whether I have served Her Majesty faithfully or not, your Lordship partly knoweth.

I protest unto you Lordship there is nothing in this world whereof I make more accompt than mine ancestors were never spotted in blood [never rebelled], and have always from the conquest been servitors to the Crown of England, which honour by them attained and to me descended I mean not to deface nor lose, whatsoever traitors report of me to the contrary, to whom God send short life and worse death."[6]

You see to English eyes this reads like a long self serving bit of plámás, the type of thing that up and coming courtiers say all the time with nobody taking it too seriously. But this is where they are wrong, Christopher is being deadly serious here. This is his strength, it was part of the great pride of the Nugents that they were the type of people who stood by their word and who were always loyal to their divinely anointed prince. He isn't looking up with expectant eyes for favour from government officials, he is looking down on them from the dizzy heights of the true and honest service of his ancestors. The upshot is that for him loyalty to the Queen, the Pale and the Norman lands of Westmeath, had nothing to do with how he was treated, or expected to be treated, by the government in Dublin. He was going to be loyal to what he saw as his true monarch and that was that. And in fact it ties into the deep religious faith of this family which comes across very clearly from the surviving records, as Christopher outlines in some strong words directed at Hugh O'Neill:

> "And many of us, having heard and read a good deal more than he did, could never find in scripture, General Councils, by the Fathers, or any other authentical authority, that subjects ought to carry arms against their anoint[ed] Christian prince for religion or any other cause;"[7]

So in some ways this family, and many of the other Normans of Meath, were in a strange middle world as the 16th century progressed. In a sense they were caught between two power blocks that actually understood each other quite well: the Gaelic Irish and the New English. Walsingham and Wallop and all these other Tudor officials were in practice I think acting like pirates in Ireland bribing, killing, imprisoning, and stealing land entirely to their hearts content at this time while the Gaelic Irish and their poets and harpists knew exactly what they were doing (although many were not slow to jump into the protection and enjoy the wealth of those same pirates.) But the Nugents and others were left sincere in their attachment to the Pale and its institutions, although they now had no real say in how they were run, which were gradually taken over and run in the interests of this pirate clique. For a long time they just floundered around, still proud of their by now abused and manipulated loyalty while being slowly crushed between those two powerful parties. One of the Nugents wrote about this in a Gaelic poem referred to in the 1650s:

> "Saroil ōaṟ scuṟ a seléiċ Sall
> Iſ soill ōáṟ bfrosṟaó ōáṟ bfeaṟann
> ōon ċṟonne ce beaus áṟ ċuro
> maṟ uḃall cuinne a camuro."

"The Irish put us to English hands,
The English driv'd us from our lands,
Betwixt them both we have no ease,
Like an apple tossed between two seas."[8]

But of course in time the crunch came and it came over religion. Religion was clearly very important to the Nugents and to many of the Old English. The family had founded the Dominican [9] and the Capuchin [10] friaries in Mullingar for example, they had protected the anchorite at Fore abbey and had lovingly preserved St. Fechin's crozier from the same place,[11] they frequently harboured the Bishops of Meath and sometimes even the Bishops of Kilmore, were probably the most important family connected with the Capuchins and the Jesuits – the two great Counter Reformation orders –, had proudly retained some relics of the martyred Franciscan Bishop Cornelius O'Devany,[12] and had always protected the Franciscans in Multyfarnham who continued to openly practice their religion only a days march away from Dublin Castle. This was noted by John Lynch who says:

> "It is indeed worthy of record that the religious of
> Multyfarnham, placed in the possession of Richard
> [Earl of Westmeath], clad in no other habit than
> that of their order while residing openly in that
> monastery after the Catholic religion had been pro-
> scribed in Ireland."

This very highly regarded historian does not mince his words when describing the role the Nugents played in defending the Catholic religion:

> "I should never make an end if I should endeavour
> to produce in this discourse all the Nugents, even
> of one family of the Nugents, who displayed not
> merely their own steadfastness in the Catholic reli-
> gion but further an example of the greatest piety.
> From these three or four the reader may form a
> conjecture of the rest. For 'in the mouth of two or
> three witnesses every word is established.' This
> only I will add that the most vehement tempests of
> persecution which have now agitated Ireland for a
> hundred years have not dashed any of the Nugents

of any note, or scarcely one out of all the families
of Nugents, onto the rocks of heresy or given his
name over to the adversary."[13]

Their attachment to the old religion I think partly reflects again their almost romantic and idealistic feudal notions and loyalties. You see in their elaborate, and fiercely defended, natural order the monk in his cloister reciting his ancient office is simply not somebody subject in his theology to the whim of any politician or nobleman. For them it was supposed to be a genuinely divine matter and they just couldn't stomach the sort of arbitrary changes that the English government wanted to introduce in the 16th century. You can see some of this idealism in one of William's Gaelic poems:

"ir créao bairrlim bán manać
o'airling ı n-ár allṁaṗać."

"in my dream it was a troop of slender-handed
white monks that I saw in conflict with the foreigners."[14]

Hence in a nutshell when the English government moved to establish the Anglican religion it had to clash on the one issue where the Old Norman families would never compromise on, their faith.[15] Their open support for Multyfarnham for example just couldn't be tolerated by a government hoping to establish its authority across the whole country. So the only real question left is would the power of these Norman lords bend or break to the prevailing power. The interesting thing is that 'bending' to this power doesn't seem to have been an option that this family explored much, they seem to be a genuinely courageous lot who did not give in easily to bullying from the state. The Aphorismical Discovery for example talks about the "brave family of the Nugents",[16] and F.X. Martin's opinion of Lavallin Nugent was that:

"The evidence from the beginning to the end of his life
never suggests that he was at any time swept by
fear...There was steel in his personality."[17]

While George Carew remarking on John Nugent said that "he was so valiant and daring, as that he did not fear anything."[18] So simple intimidation just didn't work in this case although apparently it usually did as the Lord Deputy remarked in 1590 while talking about the Nugents:

> "And being of great credit through the Pale for their kinred, affinities, possessions, wits, and courage, specially the Baron and his brother, of whom we may forbear to speak. They are dangerous men to be abroad (this being time) if the Spanish do purpose anything at all against this state. And being laid up we think the enemy will be thereby both cut off from intelligence and also disappointed of great instruments, yea perhaps the head their party here...[if they are imprisoned it will] abate the courage of the ill affected in the Pale (a kind of people easily appalled, being but laid too.)"[19]

Their staying power in the face of state intimidation really came across strongly at the time of William's court case. After all William was then under attainder for treason, which is almost like being out on bail for a capital charge, and yet instead of keeping his head down he takes on the state, including the powerful Lord Deputy, in this massive legal proceeding. Its not surprising to find then that at one stage the Lord Deputy threatened him in "a great rage" that "by the son of God if I had treason against thee I would hang thee by the neck."[20] But this just didn't work, they weren't going to fold that easily.

Of course the next question is why didn't the state just crush them like they did the Geraldines with a few choice executions and confiscations? In practice they tried that in 1580 and it didn't work because when they eliminated what they thought were the leaders of the family others emerged to take their place and were at least as much a nuisance as the few they had executed! So a smug government must have been delighted with itself in the 1581-3 period with the judge Nicholas Nugent, a recognised leader during the cess period, executed, the Baron in jail, and William in exile. But all that happened was that James, William's uncle, emerges and sneaks off to England to plead their case, John Nugent, the judge's old servant, pops up with a long discourse on the proceedings that he tries to get widely read, and William's wife and mother in law – and her father – are pestering the Dublin government constantly looking for some justice. I think therefore that the Nugents were so clannish, and their lands so dispersed among the different families, that the government could not hope to deal a single blow to them in the style of their crushing of the Earl of Desmond.

Failing to deal a blow by those means, I think a kind of covert war developed between the state and this family, with the state aiming to undermine them via a number of more subtle and modern means than maybe readily apparent.

This involved firstly an attempt to undermine the various members of the clan financially. The theory here, I guess, is that removed from the security of independent means it was felt that they would be more amenable to government pressure, although it didn't really work out quite like that. You can see this first in the trumped up tax assessments of the cess period, where the sheriff charged the Nugent estates in the Barony of Corkery an inflated sum for allegedly refusing to come to the 1577 hosting, causing massive distress as described by Richard of Donore in that year.[21] According to a letter written by William's uncles (Lavallin and James) and Sir Thomas Nugent of Moyrath the effect was that

> "we be undone (as already we are)...If we have deserved cause of misliking (which is a thing we never intended) our bodies are here, in prison, use your punishment that way till you be satisfied, but good my lord let not altogether we be made beggars for we be gent. and not the least of our calling where we dwell. And though not for our own sakes, yet for God's sake let you poor tenants and followers have no less favour than the rest of our neighbours. The wasting of our inheritance (whereof we see great likelihood) ..."[22]

Then after the supposed rebellion in the 1580 period the family were compelled to pay huge fines in some cases to purchase pardons.[23] William's wife describes this:

> "And where it is laid down that she offered a counsellor 500 pounds for her life [in fact she probably had to pay the sum as a fine], she protesteth before

God, she never did neither may your Lordships think that she was able to do, by reason that herself was then a prisoner, her goods (which her husband had sold before to a merchant for payment of debt) being given to one of Lord Grey his men, her poor inheritance seized to her majesty's use for her husband's offence, and she left without anything..."[24]

All the various branches were hit by this like the Baron himself, as he notes in this letter with just a hint of sarcasm:

"my charges more than my small living can maintain, and the same living wasted torn and mangled by such as her majesty sendeth thither to defend her subjects and not to offend them."[25]

This was certainly a deliberate policy on the part of the state (whether its victims fully realised this or not) as you can see from this letter from the Irish administration to London showing the government knew, or at least presumed, that they could exploit this artificially created poverty:

"And likewise to the Lord Justices here for then trapping of William Nugent, wherein for that money will be the aptest mean to finish this work, the rather for the universal poverty of Nugent's kinred and allies in the Pale, there will not want fit and willing instruments to undertake the matter."[26]

This kind of engineered financial pressure is to be seen in this history throughout, even in 1605 Delvin is outlining how he is been cheated of rents from Longford not because of genuine grievances by the O'Farrells but because that family was stirred up by one Sir Francis Shane that he seems to suggest was actually a government agent.[27] It is not surprising to find then that in 1607 Chichester is complaining that he has to pay for the Baron to get to London to see the Council because the Baron is too poor to pay his own way there.[28] Sometimes it seems that the government even reverted to forgery to keep up the pressure e.g. the important Fore properties were denied to the Baron on the basis of a supposed prior lease which it was later discovered was: "lately forged ... manifestly counterfeited."[29]

Another simple practice was jailing people on spurious legal pretexts or sham accusations of involvement in rebellion. You can see this in 1575 when Thomas Nugent was shocked at being thrown in jail on the basis of an obsolete law that claimed he was liable to the debts of a person the state asserted was his servant.[30] A large number of Nugents and their allies were thrown in jail at the time of the cess for no obvious offence with some (like the Baron of Delvin) staying on "for the longer restraint."[31] Richard of Donore was held for two years in the early 1590s without even knowing the charges against him.[32] They also spent time in jail on false allegations of rebellion, which were reinforced by the usual small army of government agents that can always be coerced into giving false testimony in court. Again William's wife Jenet Marward explains it happening to her after she had been arrested:

> "Being then a prisoner...means were sought for finding matter to accuse her of treason and at last John Cusack and one Pers Conegan were found to accused her of treason...But yet neither of her accusers was brought before her, to justify their falsehood for as it is well known what John Cusack is, so the other is but a very base creature, and drawn to accusing of her only for safeguard of his life as himself hath confessed since his breaking out of prison."[33]

Of course these agents are just faced with the normal choice of giving false testimony on behalf of the state or face charges themselves, that this was a very common practice we can see from the evidence of Rory O'Donnell in 1607, who says many people were given this option:

> "Ferighe O'Reille [?Kelly] being condemned to be hanged at Athlone for some crime, by a messenger secretly sent by the Lord Deputy who arrived just as the said Ferigh was to be hanged and offered him his life and large rewards if he would charge the Earl [of Tyrconnell] with treason..."[34]

The judge Nicholas Nugent was of course hanged on this kind of evidence [35] while the Baron of Delvin was constantly in and out of jail on charges like this and you can read as well the interrogation of James (William's uncle) as he hotly refutes such accusations while incarcerated in the Tower of London in 1581.

Then a further tactic was the spreading of slander against the family. They did this to create confusion in their supporters, or potential supporters, who might not have been acquainted with the time honoured government practice of slandering dissidents. They particularly falsely accused people of involvement in the various rebellions and the effect of course was that outside observers, maybe even government officials, couldn't separate out real rebels and falsely accused ones. (This also had the effect of protecting the 'real rebels' which was also no doubt intended.) We can see in the State Papers how government officials could sometimes be quite blunt about what they wanted done on this front e.g. in 1577 the instruction is: "Nicholas Nugent to be discredited as a resister of the cess."[36]

Later in 1580 its clear that the government saw the Baltinglass rebellion as an opportunity to rid themselves of the family by falsely accusing them of involvement. What seems to have happened was that Walsingham and co. started spreading rumours that the Baron was involved in the rebellion using, it appears, people like Fiach MacHugh O'Byrne's wife to spread stories to that effect.[37] The Baron then challenged the government, at a meeting of the greater council in Dublin, to charge him or clear him of these insinuations:

> "The Lord of Delvin we know not how, breaking unto [the meeting], found himself grieved, that he, with others of the nobility was suspected and further that he was advertised from England that it was informed your highness that he was become a rebel, he desired if any man could charge him he might answer and clear himself, or else rest condemned."

Unfortunately he didn't realise that this was a trap, the slander and the meeting were designed as 'bait' to reel him in on false charges.[38] Earlier Walsingham had arranged with the Lord Chancellor that letters ("and those to have devised and that such letters would come") were to be forged which implicated him in the rebellion, then they sprung this on him when he spoke up at the meeting, so they duly arrested him and held him in jail or on bail in England for many years.[39]

A few months after this happened his uncle James had gone to London to plead for the Baron's release only to find himself imprisoned on further slanders coming from elements in Dublin who were sending letters to London complaining about James' supposed "evil practises".[40]

Then when William launched his legal fight in the early 1590s it became almost a race where William was trying to make his obviously genuine charges against the Dillons etc stick while the state was hoping to prosecute him on very similar but in this case false charges. As pointed out this kind of practice is designed to confuse and divide people as well of course as a way of falsely jailing William. Specifically the government alleged that William had aided the secretary of Brian O'Rourke, the recently executed rebel, by giving him the living of the parish of Killiagh near Oldcastle Co. Meath.[41] This was then supposed to implicate William in O'Rourke's rebellion whereas in fact William was trying to show that a powerful government clique (the Dillons, Christopher Browne and the Lord Deputy) were guilty of "animating him [O'Rourke] to move war in the province of Connaught".[42] It transpired that while the same group claimed that O'Rourke's priest was aided by William the priest himself leaked a letter from jail stating that it was none other than the Dillons that had got him that living.[43] When these false allegations were disproved by the priest the next wave of slander was directed at the priest himself. The government claimed that they had an informer in the jail who told them that he had observed the priest plotting to ensnare the Nugents with these allegations about Dillon as a ruse to get out of jail.[44] In fact that priest, Shane McCongawney, was a very heroic figure who refused to go along with any of the slanders against the Baron and William despite being

> "placed 23 foot under the earth and do lose my legs
> by reason of the weight of the irons or fetters which
> I have on me."

It seems he went through all this torture partly because he was a great admirer of the Baron, probably because of his role in defending the Catholic religion:

> "I let you well [know?] that it is for [your, the Bar-

on of Delvin] sakes that I am here without cause other than that it is demanded I should charge you with matter that would be your destruction. And God be praised I have no such to accuse you of. And I tell you further there live not persons whom I do more affect than you though I fare never a whit the better for it now..."

He was even able to warn the Nugents that the government and the Dillons had compelled the Dean of Farranan (I think in 1590) to draw up a forged Latin letter (backdated to 1577) in which they hoped to implicate the whole clan in treasonous activities.[45]

As you can see the state responded to William's initiative by throwing up a blizzard of slander that must have taken some toll on William's support base. All the same when the government drew up a list of people they believed would go witness in court against William all they got was the usual Dillons and Plunketts, Elizabeth Nugent (married to Robert Plunkett of Ballymacad) and amazingly Jenet Marward, William's wife (who's mother was a Plunkett). It is genuinely noticeable how few members of this clannish family the government were able to shake away from allegiance to William and the Baron. The Baron was quite clear as to why these slanders were directed at them, here he is referring to slanders like this which were supposed to implicate him in alleged treasons involving Dr. Creagh:

"But malice is the cause and ground hereof. And why? For that I with others of my sort delivered up certain articles of treason, wherewith Sir Robert Dillon stood charged to his Lordship...and the ungodly practises used to overthrow myself and my poor brother (wherewith you shall be acquainted hereafter) do plainly manifest the same. This one thing we have yet to comfort us, that our vexation and troubles do grow for doing Our Majesty's service, which for his [Lord Deputy's] sake or any man's else living I will never desist from, inform what he list [likes] and as often as he will."[46]

This whole slander tactic continues throughout this period. For example in 1624 the government in Dublin petitioned the Council in England to hold the Earl of Westmeath in London for as long as possible so they could have time to spread around rumours that he had become Protestant and an ally of the state. The King himself got so fed up with these slanders against Westmeath that he demanded that the government in Dublin refute them and punish whoever spread them (which would be the government itself of course). Probably the King was referring to the claim that Westmeath wanted to crown himself king of Ireland which was spread about to discredit him in the eyes of the King, as the writer of the Earl's entry in the new DNB has pointed out.[47]

Sometimes as well the slander took on a more subtle appearance. For example during the court case the Dillons and the government on the one hand tried to spin it that William was launching a kind of legal rebellion, like in this from Sir Robert Dillon 7 Jan 1592:

> "who ["mine adversary I mean William Nugent"]
> hath, and in mine conscience to the uttermost in his
> power, still doth practice the overthrow of this
> state, and also to shadow the trial of his demerit
> against her Majesty"[48]

And on the other hand they tried to spin it that he was only motivated in seeking a kind of blood thirsty revenge for the death of his uncle, by even accusing him of plotting Sir Robert's murder. William had to defend himself from these slanders by pleading with the state to take his charges seriously on their merits, and not assume that he was motivated by some kind of vendetta:

> "that the pretended malice he should bear against
> Sir Robert Dillon may not hinder the proceedings
> by way of justice against him."[49]

Still this wave of slander probably succeeded in putting off from supporting him those people who were unacquainted with these government tactics.

Another way of pressurising the Nugents in this covert war was to go after family members in order to intimidate their principal targets. In 1580, for example, they tried to seize William's infant children in order to intimidate him. Then when they failed to seize his son that way they seized his uncle's son and only released him on condition that he found and delivered up William's infant son. This obviously made life very difficult for William as Elizabeth Hickey points out:

> "To William this was a three pronged ultimatum; Either his wife gave up the child; or his uncle [the judge] was financially ruined [paying the bail money for his son Richard]; or the young man Richard was kept a hostage in the Castle..."[50]

The judge was then tasked by the state to get William's son but he didn't pursue that with the required vigour which led him to face treason charges and his eventual execution. It appears that he looked the other way when William

> "(fearing by likelihood the example of cruelty shown to children in like case) took away the child from the place where he was."[51]

But the Lord Deputy was not to be denied and bluntly told William's wife:

> "but seeing (quote he) we can not lay hands on him we must lay hands on them that be nearest unto him, which are his wife and children".[52]

and with that threw her in jail. Of course this is an ancient tactic and I guess the truth is that William probably expected it and had no choice but to carry on anyway. But the state continued to apply pressure that way even up to the outbreak of the 1641 rebellion. For example in 1619 it was decreed that all the Catholic noblemen in Ireland must hand over their eldest sons and send them to England.[53] The subtext here of course is that the government could always seize the heirs as hostages at any time and this unfortunately is exactly what happened to the Earl of Westmeath in 1641. His grandson and heir was seized and detained at Chester by the parliament to intimidate the Earl who tried to persuade the Earl of Clanricard (a close relative of a parliamentarian general) to work for his release.[54]

Finally we might make note of a further practice of the state, that was kept very quiet, which is the use of poisons and assassins to deal with any troublemakers. No doubt it was much more common than we can make out from the available state papers for obvious reasons. During the height of William's legal war he became violently ill in circumstances that remain obscure but which we may speculate about.[55] His father in law, who was a leading member of the Pale nobility as the Baron of Skyrne, was murdered by a man who is later identified as a government agent.[56]

But despite all this pressure the Nugents remained aloof from most of the rebellions that did occur throughout this period apart from some events (mostly over hyped) in 1580, 1602 and 1607. This I think requires further explanation in the sense that it must be shown why they would not wish to join these revolts if they were being treated so badly by the English government in Ireland.

You first must consider the great faith and pride that the Nugents probably had in the institutions of the state as they existed at this time. They I guess were for a long time simply naive about the way that those institutions and people had been corrupted by elements like Walsingham's intelligence agency. So for example when Christopher wrote his famous declaration of loyalty saying, as pointed out above: "that mine ancestors...have always from the conquest been servitors to the Crown of England" he no doubt felt it would stir the good lords of England to rally to his defence while instead what happened was that Walsingham wrote on the back of the letter: "Delvin's lands good to plant English men on."[57] A clear statement of his intent to undermine the Baron to confiscate his lands and a typically cynical riposte to all this talk of feudal loyalties.

So much for the ancient rights of appeal to the monarch, another field that the Nugents probably had faith in was the law courts. Hence when the Baron of Delvin returned to Ireland c.1586 he quietly tried to reclaim his lands by bringing ejectment orders in the Court of Chancery in Dublin against those who had stolen his lands in his absence, as he explained to Burghley in 1591:

> "Every term I am in Dublin, following the law to
> recover certain lands taken from me during my late
> unfortunate troubles."[58]

He had to take a huge number of these cases over many years and you can see here the unspoken faith in the justice system, as opposed to taking any hot headed arbitrary action which no doubt some must have recommended to him. After all this legal system had evolved in Norman Meath over the centuries during which the Nugents had played quite a leading role in Pale politics, so like everything else about the Pale it was their system of justice, they were proud of it and trusted it. Even in Meath to this day the courts are administered under the shadow of Hugh de Lacy's great castle at Trim, an ancestor of this family. This was also a period when the legal system, and the law as laid down by parliament, became a powerful yardstick for people's moral judgements, it was rising as religion was declining as a factor, in England at any rate. For example Carte, referring to the period up to 1640, refers to

> "...that time, when everything was sacred, and swallowed implicitly, which bore the name of Parliament."[59]

This kind of sentiment is echoed by Thomas Nugent, William's uncle, when he petitioned the Lord Deputy, confident that he would get justice:

> "good my lord be not offended that I do seek the benefit of the law for your honour are bound to maintain it, as I a free subject inheritable to have it, and without it I know not how I may live."

But maybe the problem with this law-as-a-religion type concept was that it only served to place people into the pockets of the corrupt politicians who were making and administering the laws in Ireland at this time. Unsurprisingly the reality was that the government, unknown to Christopher, was even prepared to stoop to forgery to deny Delvin any justice in those courts.[60]

Then you have the ancient practices of organising a petition to the monarch to try get relief from the arbitrary actions of the English governor which was what the Baron – and his uncle the judge – had tried to do particularly at the time of the cess.[61] There again the meetings that were organised were actively disrupted by people bought off before hand by Walsingham who had secretly advised the Lord Chancellor before these meetings to "make choice of fit persons to deal underhand with" to haywork it "by good persuasion" with those people before the meeting.[62] But the Baron probably didn't know this as you can see from the account left to us by his cousin the Baron of Howth who laments the disruptions caused at the meeting without ever suspecting the hand of Walsingham's intelligence agency orchestrating it.[63]

So you can see that it took some time for the Baron to realise the extent of corruption that was around him, he probably just underestimated the power and ruthlessness of the clique that had quietly undermined those institutions that he trusted so much.

The second thing to remember on this score is that this family had probably built up a lot of inside information on the wider European political scene and possibly that information caused them to be very cautious and wary in their dealings with countries like Spain and the Vatican. You see the conundrum here is that they knew that the native forces in any rebellion would inevitably be overrun by the English army unless they could get help from the powerful Catholic countries of Europe but my guess is that people like William, who had many dealings with these powers, found them too cynical to be trusted in saving the Catholic Irish. For example according to his statement of 1584 [64] he found that Spain and the Vatican followed a policy laid down by the Duke of Guise who seemed to be part of a spiders web pulling strings across Europe. Guise had this power presumably because he was the head of a semi secret body at that time called the Holy League. So far that is mostly predictable but William's references to the way that the Scottish court seemed to be part of this same spiders web is very interesting. Because what is not said there is that at the same time as the Scottish court cooperated with England's enemies that country was basically under the control of powerful figures in England. The then King of Scotland, James VI, had a pension from Elizabeth for example.[65] Some time before 1584 Mary Queen of Scots obviously had to flee Scotland because of a revolt "secretly instigated by Elizabeth's Ministers."[66] This was after James himself had been kidnapped by Scottish nobles who were also acting secretly on behalf of the English government.[67] In fact Queen Elizabeth's intelligence agency had such powerful, yet secret, control over this small neighbouring country that they could manipulate it to carry the blame for some measures that the English government wanted taken. For instance about 1583 the English government was able to counter international pressure to release Mary Queen of Scots by pointing out that the Scottish government didn't seem to want her back. The Scottish government had come to that conclusion only because:

> "at present when her [Elizabeth's] creatures had acquired possession of the government [of Scotland], she was resolved to throw the odium of refusal [to allow back Mary] upon them."[68]

So she got her ambassador to Scotland to open public negotiations to bring back Mary while secretly getting her agents who controlled that government to reject the request. Handy thing being able to manipulate a whole country like this! As noted this occurred around 1583 which is just around the time that William is dealing with Scotland. This control over Scotland is also in evidence in 1588 when it is said that "most of his [James'] ministers and favourites were her pensioners."[69] The powerful Master of Grey that William mentions has a very interesting history in this context as well. In 1586/7 he was sent to England to plead for the life of Mary but secretly he is reported to have urged Elizabeth to kill her. Which shows I think that who he was really working for might be a more complicated question than first appears.[70] As you can see there is a powerful amount of cynicism in Elizabeth's foreign policy. Just like in modern times it was important to keep the ordinary people misled about her real intentions, as you can see from the measures she took before deciding to execute Mary:

> "...but even in this final resolution she could not proceed without displaying a new scene of duplicity and artifice. In order to alarm the vulgar, rumours were previously dispersed that the Spanish fleet was arrived at Milford Haven; that the Scots had made an irruption into England...that there was a new conspiracy on foot to assassinate the Queen" etc.

To clarify then the point about Scotland is that if these English power brokers had such a hold over Scotland then how could that country be so much a part of the Spanish and French conspiracies against England? Maybe there are wheels within wheels here.[71] Somehow these international alliances seem possibly to include people in England itself. Remember there is a lot of Spanish gold floating around here and it is even rumoured that Sir Robert Cecil (Burghley's son) was receiving bribes from the Spanish government.[72] Anyway its very difficult to figure out these international machinations at this remove but I think it is likely that a more knowledgeable William and the later members of this family must have been reluctant and too suspicious to get intertwined in these international intrigues.

This suspicion of ulterior motives on the part of potential allies also extended to the people that were involved on the ground in rebellions in Ireland. Remarkably William in his court case had shown that many of the rebellions that had occurred in Ireland prior to 1590 had been aided and abetted by a powerful faction in the Irish administration which in turn was allied to powerful people in England like the intelligence agency chief, Walsingham, and Sir Henry Wallop. He found that Sir Robert and many other Dillons, using Christopher Browne as a go between, had encouraged Brian O'Rourke to rebel. William also proved that the same group were behind other rebels like Teigh Keigh O'Kelly and Brian Mac Ferale Oge.[73] Of course informed opinion on that score had always been floating around, like this later reference from the 1640s:

> "I have seen some minutes of the Council Board [equivalent to Irish Cabinet minutes], where Sir C Coote, when Sir Luke Fitzgerald misdemeaned himself before the Board by uncivil words to a member of it, let him have the line(?) and would not reprehend him, in hopes that he would go into rebellion, for he saw he would do so, and said the more that were in rebellion, the better."[74]

The English government had various hidden motives in fostering some of these rebellions like for example in getting a pretext to send in troops to confiscate Irish held land. Another reason is that elements in the English army in Ireland probably needed the excuse of continuous rebellions to justify being paid as a standing professional army, at least this seems to be what William's brother Christopher felt when he complained of:

> "The privy plot between the Captains, which consisteth at times of discharge in moving of war by

thrusting out such of the Irish as otherwise would
be content to live quiet; for no longer war no
longer pay."[75]

But I think the fact that William accused Sir Robert Dillon of
wanting to destroy the aristocracy shows that he felt that this alliance between the state and the rebels was part of a deeper and
more comprehensive plan to make England and Ireland a kind of
Venetian style republic. In one of the charges he makes against
Dillon he says:

"Sir Robert Dillon said it were good for Ireland
that there was never a nobleman in it and no harm
for England if there were none there either."[76]

We can really only guess what all this means, presumably the
thinking of people like Walsingham and the Dillons was that rul-
ing Ireland and England would be easier without any of these independent minded nobles to interfere in the conduct of government policy. In any case you can see that with this legacy of
secret state backing for rebels, the Nugents were that bit warier in
dealing with the various revolts in Ireland from 1590-1641. Imagine their suspicion of Hugh O'Neill for example, a person well
known as being a particularly loyal agent of the English government for most of his career. He was also allied to the Dillons by
e.g. furnishing a statement in support of Sir Robert Dillon during
the court case which denied that he had got permission from
Dillon before he had executed Hugh Gavelagh.[77] He had earlier
'captured' and handed over John Cusack, the government agent
who's false testimony had convicted Nicholas Nugent, a piece of
service that the Nugents were not likely to be grateful for.[78] So
you can easily see their misgivings as they survey the scene in
Ireland at the time of the 9 years war.

The 1641 rebellion was another one of these mysterious and
suspicious rebellions, where we can see now that the decision of
the Earl of Westmeath not to participate in it initially, was based
on a deeper understanding of the dark forces assisting that rebellion than I think most people now realise. For example the
Capuchin, and senior adviser to the Papal Nuncio to Ireland, Fr.
Richard O'Ferrall remarked about the originators of the rebellion:

"By using both the Prefects of Ireland [The joint

acting viceroys, The Lord Justices Parsons and Borlace, "two cruel and pitiless Knights"[79]] and the King's Ministers, who were then Puritans, the Parliamentarians were the invitors and instigators of the Catholics into this orchestrated [80] war in Ireland."[81]

The Parliamentarians of course were supposedly the great opponents of the Irish rebels and undermined the King accusing him of being 'soft' on these rebels and sympathetic to the Catholics. After the rebellion they flooded the media at the time with lurid accounts of it which later was used to justify Cromwell's revenge on the Irish, while all along it looks now that they were secretly the ones behind the rebellion, and anyway they were themselves in revolt against the King and most people agree had also secretly backed the Scots revolt.

The circumstances of the rising are therefore maybe a bit more complicated than is normally supposed, and some incidents, like this one, related in the Aphorismical Discovery about the state giving out arms to the rebels, are possibly worth a second glance:

"and those that received the said arms from the state as aforesaid, were the very first that showed themselves against the state pursuant to the former oath."[82]

That oath of course was the one they took to rebel and seize Dublin Castle etc. When you consider that the same author had earlier stated that the Earl of Ormond, the then head of the British Army in Ireland, also took that oath, and was a willing participant in the conspiracies, then you can see that the state must have known they were giving arms directly to those who were rebelling rather than to those who wanted to hold aloof.[83] This is particularly true of Westmeath where the Earl of Westmeath was denied any arms or protection but people like Robert Nugent of Carlinstown, the most prominent Old English figure at the subsequent siege by the rebels of Drogheda, were given arms by the state.[84] I think, and many Irish thought so at the time,[85] that the state wanted the rebellion to spread and to succeed because of various reasons including international considerations (e.g. the rebellion put paid to any idea of Stafford's army going to Spain which suited Cardinal Richelieu's France) and to provide a pretext to send in a Parliamentarian (or a Scottish) army to clear the Catholics off the good land and confiscate their estates. Which is obviously what eventually happened and apparently one of the Lord Justices was bragging that they had just such an intention in the months before the rebellion:

> "and that the said William Parsons...[et alios]...did declare...that Ireland could never do well without a rebellion, to the end the remain of the natives thereof might be extirpated."[86]

Then in December 1641, after the rebellion took place, the Lord Justices wrote back to London gloating over the "defection" of the Pale gentry to the rebellion:

> "their discovering of themselves now will render advantage to his Majesty and this state...those great counties of Leinster, Ulster and the Pale now lie more open to his free dispersal and to a general settlement of peace and religion by introducing of English."[87]

The Earl of Westmeath must have known of these undercurrents at the time and you can see more clearly, I hope, why he decided not to support the rebellion initially.[88]

Hence the motivation and pressures on this family at this time were a lot more complicated than is sometimes obvious when reading the history of the period.

Note that where just a date is listed (e.g. 'see under 1667') that refers to an entry under that date in Appendix E.

1. See under 1667. Incidentally I appreciate that the prominent role that the Earl of Westmeath and Christopher had throughout this period is not much in evidence when reading most history books of that era but it does come across when you read the state papers etc. As Richard Nugent, the transcriber of many of these state papers and uncle of the World War I General, himself said about Christopher: "There is in fact hardly any career in Irish history more interesting or more checkered, or so little known."(Lady Rosa Mulholland Gilbert, *Life of Sir John T. Gilbert* (London, 1905), p.292.) One modern scholar concedes though that:
"In terms of time spent in prison the Nugents were easily the most politically active family in the Pale." (Fionnán Tuite, *Familial feud in early modern Meath,* an article in Robert Armstrong and Tadhg O' hAnnracáin ed., *Community in Early Modern Ireland* (Dublin, 2006), p.77.)

2. Printed in J T Gilbert's, *Facsimiles National Manuscripts of Ireland* (London,1882), IV.

3. *Supplementum Alithinologiae* p.87 and 185 quoted and translated by Charles O'Conor *Historical Address* p.148 transcribed at PRONI D/3835/A/2/1.

4. Examination of Walter Cusack. PRONI D/3835/A/5/61 Walter and Robert are brothers of the leading Catholic cleric Christopher Cusack.

5. See under 1582.

6. Basil Iske [Elizabeth Hickey], *The Green Cockatrice* (Dublin, 1978), p.12 and p.90.

7. See under 1599.

8. The original Irish and the English translation is given in Robert O'Connell's, *History or Annals of the Irish Mission of the Capuchins, up to the year 1655(?),* authenticated 26 Sept. 1654 Ms Bibliotheque Municipale Troyes MS 706 liber 10 p.562 NLI M/F Pos 803. We know it is by a Nugent because of this reference in a letter by the great historian Charles O'Conor of Belnagare:
"One of his Lordship's [Robert Nugent of Carlinstown] ancestors lamented the public misfortune in a fine Irish couplet. Between these parties, said he, we the Nugents, are sufferers by both. We resemble an apple tossed on the sea surges. But this apple braved the waves and no storm could sink it [referring to Robert]." O'Conor letters Vol. II p.275.
From the transcript copy, in the Capuchin Archives Dublin, of Fr O'Connell's work you get the original Irish of the poem, and his translation of that into Lat-

in (the English given in the main text is from a translation added into the Troyes manuscript by a later hand):

Anglorum numero ascribit nos priscus Hibernus,
Et nostros Angli depopulantur agros.
Scilicet in terris quamvis sit portio nostra
Parva; sumus pomo, quod fugat unda, pares.

9. p.725 of *Monasticon Hibernicon* by Archdall, and *Historie Monastique d'Irlande* (Paris, 1690) p.213 transcribed at PRONI D/3835/A/2/1,40.

10. Notes on Meath church history by Fr. John Brady transcribed by Michael Conlon (whom I'd like to thank) p.C iii 591 p.227. See also an article by Terence O'Donnell, *Andrew and Catherine Nugent,* in the Franciscan College Annual.

11. From the above notes C ii 566 p.227 quoting Patrick Lynch, *The Life of St.Patrick* (Dublin, 1810), p.302 we get this list of the anchorites, starting from William's time: Patrick Beglin, Rev. Patrick Clonan, Rev. Mr. John Nugent, Rev. Charles Fagan, and in 1719 Rev. Mr George Fleming who died a few years later and was the last. Fleming was said to have died in 1741 (Isaac Butler, *Itinerary of Journey through the Counties Dublin, Meath and Louth.",* (1744) Armagh Public Library.)

12. He was executed on 1 Feb 1612 as witnessed by the Earl of Westmeath who no doubt took possession of his body in order to preserve the relics. (George Birkhead, *Newsletters from the Archpresbyterate of George Birkhead* (Cambridge, 1999), p.146.) They showed them off to the Pope's representative during the Confederate wars. (Monsignor Dionysius Massari, *My Irish Campaign* (Dublin, 1917), Catholic Bulletin no.7 p.114.) For the Bishop of Meath see the earlier references to Thomas Dease the poet, and then later in the same century they protected Thomas' nephew Oliver Dease who was the Vicar General of the Diocese. As regards the Bishop of Kilmore (Kilmore diocese obviously covers Co.Cavan etc):
"The Bishop [Richard Brady, Bishop of Kilmore] is most secretly harboured by the Nugents, especially by the Baron [of Delvin] himself." (C.S.P.I. 13 May 1591 Dublin Fitzwilliam etc to Chancellor Hatton and Burghley)
As regards the Counter Reformation orders:
Capuchins
Including the aforementioned Fr Lavallin Nugent of course, who founded the Irish Capuchin Province (a very important figure, at one time he was even offered the job of Archbishop of Armagh), and Fr Luke Nugent, the superior of one of their houses in France in the 1640s, and Fr Francis Nugent, a brother of Sir Thomas Nugent and relative of both the 2nd Earl of Westmeath and his wife the Countess, who was, along with his brother, central to the creation of an alliance between Owen Roe O'Neill and the Old English prior to Cromwell's entry to Ireland. There was also Fr Lawrence Nugent, a very prominent

Capuchin who was in Ireland in 1617, and Fr Anthony Nugent, who I think founded the Capuchin monastery in Drogheda, and Fr Peter Nugent, a nephew – via his father – of the widow and leading Catholic Catherine Nugent, who founded their monastery at Mullingar. Actually the then serving Earl of Westmeath renounced his titles and wealth and became a Capuchin towards the end of the 17th century. This gives you something like almost a third of the prominent Capuchins of the Irish Counter Reformation being members of this family. (Fr Robert O'Connell O.F.M.(Cap.), *Historia Missionis Hibernicae Capuccinorum* (Charleville, 1654), original Troyes Ms 706, this from a transcript in the Capuchin Archives Dublin passim.)

Jesuits
Surely the most important Irish Jesuit of the Counter Reformation was the aforementioned Fr Robert Nugent ("he was regarded within and outside the Jesuit Mission as one of the most prudent and inspiring spiritual directors of his time") until his death in Inishbofin in 1652, and his brother Nicholas who, as pointed out earlier, was jailed from 1616-1619, during which he was visited by the Lord Deputy and his wife ("both of whom tried to shake his constancy"), was the superior in Galway for a time in 1641 and died in Opporto in 1656. There was also Fr Gerard Nugent, of the Bracklyn family, who was born in Meath in 1615 and was a priest in Wexford in 1645, PP in Maynooth in 1672, mentioned in the context of the Titus Oates plots and died in 1692. Also Fr Dominic Nugent of Dysart (1641-1725) ("an expert linguist who spoke fluent Irish, English, Flemish, German and French; he also composed and set to music a collection of German songs" (Jeremiah Sheehan, *Worthies of Westmeath*, (Moate, 1987), p.87)), lecturer in the Irish College in Poitiers 1671-1678 and later PP of Dysart and Churchtown in Co.Westmeath. Lesser known Nugent Jesuits include: Fr Christopher Nugent who was born in Ireland in 1603 and who served in Seville until his death in 1627; Fr John Nugent who died in Evora in 1632; and another Fr Nicholas Nugent who was born in Kildare in 1629 and who started a religious dispute in Wexford in 1671 for which he was jailed in trying circumstances.
(From the typescript obituaries of the Jesuits in the possession of the Jesuit Archives in Dublin.)

13. For Lynch see under 1667. Old traditions about their defence of the Catholic religion actually lingered in the North Midlands area for much longer than you might imagine. In the 1930s it was noted that "it was one of the Nugents that rang the first Catholic bell after Emancipation" in recognition of their role. (Folklore Library UCD Vol 720, p.43 Faughalstown school) It should be pointed out though that Lynch is partly motivated to defend the Nugents because Robert Nugent SJ had been accused by the Capuchin O'Ferrall of betraying Rinucinni, and it is O'Ferrall's pamphlet that he is trying to refute. But I think he is sincere in his assessment of the 'patriotism and catholicity' of the Nugents which he describes over many pages.
Some further notes showing the family's great interest in protecting the Cathol-

ic faith – which of course some now feel was the backdrop to many of Shakespeare's plays:

When the Baron of Delvin, the eldest son of the Earl, died in 1626 his funeral was almost only attended by other Nugents because the other families were afraid of attending the explicitly Catholic service. (Brendan Scott, *Religion and Reformation in the Tudor Diocese of Meath* (Dublin, 2006), p.136.)

Three members of a jury panel refused to punish those Catholics who didn't attend Protestant service and so were prosecuted before the Court of Star Chamber in Dublin in 1614. When pressed by the judges in Longford "11 of the Jury confessed that they were agreed to make presentment according to the evidence, but the said William Farrell, Lysaugh O'Ferrall and Edmond Nugent wilfully and obstinately refused to join in the same, and being examined by his Majesty's Sergeant at Laws, by order of this Court, the reasons why they refused to join with their fellow Jurors, as also questioned withal by this Court [the Star Chamber] upon hearing the Cause, could make no other answer [or] excuse but that it was against their conscience, and the said Edmond Nugent further said that what he did was well done.
Whereupon the court proceeding to censure it was ordered, adjudged and decreed by this honourable court that the said William O'Ferrall, and Lysaugh O'Ferrall shall pay to his Majesty for a fine each of them the sum of £20 a piece, and imprisonment during the Lord Deputies pleasure.
And the said Edmond Nugent for his contemptuous and insolent speeches in the face of the court shall pay to his Majesty for a fine the sum of £40 and committed close prisoner during the Lord Deputy's pleasure. Dated at his Majesties Court of Castle Chamber the 16th of November 1614 and in the 12th year of his Majesties reign in England, France, Ireland and Scotland" (Jon G. Crawford, *A Star Chamber Court in Ireland* (Dublin, 2005), p.519-520.)

"Probably the most blatant example" of a religious house that defied the suppression of the monasteries was Multyfarnham. The surveyors "declared in 1540 that no one wished to purchase the chattels of Multyfarnham, but undoubtedly that was because the protecting hand of the Lord of Delvin lay upon them, and because Sir Thomas Cusack, who watched over crown interests in this area, was not prepared to antagonise him." (Brendan Bradshaw, *The Dissolution of the Religious Orders in Ireland under Henry VIII* (Cambridge, 1974), p.141.)
The Queen herself wrote an indignant letter to Bishop Jones in Dublin in 1600 demanding that they take action against Multyfarnham (Brendan Scott, *Religion and Reformation in the Tudor Diocese of Meath* (Dublin, 2006), p.109.) That probably provoked the raid on Multyfarnham that was intercepted by the Nugents who fought a battle against the government troops and rescued the friars. Its mentioned in the Alithinologia book infra Appendix E under 1667.

An account by the Spanish Ambassador of a meeting between the Irish Catholic leaders and the King in 1614:

"Then the Archbishop of Canterbury spoke to them with such severity that the Baron of Delvin...could not endure it and, going on his knees, he interrupted the Archbishop's discourse..." saying basically that "since being a Catholic was considered such a treacherous crime" that he would prefer to go abroad and give up all his estates than to be classified as a traitor at home in such circumstances (Micheline Kerney Walsh, *Destruction by Peace* (Armagh, 1986), p.334). At the same time Sir Christopher Nugent described to the King the "fraudulent nature of the passage of the anti-Papist laws in Ireland" (Patrick F. Moran ed., *The Analecta of David Rothe, Bishop of Ossory* (Dublin, 1884), p.265).

The "Principal Disturbers of" the Parliament of 1613, when the Catholics put up some strong opposition, even replacing the speaker etc, lists 17 names of which 3 are Nugents:

The Baron of Delvin – 'turbulent'

Gerald Nugent – "Busy and one of the preferers of the first slanderous petition"

Sir Christopher Nugent – "Another ringleader and a countenance of the first disobedience; a procurer of others to disturb the Parliament by false informations."

(Calendar of Carew MSS 1613 p.275).

The latter was "Sir Christopher Nugent, a lawyer and an obstinate recusant" (James Willis, *Lives of Illustrious and Distinguished Irishmen* (Dublin, 1840), p.335 quoting Carte's *Ormond.*), a brother of the first Earl, and William's nephew, he was educated at Cambridge, later lived at Corbetstown, and helped the Franciscans to survive at Multyfarnham where he is buried. (Fr Brady in *Irish Book Lover* vol.XXIX March 1945, p.90-91 quoted in Fr Terence O'Donnell OFM, *Franciscan Abbey of Multyfarnham* (Multyfarnham, 1951), Appendix V.)

14. 'Dorcha an Lísi ar Loch Éirne', transcribed by Pádraig Ó Fágáin, *Éigse na hIarmhí* (Baile Átha Cliadh, 1985), p.77.

15. Christopher was so much out on a limb in his defence of the Catholic religion that one of the charges against him put before Burghley was that "all the noblemen of this country do go to [the Established, Anglican] church, I [meaning Delvin, he is here writing back to Burghley refuting the charges] only excepted."(Lord Delvin to Lord Burghley Clonin 13 Sept 1592 PRONI D/3835/A/5/64.)

16. See under 1641.

17. F.X. Martin, *Friar Nugent* (London, 1962), p.145.

18. Sir George Carew (edited by Standish O'Grady), *Pacata Hibernica* (1896), Vol I.

19. See under 1590.

20. See under 1592.

21. See under 1577 also other letters PRONI D/3835/A/4/62-61.

22. 6 July 1577 PRONI D/3835/A/4/63.

23. For example Lavallin Nugent and Edward Nugent "gentlemen of ancient living paid Mr Fenton for their pardons 400 pounds" (prob 1582 PRONI D/3835/A/5/25.

24. prob June 1583 PRONI D/3835/A/5/29. The above reference showed that on some grounds she had to pay 500 pounds.

25. Delvin to Burghley 29 Oct 1583 PRONI D/3835/A/5/30.

26. G. Fenton to Lord Burghley 21 Jan 1583/4 ibid.

27. He said that Sir Francis Shane was the son of one Nicholas Shane some-time smith of Ardrath, the obvious implication being that nobody could rise in status like this without state backing: 20 Sept1605 PRONI D/3835/A/6/392.

28. 4 June 1608 PRONI D/3835/A/4/559.

29. Robert Legge to Lord Burghley 27 Jan 1586/7 PRONI D/3835/A/5/44.

30. See 1575 .

31. Privy Council to Lord Deputy from Greenwich 18 July 1577 PRONI D/3835/A/4/60.

32. 22nd Dec 1591 his petition to the English Privy Council PRONI D/3835/A/6/422.

33. See 1582.

34. See 1607.

35. See the DNB under Nicholas Nugent.

36. CSPI p.296 6 April 1581 where I think it is Adam Loftus looking for credit for his earlier efforts at slandering the judge.

37. Lord Chancellor to Walsingham 27 Nov. 1580? PRONI D/3835/A/4/215.

38. The historian Richard Nugent in his papers in the PRONI (D/3835/A) details countless examples of these kind of charges been laid against Christopher which he thinks, after his exhaustive research, were pretty much all lies. There are too many examples to detail here. During the nine years war Christopher even alleges that some of the O'Neill's spread false stories that he had gone over to O'Neill in order to discredit him in the eyes of the state. I think there is no reason to disbelieve him about this and you can appreciate his frustration in constantly having to fight against charges that he supported O'Neill while the rest of the time actually fighting O'Neill! He got fed up with this at one point: "yet the devices and idle plots of every runaway fellow of them [the rebels] will be heard with greater attention than mine whose whole study is with the hazard of my life...wherefore I could wish that actions were preferred in her Majesty's service before the brabblings of such as never yield any other fruit." (Delvin 27 Jan 1599 PRONI D/3835/A/5/116.)

39. See under those years in Appendix E for these references.

40. "For he left no good practises behind him" State Papers PRO 63/86/14.i. and CSPI p.323 6 Oct 1581 has 'evil practises'. He clearly refutes all that successfully during his interrogation.

41. PRONI D/3835/A/59 5 Feb 1591/2.

42. Quoting questions that the Barons Delvin and Howth wanted to ask of Sir Robert Dillon prob. Oct 1592 PRONI D/3835/A/5/75. In a letter endorsed on the 21 Oct 1592, the same writers had written to London complaining that Dillon "wrote to O'Rourke wishing him to move war upon the parts of Sir Richard Bingham's government, undertaking that the same should not be ill taken by the Lord Deputy nor the State."(PRONI D/3835/A/6/399)

43. Specifically Alexander Plunkett of Moat near Oldcastle, an ally of the Dillons, turns up on both fronts in the sense that he accuses William of planting the priest in Killiagh (12 Dec 1592 PRONI D/3835/A/5/82) while the priest said that it was Alexander who got him the position. The government had threatened the priest to try to get him to go along with these false allegations and slanders but he refused (PRONI D/3835/A/5/75).

44. PRONI D/3835/A/5/68.

45. See the Calendar under 1592 for these references from the priest. See also under 1577 for the Parma letter which implicates nearly all the various Nugent families of Westmeath as you can see from the letter attached to it which is under 1590.

46. The list of potential witnesses is from 7 Feb 1592/3 PRONI D/3835/A/5/84

, the quote from the Baron is from C.S.P.I. p.576 13 Sept. 1592.

47. See under 1624 in the Calendar.

48. PRONI D/3835/A/5/59.

49. The reference to the supposed murder plot: Cockatrice op.cit. p.101. Unlike Mrs Hickey I don't believe that there is any truth to the allegation conveniently timed to discredit him. The quotation is from C.S.P.I. p.428 William Nugent to the Privy Council 24 Oct 1591.

50. ibid p.60.

51. The quote is from Jenet's petition and for the account of the judge's actions see the report on his trial, both references are listed under 1582.

52. ibid.

53. Archiv. Hibern. Vol VI 1917 p.51.

54. *Memoirs of Clanricard* as printed in the 18th cent. c.p.80.

55. Cockatrice op.cit. p.153.

56. John Cusack, see the trial report under 1582.

57. See under 1580 and also Cockatrice op.cit. p.12.

58. Cockatrice op.cit. p.98.

59. Thomas Carte, *Life of Ormond* (Oxford, 1851), Vol I p.217.

60. As pointed out above, see under 1587 for the forgery reference. The court cases he took can be seen in the Catalogue of Chancery Pleadings in the National Archives. The Thomas Nugent quote can be seen at 1575.

61. See under 1578 for a description of the Baron's (and his uncle the Judge's) central role in the Cess petition.

62. See under 1577.

63. The Baron of Howth's account is in the Book of Howth.

64. Under that date in the appendix.

65. David Hume, *The History of England* (Edinburgh, 1839), p.45.

66. ibid p.36.

67. ibid p.35.

68. ibid p.37.

69. ibid p.70.

70. ibid p.55.

71. I was going to add in something here but forgot to. Now I have forgotten what I was going to say in it. Drat...lol

72. John Maclean edit., *Letters of Sir Robert Cecil to Sir George Carew* (Westminister, Camden Society, 1864), p.68.

73. See under 1592 in the appendix. Notice the connection to Wallop and a connection with Sidney is evident under 1583. The overall pattern of alliances becomes apparent as you read the State Papers. In general, and taking the whole period into account (say 1570-1620), although of course there are shifting alliances, nonetheless it goes something like the Nugents allied to: the Barons of Howth – Viscount Gormanston – John Cusack of Troubly – Patrick Bermingham of Corballies – sometimes Maguire and O'Donnell – Turlough Luineach O'Neill – Sir Richard Bingham – Sir John Perrot – Nicholas White Master of the Rolls – Burghley – and until his death in 1583 the Earl of Sussex. Then on the other side you get: nearly all the Dillons – Hugh O'Neill – Sir Henry Wallop – Walsingham – Sir Robert Cecil, Burghley's son – Adam Loftus Archbishop of Dublin and Lord Chancellor – Black Tom Earl of Ormond – Mountjoy – Christopher Browne – Alexander Plunkett of Moate near Oldcastle Co. Meath.

74. Nicholas Plunkett of Donsoghly, *A Treatise or Account of the War and Rebellion in Ireland since the year MDCXLI* (written early 18th cent.), NLI Ms.345 p.251.

75. 'Articles for reformation of certain abuses in Ireland' by the Baron of Delvin 26 May 1584 PRONI D/3835/A/3/14 (see John Gilbert *Account of Facsimiles of the National Manuscripts of Ireland* (London, 1882), Vol IV c. p.xxxiv).

76. Under 1591. And under 1582 you can see this statement from John Nugent of Skurlockstown: "The Baron [Dillon] whom they [the lords of the Pale especially Westmeath] knew to be so far from favouring the noblemen as [they] themselves in common phrase usually term him the canker of nobility."

77. Cockatrice op.cit. p.104.

78. ibid p.61. Even the Annals of Loch Cé under 1582 recognised that Cusack was lying: "Nicholas [Nugent], son of Christopher, son of the Baron, was put to death in Muilenn-cerr, and Nicholas Cusack was put to death along with him; and it was John Cusack that made the false charge on which all the good heirs of the Foreigners were put to death before that."
(http://www.ucc.ie/celt/published/T100010B/index.html)

79. As described in the Gaelic diary of Fr. Toirdhealbhach O'Meallain. (William Nolan and Henry A. Jefferies ed., *Tyrone History & Society* (Dublin, 2000), p.366.)

80. Literally "going to be hastened war..."

81. Richard O'Ferrall OFM (Cap.) and Robert O'Connell OFM (Cap.), *Commentarius Rinuccinianus* (Dublin, Irish Manuscripts Commission, 1932-49), Vol.V reprints O'Ferrall's 1658 report to the Cardinals in Rome from which: "Et ab Iberniae Praefectis et Ministris Regiis nunc Puritanis, Parlamentarii ad accelerandum bellum in Iberniae Catholicos fuerint invitati et instigati."

82. John Gilbert, *A Contemporary History of Affairs in Ireland from 1641-1652* (Dublin, 1879-80), Vol I p.12. The Lord Justices admitted in a letter back to the King that they gave out arms for 1,700 men and only got back enough for 950..."so as those whose loyalty, we had reason to expect would help us, are now through their disloyalty, turned against us, and are strengthened by our own arms."(14 Dec 1641 NLI MS.2542 p.63 Letters of the Irish Council to the King.) Bellings also remarks that this is what happened with the arms the state gave out (John Gilbert ed., *History of the Irish Confederation and the War in Ireland, 1641-1643* (Dublin, 1882-91), Vol V p.38).

83. As pointed out he is named by the author of the Aphorismical Discovery as one of the conspirators (John Gilbert, *A Contemporary History of Affairs in Ireland from 1641-1652* (Dublin, 1879-80), Vol I p.12.), also he is stated to be an ally of Sir Phelim's and the rest of the conspirators in this book published at the time: *The Petition and Declaration of Sir Phelim O'Neill*, printed for W.Neal 1641.

Furthermore the significance of this deposition is that most of the big Pale lords were by this stage out of favour and the only significant figure left, who could be everyday whispering in the ear of the Lord Justices, is Ormond:
"And this deponent further saith, that on December 19th, 1641, he, the deponent, heard Sir Phelemy [O'Neill] in his own house say, that if the Lords and gentlemen (meaning Popish) of the other provinces, then not in arms, would not rise but leave him in the lurch for all, he would produce his own warrant signed with their hands, and written in their own blood, that should bring them

to the gallows, and that they sat every day at council board, and whispered the Lord Justices in the ear, who were as deep in that business as himself." (The Deposition of Dr Robert Maxwell, rector of Tinane, in the county of Armagh in M. Hickson edit., *Ireland in the 17th century* (London, 1884), Vol I p.326-335.)

This also tallies in with the statements of the Earl of Antrim which implicate the Earl of Ormond in these conspiracies during the summer of 1641, for which see his deposition (G Hill, *An Historical Account of the MacDonnells of Antrim* (Belfast, 1873), Appendix XIV p.448-451.), an article on him by Jane Ohylmeyer (*The 'Antrim Plot' of 1641 – A Myth?*, History Journal 35,4 (1992) p.905-919), and the statements of Thomas Trant, Timothy Miller, George Stockdale, Anthony Enos, Willington, as well as a letter of his wife's dated 11 March 1641 which mention a meeting between Rory O'More and Antrim, all of which implicate Antrim as involved with the rebellion (this letter and these statements from Geraldine Tallon ed., *Court of Claims, Submissions and Evidence 1663* (Dublin, 2006), p.396-401.)

He even drew suspicion from the Parliamentary party in Dublin as you can see from this pamphlet published at the time:
"The first thing that I propounded to clear to you is the great trust and confidence the Rebels from the beginning reposed in him [Ormond]. To make good which, though there be many more than probabilities to entice a reasonable man to believe he was acquainted with the first design and plot of the Rebellion, and there be some (that when time serves) can tell what advice and counsel he gave for the execution of it; having resolved with myself to bring nothing before you but what carries the light of the sun along with it: I shall as pregnant as proof can be desired." He goes on to describe how Ormond deliberately allowed the rebellion to spread and wasted the strength of the army which could otherwise oppose it. (p.19-32) The pamphlet is then mysteriously cut short in an unfinished state. (Adam Meredith ["one of Sir Robert Meredith's sons"] *Ormond's Curtain Drawn* (London, 1646), p.19 Thomason Tracts E513(14). The authorship quote is from the Earl of Anglesey and I don't think it is by Sir John Temple because he is mentioned in it in the third person.)

Even Henry Jones admits that the rebels had always understood that Ormond was one of their number and they were shocked to realise that he was now on the other side. (Dr. Henry Jones, *A Remonstrance* (London, 1642), p.31.) He was probably operating as an agent provocateur encouraging the Irish to rebel, claiming the King wanted it, while doing the Parliamentarian's bidding in spreading the revolt. He wasn't the only one at it either as you can read in this deposition from Hugh O'Connor of 11 Feb 1642/3:
"Who being sworn and examined about Christmas 1641 he this Examinant, with others of the gentry of the County of Roscommon, were persuaded and prevailed with to join in the present rebellion by Hugh Oge O'Connor and certain others employed (as they said) by Sir Lucas Dillon for that purpose. Affirming unto him this Examinant and the rest of the gentry of the County afore-

said that Sir Lucas Dillon well knew it to be the King's pleasure that the said gentry should take up arms, for that the Puritan Parliament of England would otherwise destroy them. And with all further alleged that they should within one quarter of a year see his majesty himself and the said Parliament in arms, the one against the other. Yet afterwards the said Sir Luke repaired unto the Lord President of Connaught and professing his fidelity obtained his lordship's protection, under colour whereof he the said Sir Luke played on both hands" (Depositions Roscommon TCD MIC 830 p.9).

84. For Robert see John Lodge, *Peerage of Ireland* as updated by Mervyn Archdall (Dublin, 1789), Vol III p.322.

85. Since this account of 1641 is not the usual one given I thought I would quote some contemporary sources to back up this version of events.

First up is Dr. George Leyburn, a leading English Catholic and friend of the Queen's, who was sent by her to try and persuade Ormond not to hand over Dublin to the Parliamentarians in 1647. He was also in jail in 1644 with General Monck, which could have been a fruitful source of gossip on the origins of the rebellion, which he relates here:
"And now to say something of the Supreme Council, or the Confederate Catholics, I must draw a little higher towards the spring that so the reader may the better judge the whole. The predominant faction in the English parliament, knowing no so likely Impediment to the designs they had in hand, as that which might proceed from the Catholic party, which though not very great in England, in respect of their numbers, yet was numerous in Ireland, the 100th Irish man not being a Protestant, and abominating all of that religion, had no so good way to affright the King from making use of that assistance, as by all means they could possible, to thrust the Irish into rebellion, and then to accuse the King, the Queen being a Catholic, as the author of it; from whence divers things would follow.
1st, that they should, with the help of their Scottish friends, have a good occasion to destroy and extirpate that people, possessing themselves and their party of their lands; as also [extirpating] the Catholic religion in the three nations."
Leyburn is pointing out how they would use this to scare the King into doing what they asked and encouraging him to distance himself from the Irish Catholic party which would otherwise be of great assistance to him. Notice too that the King probably did contemplate some kind of revolt against the Parliament, which then morphed into the Irish rebellion, so this means that the Parliament probably had serious blackmail information on him which would 'prove' his involvement in the Irish uprising. The blackmail is then obviously used against him:
"Secondly, the King having this principle infused into him, that nothing was so necessary to his safety, as the clearing himself and the Queen from that Imputation [of the accusation that the Parliament spread of his involvement in the rebellion], would be so far from seeking assistance that way, as he should not

dare to refuse join with them, in such Acts of Parliament as they should propose to him, for the better perfecting those designs; provided the pretence were the repressing or punishing of that rebellion, by which it would come to pass that they would levy what forces, or raised what monies they pleased, which afterwards they might convert to what uses they thought fit.

And all this, as things were disposed, was no hard matter to compass: For the Irish had not enjoyed such a pleasant bondage under the English, but that they had contracted ill-will enough against their masters, besides which, other things contributed."[i]

Probably the most highly regarded Irish Catholic historian of that time is Fr John Lynch who lived through the whole rebellion and its aftermath in Ireland, and writes in *Cambrensis Eversus*:

"Those foreigners [the New English] spared no dignity or injury to goad the natives into rebellion, that there might be for themselves a rich harvest of confiscation...Chichester is said to have concocted a rebellion of this kind, and it is certain that before the commencement of the late war in Ireland, Vincent Gockings, a baronet and Englishman, wrote to the Lords Justices, ...[with a proposition in which he noted that] if the Irish were thus goaded into rebellion, their properties, he said, could be confiscated, the King would acquire many estates, and a wider field for the establishment of fortresses. About the commencement of the late war, the government of Ireland was vested in a duumvirate, William Parsons and John Borlace, who could easily have suppressed the rising flame in its infancy, but they deliberately fanned it into a fury, that the estates of many of the nobles might be forfeited to the crown...[Meaning the Lord Justices' as entrusted with the care of Ireland by the King:] Not dogs or shepherds were placed over the flock...to defend, but wolves to devour them.

The following is the substance of a passage in a work styled *The History of the Independents*. In the beginning of the Parliament of 1640, the Independents, that is the schismatics, publicly demanded that the Irish Papists should be extirpated, and their lands conferred on the conquerors: the enactment that was made to that effect compelled the Irish Papists to massacre the English protestants. The design of the Independents was to make the Papists and the Protestants waste their strength by mutual massacre, and thus facilitate the overthrow of Protestantism in England."

The Independents represent a group of disparate Protestant sects, initially allied to the Presbyterians in overthrowing the King, and opposed to the Anglicans. Oliver Cromwell was a leader of the Independents, he who is back in Ireland these days! Notice the cynicism implied here, the implication is Cromwell must have known that his own group had fostered the rebellion that he made such a big deal out of revenging. Incidentally this bit by Lynch was quoted by the authors of the *Commentarius Rinuccinianus*[ii] and they note approvingly that "the former [Lynch] was an eyewitness to a great part of the things acted out in Ireland at that time." This I think shows that the above account from the Independents book was also their view of what happened in 1641. Lynch continues:

"They also prevented an army of 3,000 men, which had been collected by Stafford, from going over to serve in Spain, though they had no other means of support, and had been expressly promised by his Majesty to the Marquis of Valada and Malvez, the Spanish ambassadors. These soldiers, thus disbanded and left without resource, were the first authors of the troubles. The Independents who perpetrated these acts were the real authors of the Irish rebellion, and must answer for the blood of more than 10,000 Protestants slain in the war. Moreover they forced the King to drive the Irish to despair by giving his assent to their [meaning the Parliamentarians] bill, which confiscated all their property, and handed it over to those who would venture money for the payment of the troops deployed for the conquest of Ireland...

The origin, then, of the tempest of war in Ireland, is traced with certainty to its true authors...there can be no question that the Irish war was not commenced by the Irish, but by the English."[iii]

Nicholas Plunkett (1629-1716/18) of Donsoghly Co. Dublin was a prolific author on Irish history of the 17th century, he wrote the highly regarded *Light to the Blind*, *Jacobite Narrative of the War in Ireland* [iv] and numerous other works.[v] Although very young at the time he participated in the wars of Ireland at this period e.g.:

(a) he worked with the Duke of Ormond, had knowledge of his ciphers, and went back secretly into England on his behalf in the 1650s;[vi]

(b) he fought at that battle in Wexford where Antrim's Scots under Glengarry were defeated, before that battle he was a mediator between the two sides and saved the life of Glengarry.[vii]

(c) he also had important family relations which must have helped him build up a picture of what happened in 1641, including his granduncle Colonel Richard Plunkett who was one of the main figures involved in the early plotting,[viii] and his more distant relative the famous Sir Nicholas Plunkett of the Fingal family who he certainly knew because he witnessed a deed for him in 1670 [ix] and he apparently incorporated some of Sir Nicholas' papers in his own account of 1641.[x]

So we are very privileged to hear his thoughts on what really happened in 1641:

"The rest [of the rebels] were brought in gradation [to join the rebellion] necessitated on one side by the preposterous and designed severity of the Lord Justices, and wheedled in on the other by the persuasions of the Irish clergy of Ulster."[xi]

"But the [English] Parliament foresaw this [the transporting of Stafford's Irish army to Spain] would hinder the Irish in their designed rebellion in Ulster and reprimanded this motion of the King and allowed none after disbanding to go out of the Kingdom."[xii]

"The bloody massacre of Ulster, a massacre they [the Parliamentarians] might have prevented [but] they rather designed it by their provocations managed by their wicked engineers [the Lord Justices] in Ireland and were well content to sacrifice so many of their own brethren to facilitate their own design on King and loyalist."[xiii]

"Here now was Clotworthy's practises amongst other things plainly denoted...who joined with the black policies of those days to blow up the Ulster men into those horrid flames of a bloody revenge and having so blown them up into worse than Bachanals they removed all obstacles (particularly Stafford) that might suppress the flames from devouring those undistingushed multitudes that stood in their way."[xiv]

"I must without partiality suspect him [Owen Connolly who had been, and Plunkett suspects still was, a servant to Sir John Clotworthy] to be all along in the nest with O'Neill and Maguire, a spy to the Presbyterian junto [the English parliament] and a decoy to wheedle in the rebels to the preparation of that most abominable and fatal cruelty and revenge [the rebellion and the supposed massacres] which that Junto for their own wicked interest and the King's ruin permitted to take hold."[xv]

Another leading figure at this time was Dr Nicholas French the Bishop of Ferns who wrote about the early days of the rebellion:
"But the plot of those crooked ministers of state was to involve all the Catholics in the business and thereby to find a colour of confiscating their estates."[xvi]

Even the Earl of Clanricard, the later viceroy, had this to say about the Lord Justices a few months after the rebellion broke out: "And since the distempers began they (Lord Justices) had so disposed of affairs, as if the design was laid to put the whole kingdom into rebellion."[xvii]

This is by Peter Walsh, a close friend of Ormond's (and hence any specific role by Ormond in these events he will gloss over) who was in the thick of all the religious controversies during these years, writing in 1660:
"the Lord Justices (who, by their words and actions, not only expressed their unwillingness to stop the further growth of those distempers, but meant to increase them, and were often heard to wish that the number were greater of such as became criminal)...[referring to the early days of the rebellion:] So as thus far we may observe, who they were that widened the wound, instead of staunching the blood...[after the rebels had taken Drogheda:] Now it was that the times began to favour the design of the Lords Justices and party in the Council, which was as forward as they, to foment the distractions."[xviii]

This is the opinion of an English MP in 1680, and one of the leading historians of the time, Dr. John Nalson, who says that in addition to merely negligent administrators: "so there were others in Power, who were so taken up with the contemplation of forfeitures, that they rather increased the fuel, than took care to suppress the flame."[xix]

We now defer to the views of Hugh Reilly, the Cavan barrister that was appointed Chancellor of Ireland in the exiled court of James II in 1693:
"The Lord Justices, and most of the Council, were not a little pleased at this re-

volution [the rebellion], and swallowing already in hope the estates of all the Catholics in the kingdom, which they had long gaped after, did now resolve to leave no stone unturned, fully to compass that design...[They issued proclamations against the rebels but] this was only for show, or as the saying is a copy of their countenance, for their true intention was to involve the inhabitants of the other provinces also in the same crime, so as to bring them under the lash of the law and therefore they took no care to suppress the Northern insurrection, [so] that the contagion might spread and infect the whole kingdom."[xx]

Footnotes

i. George Leyburn, *The Memoirs of George Leyburn* (Edinburgh, Clarendon Historical Society, 1886), p.13.

ii. Fr. Richard O'Ferrall and Fr. Robert O'Connell, *Commentarius Rinuccinianus* (Dublin, Irish Manuscripts Commission, 1932-49), Vol.I p.250.

iii. Original in Latin (1662, St.Omer) this from Matthew Kelly ed., *Cambrensis Eversus* (Dublin, 1848-52), p.255 in Orig and in translation p.77, p.88, and p.89.

iv. Which you can read here: http://www.ucc.ie/celt/online/E703001-001.html .

v. See Eamonn O Ciardha – whom I'd like to thank – , *Ireland and the Jacobite Cause 1685-1766, A fatal attachment* (Dublin, 2002), p.35,93,105,107,138,156.

vi. NLI MS.5065.

vii. J.T. Gilbert ed., *History of the Irish Confederation and the War in Ireland, 1641-1643* (Dublin, 1882-91), Vol III p.115. He has to be the mediator mentioned earlier by Bellings because that would be the only way that he could have known Glengarry before the battle.

viii. See the history of the Plunketts in John Lodge *Peerage of Ireland* as updated by Mervyn Archdall (Dublin, 1789).

ix. Analecta Hibernica no.20 p.155.

x. HMC Rep.Vol II 1871 Appendix p.189.

xi. Near the beginning of NLI MS 346.

xii. ibid p.147.

xiii. ibid p.595.

xiv. ibid p.596.

xv. ibid p.861.

xvi. Dr. Nicholas French, *The Bleeding Iphigenia* (originally Louvain, 1679), republished with the rest of his works as *The Historical Works of Dr French* (Dublin, 1829), Vol I p.45.

xvii. Fol.63 letter of 23rd Jan 1641/2 quoted in Dr John Curry, *A brief account of the most authentic Protestant writers of the Causes, Motives and Mischiefs of the Irish Rebellion* (London, 1747), p.55.

xviii. From his 1660 pamphlet a *Brief Narrative...* which was reprinted by Dr John Curry in *A brief account of the most authentic Protestant writers of the Causes, Motives and Mischiefs of the Irish Rebellion* (London, 1747), p.77.

xix. John Nalson, *An Impartial Collection of the Great Affairs of State* (London, 1683), Vol. II p.629.

xx. Hugh Reilly, *Ireland's Case Briefly Stated* (first published 1695 this edition London, 1768), p.15. Also known as *The Impartial History of Ireland*.

86. John Gilbert ed., *History of the Irish Confederation and the War in Ireland, 1641-1643* (Dublin, 1882-91), Vol II p.230 no.6 in a statement from the Confederation of Kilkenny 1642/3.

87. Harold Christopher O'Sullivan, *Land ownership changes in Louth in the 17th century* (TCD thesis Oct 1991), quoting Robert Dunlop *Ireland under the Commonwealth* (Manchester, 1919), Vol I p.cxix-cxxi.

88. You can see his opposition to the rebellion described by Fr Patrick Hackett O.P. in his 'Aphorismical Discovery', who attributes it to the influence of Bishop Dease, under 1641. A lot of people in Catholic Ireland were looking at him to see what he would do at this time, like Thomas Carew who writes about his renewing political troubles in his old age:
"Richard Nugent Earl of [West]meath, by the recollection of all men, was a most worthy person on account of the glorious acts he had carried out, after which, in his old age facing death, he had gratified the thresholds of St. Peter and St. Paul of the Apostles and kissed warmly the feet of Popes, and finally coming back into Ireland he could have rested with a happy end" instead of getting involved once more in politics. (Thomas Carve, *Lyra sive* incorporating *Annales Hiberniae 1148-1666* (Salzburg, 1666), under 1640 p.325.)

APPENDIX E

Calendar of Original Documents 1575-1664

The spelling and punctuation are in some cases modernised, otherwise these are the original words. Dates are unchanged from that written on the original document consulted, only placed in the Jan.-Dec. year.

1575

Thomas Nugent to the Lord Deputy July 25 1575 PRONI D/3835/A/4/80 and A/3/5 p.103, from Bodleian Carte Papers Transcripts PRO Vol LV p.167

I believe this is William's uncle who is outlining how he was suddenly arrested on ludicrous charges relating to debts incurred by a person accused of being his servant. (Which debts a master is liable to according to an obsolete law of 33 Henry VI). He quotes in the original Latin Isodorus, St.Gregory, Salomon, the Magna Carta cap29, and Bracton 'one of the ancient fathers of the law.' He notes that the Lord Deputy dislikes him and writes of "the goodwill you bear to him that (as I conjecture) looketh to have the same [money] to his own use...

I did neither mean nor promise [at the earlier court proceedings], and if I had made such promise [to pay the debt] (as indeed I did not) your honour do see that it is not due upon me, and thereupon the law saith 'quod ex nudo pacto non ontur accio...

...good my lord be not offended that I do seek the benefit of the law for your honour are bound to maintain it, as I a free subject inheritable to have it, and without it I know not how I may live..."

1576

Individual and particular report of the character and biases of the several judges etc in Ireland c. June 1576 PRONI D/3835/A/5/492
"The first [Sir Lucas Dillon] esteemed but of small learning wilfully affected in his friends causes without truth or equity and not without corruption

The second [Nicholas Nugent] great allied also, of modest disposition, rather more slow to further the Queen's cause than the other. I have not heard him tainted with corruption."

[So as you can see from the way events transpired, the state felt it was in their interests to employ corrupt pliable judges rather than more steadfast honest ones.]

1577

Richard Nugent at Donore to Sir Thomas Nugent now in jail June 20 1577 PRONI D/3835/A/4/61-62

"Cousin Thomas, I have no news to lighten your mind and give you consolation in your imprisonment but that Captain Collier by virtue of my Lord Deputy's commission, or rather the sheriff in his name, hath robbed our poor country in taking up and levying those fines to Captain Collier that were forgiven, at my Lord Deputy's suit and request, especially all your poor tenants are made very poor, for in every town of yours they took a prey of garrons, or sheep or kyne, for no kind of cattle could escape them. Also their kerne were cessed for the most part upon your land. It was a rueful sight to see when they took all the garrons they could catch and their distresses, how they were constrained to sell their little kine for half their value, some others to mortgage their pots and pans and little household stuff, for they said if they had not presently redeemed their distress they were never like to ransom them in good cause again. Out of the 20 acres they paid a noble sterling and the wastelands they were fain to pay. I have no more to say, but that the poor inhabitants do so sorrowfully complain, as they would never know what to do, for live they can in no sort with what they might they have paid and ransomed their pledges for the most part. Let my Lord of Delvin, cousin, understand what is done, the sheriff hath been too extreme in executing his authority, and no marvel for he had a share with the captain and so had the cessor also. As for the things I spake with you etc...Your cousin Richard Nugent."

[Thomas was in jail along with James and Lavallin Nugent, three of William's uncles.]

Walsingham to the Lord Deputy 2 Nov 1577 PRONI D/3835/A/4/55

Advising him that before he meets the opponents of the cess he might like to "make choice of fit persons to deal underhand with" to fix it "by good persuasion" with those people beforehand.

1578

Lord Deputy to the Privy Council 18 Feb 1577/8 PRONI D/3835/A/4/51-52

Describing the meeting about the cess where he imprisoned a lot of the ringleaders.

"The Baron of Delvin, who at that time and ever since in effect hath been the Speaker for the rest, seeking by cantelous and subtle evasions to colour his speeches, would in conclusion come to no direct position. [Because they were waiting for an answer back from agents they had sent to England]...Relying (as it should seem) wholly in respect of nobility to the Baron of Delvin and in respect of learning to [judge] Nugent the second Baron."

1580

An endorsement of a letter, of the Baron of Delvin's to the Chancellor, by Walsingham 5 Aug 1580 PRONI D/3835/A/4/212

"Delvin's lands good to plant English men on. "

Lord Chancellor to Walsingham 27th Nov 1580 PRONI D/3835/A/4/215

Discussing how they were going to prepare a meeting of the nobility as a trap to bait the Baron of Delvin. What they intended to do apparently was to spread rumours to the effect that Delvin was implicated in the Baltinglass revolt then Delvin was expected to object at that meeting and there they would spring forged evidence against him. They referred to letters "and those to have devised and that such letters would come."

Lord Deputy to Queen Elizabeth 22 Dec 1580 PRONI D/3835/A/2/5 p.175

"Delvin surely hath been the carrier of the Earl [of Kildare] into this mischief, whose obstinate affection to Popery hath now approved him unsafe to himself, unsound to friend, disloyal to prince, and false to God such is the yield of such seed, which would to God were not so plenty in this land."

From the Irish Council 23 Dec 1580 PRONI D/3835/A/4/216
At the assembly of the nobility: "the Lord of Delvin we know not how, breaking unto, found himself grieved, that he, with others of the nobility was suspected and further that he was advertised from England that it was informed your highness that he was become a rebel, he desired if any man could charge him he might answer and clear himself, or else rest condemned." They in fact did arrest him with the consent of even the Earl of Kildare. Then they discussed evidence against the Earl and arrested him as well!

1581
Nicholas White [Master of the Rolls, writing to his good friend:] Lord Burghley 22 April 1581 PRONI D/3835/A/5/5
"...who [judge Nugent] I assure your honour is (to my knowledge) a dutiful man to her Majesty and well known here to be both learned sober and wise."

Interrogatories administered to James FitzChristopher Nugent in the Tower of London replied to on 30 Dec 1581 PRONI D/3835/A/5/9-10
"1) Imprimis did you ever receive any letter from James FitzMaurice after his last entry into rebellion, or from any other rebel touching your aid to be given to them.

He sayeth that he never received any letters from James FitzMaurice after his last entry into that realm, nor ever knew him, or had anything to do with him, or any other rebel nor was ever required to give any assistance to any of them.

2) Item how many such letters have you received from whom, when, where, and by whom.

To the 2nd he answereth as before.

3) Item what were the contents of any those letters as near as you may remember, and what is become of them.

To the 3rd he answereth as before.

4) Item whether did ever answer any of those letters and how ye answered the same.

To the 4th he answereth as before.

5) Item about what time and how long since is it that William Nugent brother to the Baron of Delvin entered into actual rebellion against her Majesty and what moved him so to do.

He saith that about 4 days before Christmas was 12 month the Baron of Delvin was committed to Dublin Castle and thereupon Brian FitzWilliam and Thomas LeStrange, sheriff, were sent to search his house. Whereupon William Nugent the morrow after came to the farthest part of the country and sent for this examinant and divers other gentlemen and told them of the said Baron's commitment and search of his home; and also that the country was to be run over by soldiers. Whereto this examinant answered that he thought it was not so and told him that before, in the time of Sir William FitzWilliam's, the Earl of Kildare the Lord Louth, the Baron and the said William Nugent were committed and after delivered and so might they be now; hereupon the examinant returned to his house. Viz about 1 or 2 days after, Nicholas Nugent brother to this examinant and one of the Judges in that realm fearing stir in the country came thither as he thinketh of himself; and sent for this examinant who both going to Sir Thomas Nugent's lands adjoining to O'Reilly's country persuaded the said William to go to Dublin but he would not because he had been committed before. After this came Baron Dillon accompanied with Sir William Russell and Brian FitzWilliams who assured the gent[ry] of the country that there was no such meaning. William Nugent was then in the country and had gathered certain men for his guard and came not unto them. Upon the return of Nicholas Nugent to Dublin making report of the state of the country he was sent back on Christmas day as he thinketh with a letter from the Lord Deputy to Baron Dillon to return with the army to Dublin and the said Nicholas to remain in the country and to send this examinant and William Tuite to the Lord Deputy; who having been before his Lordship were sent back with haste, and commanded to will the army to return to his Lordship as they did. And so this examinant remained in the country which remained indifferent quiet save that William Nugent stood upon his own guard having assembled about 100 persons, who as yet did no other harm but take their meat and drink upon the country and borders adjoining. Thus remained things from Christmas until about middle Lent; then the devil tempted him and joined himself with the sons of Mageoghegan that had murdered their own brother and some of the O'Connors that were rebels. The Lord Deputy hearing of this combination sent for the Baron of Delvin charging him with his brother's fact, who in the Council chamber wrote a letter unto his brother which was delivered unto him by William Tuite, being willed to send for rest of the gent of the country to join with him to persuade William to give over his enterprise. Whereupon this examinant, Thomas Nugent and William Tuite met with the said William at Ballaknock beside a water, he being a great deal stronger. There was the Baron's letter delivered unto him and they used the best persuasions they could to reclaim him and he took leisure until Monday following to answer the letter, their meeting being on the Saturday, which answer he sent to Mullingar unto them on Monday next and what it was may appear by the letter which was returned to Dublin to the Baron by the said Tuite, and is now here to be seen in the custody of Lady Delvin. On Wednesday following Sir Edward Moore came into the country accompanied with John Plunkett and Thomas Fleming and other gent on horseback and 2 bands of footmen. Whereupon the said William fled out of the country and went into the north unto the Irish where he remained until about a fortnight before Michaelmas at which time he came privily into the country and so went to the O'Connors and was there at the time of this examinant's departure out of Ireland. And more he cannot say to the 5th interrogatory.

6) Item whether were you in his company at such time as he broke out into that rebellion and how long did you and Oliver Nugent continue in company with him after he was entered into that

rebellion and upon what occasion and to what end.

He saith that sith [since] the committing of the Baron of Delvin he never was in the company of William Nugent otherwise than he hath declared before. And for his brother Oliver he knoweth not whether he were in his company or no, he never heard of it and thinketh not.

7) Item how often hath the said William Nugent been in your company, or relieved by you and at what places since he so entered into rebellion and what conferences have in this meantime passed between you.

He can say no more than he hath done already; he never had any conference with him other than is before declared, nor sent him or gave him any relief sith the committing of the Baron of Delvin and a good time before.

8) Item whether was the said William Nugent in your company at Clonin the Baron of Delvin's house, within 3 or 4 days after he was entered into rebellion. If ye, then who was with him, and what conferences had he with any and with whom and what was the cause ye had not then stayed or apprehended him.

He saith that sith the Baron of Delvin committing he never was at Clonin, the Baron of Delvin's house, in the company of William Nugent and therefore could have no conference with him nor apprehend him.

9) Item whether was the said William Nugent at Clonin aforesaid upon Christmas Eve, was [sic] 12th month, if ye, who was then in his company, how long stayed he there, to what end and what conferences had ye then with him.

He sayeth that he hath heard that William Nugent was upon Christmas Eve was 12 month at Clonin the Baron of Delvin's house; he heard that he supped there that night and dined next day and so departed. What the cause of his coming this examinant knoweth not unless to have meat being otherwise not appointed and what conference he had with any he knoweth not. This examinant was then at his own house, recovering of a disease which he had and could not come thither, yea the Baron having made great preparation for that Christmas and having invited this examinant he had answered that he could not come.

10) Item whether Nicholas Cusack of Drakestown did show you any Bill wherein was contained that the said Nicholas should be accused of treason. If ye, then where and when did he so [sic] and what conferences had you together at that time, and what did ye thereupon.

He sayeth he never saw Nicholas Cusack sith harvest was 12 month, at such time as Lord of Delvin, the Chief Baron and Sir Nicholas Malby parled with O'Rourke in the borders of his country. And this examinant saith that the said Cusack never showed him any such Bill as is mentioned in the interrogatory; nor he never knew of any such matter before he heard it here in England.

11) Item what was the cause of your coming into England and at what time and where did you take your passage out of Ireland, and what stay have you left in your country in this mean time.

He saith that the lands which he holdeth he had from his brother the Baron of Delvin's father upon condition to serve him and his heirs in their honest affairs; and that being sent for by the Lady of Delvin to her house of Kiltomb he enquired whether there was any suit made for the Baron's deliverance or no; whereto she answered no. And so upon conference what were fittest to be done for him she said that she would go over into England; so as [meaning 'if'] this examinant would go with her; for that he knew the Lord Chamberlain and others of the Council that had been deputies in Ireland. And so the said Lady repairing to Dublin procured a passport wherein the name of this examinant was mentioned as Mr Secretary hath shown. He took shipping with the Lady at Dublin where he arrived the very same day of her departure. Country he hath none, nor great lands. The care of that which he hath he committed to his wife, his brothers Oliver and Nicholas and William Tuite his brother in law and other his friends and kinsfolks. And this did he by making a will and no other means of conveyance.

12) Item whether did you tell John Shurlock or any other that any of the Cusacks, and which of them, were accused to the Council [. Did] there fare any matter and for what matter and when did ye so and when and by who, and where understood ye thereof. [sic].

He sayeth that he never knew any such man as John Shurlock nor before his being ever heard [sic] of any accusation of Cusack and therefore could not tell it to Shurlock or any other.

13) Item, when and by whom and upon what occasion did you first know of the late conspiracy practised by John Cusack of Ellistonreid and others.

He saith that until his being in England he never knew or heard of any conspiracy practised or intended by John Cusack; and heard it first by report of a servant of Justice Dillon's which [sic] came over. To his remembrance his name was John, his surname he knoweth not.

14) Item about what time was it that the Council in Ireland sent to Clonin aforsesaid for the apprehension of William Nugent.

He saith that he knoweth of no sending to Clonin but that night that the Baron of Delvin was committed as he hath declared in his answer to the 5th interrogatory. The Baron was as he remembreth and hath heard committed on Wednesday before Christmas and that night his house was searched by Brian FitzWilliams and the sheriff. The Saturday after he hath heard that William Nugent was there, as he hath declared before but whether they had any commission to take him or no he knoweth not.

15) Item what messenger was then sent from the Baron of Delvin to give knowledge to William Nugent that he should be apprehen-

ded.

He knoweth not of any messenger sent from the Baron of Delvin to his brother William to tell him that he should be apprehended.

16) Item whether was the same William Nugent with you at the same time in the house of Clonin aforesaid and what moved you to be a mean to shift the same William from apprehension and how did ye the same.

He sayeth as he hath done before that sith the committing of my Lord of Delvin he never was at Clonin in the company of William Nugent, nor ever saw him or spake with him otherwise than as he hath declared in his answer to the 5th and other interrogatories before. Nor ever shifted him away, or kept him from apprehension; nor spake to him, nor sent unto him to go away. And whether this examinant was then in the house of Clonin, Brian FitzWiliams, the sheriff and others that were sent to apprehend the said William Nugent can best tell whether they saw him there or no. All this which he hath answered he protesteth to be most true, and that he will justify the same."

1582
Statement of John Nugent [of Skurlockstown] [1] at Dublin Castle 5 Feb 1581/2 PRONI D/3835/A/5/14
"A plain discourse as well of William Nugent's rebellious acts as also of the search made for his younger son Christopher and also of his wife Gennett Marward's behaviour during the time of the rebellion, wherein Ellen Plunkett, wife to Nicholas Nugent is touched, made and declared by John Nugent hereafter particularly ensueth [meaning the account is given in detail below]. At the Castle of Dublin the 5 of February 1581.

First upon the apprehension of the Lord of Delvin, the said William Nugent being then in the Clonin, hearing say that Captain Bryan Fitzwilliams and Mr [le] Strange then sheriff was come thither to apprehend him, he made an escape and took his said wife with him to a Castle that lyeth in Lough Shilline in the Brenny [a pronunciation of Briefne, an old name for Co. Cavan],

180

which he purposed to defend against the Prince's [sic] power and had victuals sent to him thither by Edward Delahide my Lord of Delvin's steward out of the Clonin and from the neighbourhood thereunto near adjoining. Whose names I do not perfectly know by reason that I do dwell afar off; which Edward and another of the household servants of the Clonin called Pierse O'Connoghan are fled and gone out of the country for the said cause.

His wife being as he thought laid up safely he sent to his base brother Edmond Nugent who then was a horseman, and soon after he sold his horse and caused Christopher Nugent, Robert Bán Nugent, and his own brother Edmond to sell their horses which he gave them and to become kerne. And they, and two of the Fays viz. Robert and Edmond, Cahill McGillespie O'Reilly and the rest of Sleight hee accompanied the said William wherever he went.

It was spoken and bruted throughout the country, that the said Captain [Fitzwilliam] would have left a ward [meaning a government guard or garrison] in the Clonin and the said William assembled his people and was lurking about the Clonin, aforesaid, a long while to prevent him [the garrison commander, from coming out presumably.] And Richard Nugent of Donore was of the company, and as many men as he could make.

About the time of Sir Lucas Dillon Knt etc and Nicholas Nugent then Justice went in commission into the county of Westmeath to appease the war, the said William Nugent was a common procurer of all the Nugents in general to rebellion, except Thomas Nugent of Carlinstown [Co.Westmeath] and Lavallin Nugent of Drumcree that would not be led by him, until by the good exhortation of the said Sir Lucas and Nicholas they were bridled and stayed.

Until Sir Edward Moore coming into the country, the said William Nugent and his company were wont to lie at a wood called Killmemekartagh, sometimes at the Bollyroo, and Lavallin Nugent of Drumcree his wood of the Dirre, where they had great fires in the night and victuals were sent to them by the victualers of Castletown [Delvin] viz Thomas Bane, Teig O'Balwy, Edmond Browne and William Fernane.

At which time the O'Connors viz Patrick's sons, viz Teig and Brien and Lisagh O'Connors sons, Brian Mageoghan, and his

181

brother Conlo, his cousin Calvagh Mageoghan appointed Clone-faddy in Ferrebille as a meeting place for William Nugent to come unto them. And there they combined together and it was concluded between them that William Nugent, Brian Mageoghan, Sir Nicholas Eustace, and a few more should go into the North; Edmond Nugent and his company to go to O'Rourke his country [Leitrim]; and the O'Connors to remain about the great moore [bog of Allen?], of purpose to the end that they might draw the Irish lords to come and disturb the English Pale, where they remained a long time.

The said William Nugent procured his base brother Edmond Nugent to come before him into the country and to make suit for a protection. Unto the end that he might have liberty to come into the country, so as he might be a procurer of the country people to go with him. At which time Edmond Nugent, son to Gerrot Nugent, and as many men as he could make, was persuaded to go with him. And when seeing that they had heard of his coming from the North, to send to the O'Connors and they all to meet upon the great moore.

During which time John Cusack, now prisoner, wrought with the gentlemen and heirs of the Pale, that they might be furtherers of the holy cause now in hand, as they termed it. And his manner was to take a Corporal Oath of each one that made him [the initiate] promise that they would do, and be led by William Nugent, their general in what so enterprise he would take in hand. And because I was new required to be of the number of him that wrought the conspiracy against the Prince, I do not know what they pretended to do, but what I heard by the common brute of others. And therefore I refer to the said John Cusack, who knowest most of all men hereof.

When it was mentioned that my Lord Deputy would go into the North, the said William Nugent came up from thence because he stood in doubt of O'Neill, and he dispersed his people and went but a few in company. Whereof Patrick Cusack and another John Cusack were two that went with him in his company, and the rest were dispersed as follows viz [:] Cahir Reddy O'Reilly, who supplied Cahill McGillese owine [?] was always succoured in Fertullagh; Edmond Nugent, Moriertagh McLysagh and Christopher Nugent remained in the country and took meat and drink violently wheresoever they came.

It was my unfortunate chance, that as I had occasion to go to the town of Coileadogherane I went through the town of Mapestown and there it fortuned that I met Piers Boy Nugent of the same, who told me that William Nugent and Edmond McGilletane Harper lay in his barne, and he would gladly have spoken with me. To whom I made answer that I durst not go to him, and he said that I should not need to fear, by whose persuasion I went in. And amongst all other communication the said William said, that he was little beholden to his uncles and kinsmen,[2] which gave him nothing and he driven to travel into far countries, and that it should not be long so.

"And," said he, "is it possible, that you should shift 20 or 40 Baulavase [? square feet?] of rough canvas to make me a tent to lye in the night?"

"No, indeed," said I, "it is not possible for me to get so much canvass, but that it should be known, by me [meaning he couldn't procure it quietly or anonymously], but I have a caliver [a gun] and a flask which Captain Cruise gave me, and I will bring it you at night, and a small bottle to carry some acqua vita about you."

And according to promise I brought the calliver and the rest the night following.

I being in company with the said William and Edmund in the barn aforesaid, that fortuned it a little before supper John Cusack came in, being before in the English Pale. And the said William rejoiced greatly at his coming, and as he began to tell news of the Pale they stood both a little beside, and they had long communication together. And what they said I know not but John Cusack spake of Monday, and said William: "say not so, keep that to yourself", and by all likelihood it was some meeting day that was between the conspirators.

When supper was done, we went all four to a little grove of wood that lieth upon the land of Mapestown and there we lay until it was towards day. At which place and time the said John Cusack began to tell the said William that his wife was somewhat crazed, and that his uncle Nicholas, and his mother [in law] Ellen were coming upon the morrow after into the country to find out his son Christopher. And told him that the said Nicholas was bound to bring him in by a day [sic], for to submit his body to the castle. [Presumably Cusack is claiming that Nicholas, William's uncle and his wife's step father, has a day to get the child or the government will throw him back in prison.]

Whereunto the said William answered that it was less force that he should remain there awhile than that he [the Lord Deputy?] should have three pledges from him; signifying my Lord of Delvin his brother, his wife and his child.

"What," said John Cusack "well [3] ye seem to be so unkind to your uncle, that ye will suffer him lying in prison for a child, and cannot tell how long he will live."

"No, do not so," said John Cusack, "for it is the mother of the child's pleasure that the child be sent in in hope to get herself set at liberty. For I saw a letter written with her own hand of that effect, wrote her mother to the child's foster father and have you not seen it as yet?"

"No indeed," said William, "I saw it not, and if I had seen it it shall not be able to persuade me to put in the child. But in this sort: that [if] I can get my wife enlarged, and at my own will, I will be contented to send in any of both of my sons, and not otherwise."

Which argument was misliked of by the said Cusack and me.[4]

At the break of the day we removed from that place to another place called Ballyroo, and John Cusack said, "I promised to meet Ellen Plunkett [Nicholas' wife and the child's grandmother] today at Killowa, and if you will I will bring her to some convenient place where you may have speak together."

"I will be glad thereof," said William, there they concluded to meet at Richard Crosse's house in Castleton [Delvin, I presume]. And thither they came both upon the said Cusack's draught [horse] the night following, and what company they had, or how they did behave themselves, I do not know by reason that I was not present. And I refer that to Walter Porter now prisoner, who was then present. But it fortuned after that I met the said Crosse who told me that it was through the night that my mistress Ellen Plunkett came to his house, and that he was constrained to flee from the same.

"How happened it?" said I.

"It happened," said he, "that she would needs go to the great Castle,[5] and thither came William Nugent and Tadee Nolane in his company and they had conference together. And I have undone myself," (quoth he) "that I followed not Sir Edward Moore's counsel when he would have me to go to Dublin."[6]

Upon the morrow after her being at Castleton, she came as far as the wood, of Ballinvaealle [near Oldcastle Co. Meath] and there alighted. And it was my fortune to hear of my master Nicholas Nugent's coming to Dromcree. And thither I went, and being standing with him awhile there, he willed me to ride forward towards Ballinvealle to bid his wife to stay for him; and I did so. And there she delivered me the letter mentioned before by John Cusack, and she told me how my master was vexed for [meaning doubtless obliged by the state to get] William Nugent's youngest son. And thereupon she willed me to go with the letter to Hubert Fay, who as she said brought away the child from Kilkarne, and because I knew of William Nugent's mind before. I said it was but in vain for me to go thither, and that unless it pleased his father that the child would not be had.[7]

Soon after my said master Nicholas Nugent and his brother Oliver came present and then they mused what was best to do, therein. And in the end they concluded to go to John Plunkett of BallyLoghcreawe [a prominent family living nearby], he to work with one Thomas McShane ORely who is an alter [?] to William Nugent, to get the child. And we lighted on a hill above Bally-Loghcreawe, and I was sent to the said John Plunkett to require him to come forth and to speak to his cousin Ellen Plunkett that stayed for him on the hill over the town. And thither came he and found her there. And being in communication together Nicholas Nugent came thither who went awhile in the way with his brother Oliver. And after he had lighted they began to talk of the child;[8] In so much that John Plunkett said that it lay not in Thomas Mc-Shane to get the child, unless it please the father. And when I heard him say so, I said, that if you will keep counsel of me, I will presume to go to his father, and I will show him his wife's handwriting, and then I hope he will be moved to cause the child to be sent in.

This being done, I travelled so far until I came to Fower [Fore]. And I found William Nugent in Gerrott Nugent's chamber in Fower aforesaid. And I showed him his wife's letter concerning the child, who answered that he would not assent that the child should be delivered, unless he could get his wife set at liberty, which answer I repeated at my return.[9]

Soon after I received another letter by William Millar of Kilkarne, which was subscribed by William Nugent's wife, and directed to Hubert Fay, concerning the said child. And I told the said Fay of the tenor therof, who answered that one Robert Fay, by William Nugent's appointment, brought the child from Kilkarne and not he, which letter is forthcoming.[10]

Upon relation made by me of William Nugent's wants, and lack of money, Ellen Plunkett delivered me three pounds in money, which I sent to him after by Bryen mcGillehevoick [?] his footboy.[11]

Item when all practices could not find out the child, the said Ellen Plunkett disposed herself to make search for him in the Brenny, and went as far as Loughroner [Ramer], and I went with her. And there we learnt that the child was sent to a country called Fermanagh, and there as it is said remaineth.[12]

The Traitorous Acts given me to be understaned [sic], and by whom particularly ensueth:

First William Nugent told me that Maguire promised to send him 300 shot and target men upon his own proper charges, whensoever that he would attempt to do any harm to the English Pale.[13]

He told me that the Prior O'Neill and Art O'Neill, with as many men as they can make, promised to assist him in this rebellion. And he told me also that he did send unto them already, and that their answer was that they would not hazard themselves, nor their men, until the said William had begun the war and done some harm of himself.[14]

The said William told me that upon the death of James Fitzmorrish [Fitzmaurice Fitzgerald] the Pope of Rome made Sir John of Desmond General and furtherer of the holy cause, and the said Sir John gave him the same authority to be General of the English Pale.[15]

He told me it was partly through his mean that the prey of Brackline was taken.

The said William told me that he lay in an Ambushment at Killawteary for Captain Malby, thinking that by taking him he should purchase himself a pardon.[16]

['From this to the end is "written by Mr Secretary Fenton"']

He [John Nugent] saith that Ellen told him that she had talked with William Nugent in the great castle at Castleton.

He saith further that he thinketh upon his conscience that Nicholas Nugent knew that Ellen spake with William as is afore-said.

He confesseth that William Nugent told him that a little before Michaelmas last, the Baron Delvin wrote a letter to the said William of this tenor viz. "Let the poor man enjoy his sheep, or else you do him great wrong." This letter William answered in this sort viz. "if it had been a sheep that had been scabbed, it had been better he should have perished, than the whole flock."[17]

Another letter at the same time the said William showed to the examinant, containing this matter:
"the work I have taken in hand, I cannot as yet go through with it, for that neither the stones nor mason are ready, nor lime burnt. And therefore we must wait a time." This was written with William his own hand.[18]

Signed underneath with John Nugent's own hand wherewith all the rest was written. [Endorsed:] The Copy of John Nugent's Confession 5 Feb 1582 [sic]."

Footnotes to John Nugent's statement.
1. We know he is of Skurlockstown because John Cusack's account mentions a John Nugent from there as giving William a cal-liver. The Skurlockstown is probably that of Clonarny parish, Delvin Barony Co. Westmeath. This family is a branch of the Kil-lagh (Kill hech) family from Killagh parish in the same barony, for which see: Duald McFirbish RIA MS 24 N 2 p.401-8. They were often servants to the Barons of Delvin in the 17th century and doubtless earlier. John got out of jail and was "pardoned

without trial" probably by paying a bribe to the Dillons (PRONI D/3835/A/5/25). He is presumably the same person as writes the later account of the judge's trial because he is here listed as a servant of the judge and the trial account is written by "a poor old servant" of the judge's (PRONI D/3835/A/5/32 in a letter endorsed 5 July 1583). He later became an undersheriff for Co. Cavan and on 6 May 1592 he supports William by giving an affidavit in Dublin Castle during the court case. There he is described as a 'farmer'. (PRONI D/3838/A/5/62)

2. Of course John probably wants to protect them from the allegation of involvement with William.

3. recte from 'will'.

4. The writer dislikes this because he is Nicholas' servant and is worried about him. Otherwise I don't think he has much sympathy for Cusack's position. In fact it could be that the writer is being a bit coy when he talks about his 'unfortunate chance' meeting with William, it is possible he was sent by Nicholas to seek out William in order to find out about the child.

5. No doubt that still seen in the town of Delvin.

6. A sidebar added in by Secretary Fenton highlighting aspects of the evidence that he hoped to capitalise on: "William Nugent meeteth with Ellen Plunkett at Richard Crosse's house. The said Ellen is wife to Nicholas Nugent, late Justice, and mother to Jennett of Skryne wife to William Nugent. This Crosse is fled."

7. Meaning that Fay would not give up the infant without the say so of the father. A sidebar: "Ellen Plunkett delivereth to the examinant a letter from Jennet of Skryne mentioned in the 17th former article" [paragraph]."

8. Fenton again: "Nicholas Nugent and Oliver speak for William Nugent's child" which is I think an exaggerated interpretation of "they had begun to talk of the child".

9. same: "William Nugent at the house of Gerrott Nugent in Fower."

10. "Another letter from Jennett of Skryne for her child".

11. "Ellen Plunkett sends money to the traitor William Nugent." Anxious to ensnare Ellen in their net of course, she held a lot of the family's property as a joincture on the death of her former husband. The Marward lands of Skreen were estimated to yield c.130 pounds a year with Ellen getting 99 pounds of that and her daughter the rest. Notice that it is the women who own most of the property here, it was certainly not the property of their husbands Nicholas and William respectively. (Cockatrice op.cit. p.38) Hence of course the government was keen on stitching her up for treason in order to confiscate the property.

12. "Fermanagh is Maguire's Country."

13. "Maguire promised to join."

14. "The Prior Art O'Neill consented."

15. "William Nugent made General of the Pale by the Pope's authority which showeth further that this rebellion was intended before any apprehension of matter meant against the Lord his brother or himself." A touchy subject for the government because of course it is a lie. William in all probability intended no rebellion until (deliberately) forced into it by the government. John in his account doesn't show any preplanning because Sir John is likely to have bestowed the above honour on William after he had rebelled and without reference back to Rome.

16. "Practise to intercept Sir Nicholas Malby." In John Nugent's account of the judges trial he denies that this was ever a real plan at least on the part of the Baron of Delvin or the judge.

17. Showing the confident use of allusion and pseudonyms by

William and the family, to get around heavy government surveillance and censorship. Probably the Baron meant that he should come in and agree to be arrested like the rest and William replies that he cannot because if he came in now he might be compelled to confess and disastrously implicate those that helped him.

18. "This letter was written in the name of Francis Harmon and directed to Lawrence Harmon, but meant to the Lord of Delvin."

Petition of Jane Marward [William's wife] prob. June 1582
PRONI D/3835/A/5/72
"...Therefore upon the apprehension of the Earl of Kildare and Baron of Delvin, her husband having betaken himself to flight, her father in law [step father] the Justice Nugent had dealt with the Lord Gray for bringing her from her husband, with who she was then fled, great with child, which she was granted unto him, she then being brought home, and delivered of her child, news came to her father again that her husband intended to have taken her from him. Whereupon he moved his dwelling from the country to Dublin and brought your supplicant with him but left the child with his nurse in the country. In which mean time her husband (fearing by likelihood the example of cruelty shown to children in like case) took away the child from the place where he was.
Whereupon the Lord Gray [then Lord Deputy] calling her to before him told her that her husband had been dealing with the Connors and for all his eloquence they had refused him, but seeing (quote he) we can not lay hands on him we must lay hands on them that be nearest unto him, which are his wife and children and thereupon committed your supplicant refusing her of liberty upon sufficient surety for her appearance from time to time [allowing her no bail]. And this she protesteth was the only cause of her committing, without any offence or accusation that she knew going before.
    Being then a prisoner, her life and living shot at, the one for envy, the other for gain, means were sought for finding matter to accuse her of treason and at last John Cusack and one Pers Conegan were found to accuse her of treason for sending shirts, letters

and other necessaries to her husband. She was brought to the Bar and arraigned and had been like enough with the rest as the Lord Gray writes (such was the iniquity of the time) had not her Majesty's mercy prevented it, as no doubt it did many other innocent lives. But yet neither of her accusers was brought before her, to justify their falsehood for as it is well known what John Cusack is, so the other is but a very base creature, and drawn to accusing of her only for safeguard of his life as himself hath confessed since his breaking out of prison. Whereout also he was fled for fear least not being able to make his accusations good his life should be taken from him. So as neither of them she trusts are worthy of your Lord's sight to carry credit against her."

Account of the trial and execution of Nicholas Nugent by John Nugent of Skurlockstown, the author of the long confession above.1582 PRONI D/3835/A/2/12
From TCD F-3-16 folio 175 and British Museum Clarendon vol 46 no 4793
"(p.108) [Judge Nicholas] Nugent had prosecuted John [Cusack of Ellistonread] for the murder of the Baronet of Skryne, his wife's later [previous] husband,
(p.100) John Caro Cusack, a bastard by birth, and a dissolut soul all his life, began to suborne and entice some young gentlemen of the Pale, from the ancient loyalty where they and their ancestors hath long time tarried and been trained up using the crocodile tears and the mermaid's song to allure them to their destruction.
(p.113) The Baron [Dillon] whom they [the lords of the Pale especially Westmeath] knew to be so far from favouring the noblemen as [they] themselves in common phrase usually term him the canker of nobility.
(p.114) The doing him [Judge Nugent] away then was an amaze to all men's minds as the secret intertalking of men was better be a Dillonian than an honest or a true man...[goes on to say that they stuck with the Dillons because they were afraid that if they opposed them then they would be charged with involvement in the rebellion.]
(p.116) [The writer is motivated to write this account partly out of a] desire in signification of truth to wipe out the stains that the

poor country seemeth to have received by Mr Nugent's death, [and lest the Pale] should be left spotted with any taint of guiltless blood to posterity.

(p.118) John Cusack first a bastard, then after a murderer, and thirdly a traitor, should last become a perjured witness for promise of his life, and hope of good reward, is easy for every man to perceive except only Sir Henry Wallop whose opinion of John is very great, and whose sincerity in the service is such as he thinks an Irishman cannot truth but in accusing another of treason.

(p.119) It is not unknown to such as know the English Pale in Ireland what stroake [sic] the Dillons have borne there these latter years clinging to credit with the Magistrates by following their humours though never so directly. To the spoiling of this poor country in so much as you shall not find man advanced or rejected to or from any office or charge in the country but by them preferred. Which hath won unto them such fear in the Commonality, and such duty with the jurors as you shall hardly see any matter in controversy pass against him they love, or with him they favour not. I speak not this, I promise you, for that I envy their credit but the better to intimate unto you what sway they carry in the country. In so much as a beck private half a word of one of them is enough to make a juror know his intent."

Fenton to Walsingham 8 Dec1582 PRONI D/3835/A/6/321
Edmond Nugent (the Baron's base brother) and Conley Duff Mageoghegan have got a protection and are now to do some service for her Majesty at least for four months...

1583
Theobald Dillon writing I think to Malby in Connaught from Killinure 2 Jan 1582/3 PRONI D/3835/A/6/313
wanting to know when he will be interviewing Edmond Nugent...

The Lord Justices from Drogheda to Secretary Walsingham 8 Aug 1583 PRONI D/3835/A/5/29
"Right Honourable, it may please you to be advertised that yester night coming to this town we were presented with the head of Edmond Nugent, the rebel (base brother to the Baron of Delvin) who

having the night before taken the spoil of a village in the County of Longford was followed by O'Ferrall and the sheriff of the county, near unto the house of James FitzChristopher Nugent (uncle to the Baron) who came late out of England, who then rising out with them to follow the pursuit happened to light upon the traitor and (with the assistance of the sheriff and the rest that came into him) slew the said Edmond with three of his men, and hurt divers other of his company which notwithstanding escaped away by flight. Mr. Nugent is dangerously hurt in two or three places. Hereof we thought good to advertise to your honor for that we account it a very good piece of service, both in the one and the other the said Edmond being not only a very mischievous fellow of himself but also one under whose name many notable mis-chiefs were done by others. And yet until this time (by means of his great alliance thereabouts in the country of Delvin) suffered to wander up and down in those parts, being rather winked at than pursued. Thus having no further to enlarge unto your honours at this present we humbly take our leave."

[Note the great cynicism here of Walsingham and his intelligence agency. They claim to be on the hunt for notorious rebels who are 'winked at' in Ireland whereas they in fact had released Edmond from jail in order to employ him on some unspecified government business.

Looking at it it seems likely that Edmond was sent to kill his uncle (probably with the assistance of the Sheriff and O'Ferall) and that James was only defending himself. Notice how in King Lear Shakespeare departs from his sources to include an illegitim-ate Edmund. Also King Lear is written not long after the death of William's eldest son who had temporarily gone over to the side of Hugh O'Neill, the great enemy of the Baron of Delvin and his brother.]

Lord Delvin writing from Greenwich [on bail in England] to Lord Burghley 29 Oct 1583 PRONI D/3835/A/5/30
Asking him to grant him an audience with the Queen and ac-knowledging his help so far :
"You have already brought me past the current of the stream, leave not me now seeing the greatest pain is past." Not shy of out-

lining the injustice done to him which is making him somewhat cynical!:

"And albeit that mine Imprisonment hath been very miserable and strait mixed with tyrannical threatenings and ungodly practices (during my being in Ireland) my charges more than my small living can maintain, the same living wasted, torn and mangled by such as her Majesty sendith thither to defend her subjects, and not to offend them."

Ciaran Brady ed., *A Viceroy's Vindication? Sir Henry Sidney's Memoir* (Cork, 2003), p.92 and p.96.

The Lord Deputy's 1583 report on his time in Ireland:
"Sir Lucas Dillon and his whole lineage, far the best of that country breed; he and they constantly stood with the Queen in defence thereof. The chief opposers of them against the Queen were the Baron of Delvin, the cancerdest and most malicious man, both for religion and English government, (I think) that Ireland then bare.
...
For as soon as I was gone her made Nicholas Nugent (displaced by me from the second Baronship of the Exchequer and committed to the Castle of Dublin, where he found him prisoner for his arrogant obstinacy against the Queen) chief Justice of the Common Pleas;"

1584

21 Jan 1583/4 Fenton to Burghley PRONI D/3835/A/6/305
[describing William] "being of the Pale, where he wanteth neither credit not opinion with the people and of himself hath a great facility to persuade and draw."

G. Fenton to Lord Burghley 21 Jan 1583/4 PRONI D/3835/A/5/30
"And likewise to the Lord Justices here for then trapping of William Nugent, wherein for that money will be the aptest mean to finish this work, the rather for that through the universal poverty of Nugents kinred and allies in the Pale, there will not want fitt and willing instruments to undertake the matter...I think it would be to good purpose to cutt off Nugent at the least."

William Nugent and Brian Geoghegan in Paris to Cardinal Como in Rome 12 May 1584
Vatican archives 1. Vol 1, fol. 286
Illmo. et Rmo. Padrone nostro Colenmo~Eui*h*

Il giorno dell' Ascensione giunsimo a Parigi ove dopo nostro arrivo andammo a presentarei a Monsignore il Nuntio, e l'Ambasciatore di Scotia portando all'uno et l'altro le lettere di V. S. Illma. Hora stiamo attendendo quel che ci sarà imposto. Quel che di nostro paese intendiamo è che non vi è fine della persecutione; ma che di giorno in giorno ella cresce procedendo di male in peggio. Se averrà cosa alcuna degna della saputa di V. S. Illma., le ne daremo aviso di tempo in tempo; ben le supplichiamo che quando occorresse impilgarei per nostro paese procuri che per questo si il Sigre. Conallo Mora il quale sta in Napoli a servigii della Mtà. Catea. et a questo negotio sarà d'importanza grande. Con questo fine baciamo humilmente le mani dì V. S. Illma. alla quale il Sigre, Iddio conceda in lunga vita ogni contentezza.

Dí Parigi alli 12 di Maggio 1584, obligatissi servri.
Gugmo. Nugenti; Barnaba Geochagan.
All' Illmo. et Rmo. Monsigre. lo Cardle. di Como Padrone nostro Colenmo. Roma.
(*Miscellanea Vaticano-Hibernica*, Archivium Hibernicum 1918-21 Vol VII p.323.)

[What follows is just a sketch translation of the Italian. 'V.S.' presumably means 'Venerable Fathers', or some such title for the Cardinals in Rome. Also 'honourable lady' seems to mean the same, or at least stands for the Catholic Church in some sense:
"On the feast of the Ascension we arrived at Paris and then went on to present ourselves to the Monsignor the Nuncio, and the Ambassador of Scotland bringing to both of them the letters from the Honourable V.S. Now we are attending to our obligations. What we understand about our country is that there is no end to the persecution: day by day it goes from bad to worse. If things happen which the Honourable V.S. should know we will

give word to her from time to time. And we implore that when our country is pleaded for that it will be Mr. Conallo Mora who is in Naples [who will handle the negotiations], servant of (Mta) Catea, and this will be a negotiation of great importance. In conclusion, we humbly kiss the hands of the Honourable V.S. on whom God may bestow every contentment and long life."]

William Nugent and Brian Geoghegan in Paris to Cardinal Como in Rome 27 May 1584
Vatican archives 1. Vol. 1, fol. 287.
Illmo. et Rmo. Padrone nostro Colenmo.
Dopo la nostra ultima a V. S. Illma. ci appresentammo al Sig. Duca di Guisa per ordine di Monsig. Nuntio, il quale diede il carico di condurci da Sa Eccza. na Padre Claudio Mattheo rettor del Collegio de' professi della Compagnia del Giesú huomo molto intrinseco di esso Duca. Pare a S. Eccza. che ce ne partiamo per Iscotia quanto prima, et con lei concorrono ancora nella medesima opinione detto Monsig. Nuntio et Monsre. l'Ambasciatore di Scotia. Hora dunque non starà per noi di farlo, poichè così vogliono coloro a quali Nro. Sig. ci ha indirizzati per grande che sia il pericolo che ce ne habbia da seguire. Et grande veramente sarà il pericolo così nel passare, considerato che i marinari per lo più pigliano terreno in Inghiltera, come anchora nello stare in Iscotia istessa, essendo quel regno tutto in potere de ministri heretici li quali si come intendiamo usano ogni crudeltà contra gli Catolici. Con tutto ciò ajutandoci Iddio non mancheremo noi nel minimo puntiglio che sia d'accompire tutto quel che ci sarà commandato sperando che havrà da riuscire a gloria di Dio et bene di S. Chiesa: il che desideriamo do procurare con la vita o con la morte nostra. Mons. Illma. ci importarebbe grandemente che Monsre. Nuntio havesse ordine di pagare le nostre provisioni qui in Parigi perchè à riscuoterle in Roma et trasportarle qua et da qua a Scotia sarà una taccenda, et in questo mentre ne potremo ben patir bisagno, et perciò quando à V. S. Illma non par disdicevole di ottenereclo gliolo sia raecommandato. Et con questo humilissimamente le bariamo le mani.

Di Parigi alli 27 di Maggio 1584

Di V.S. Illma. et Rma.
Humilissmi. et obligatissani. Servi.
Gugmo. Nugenti; Barnaba Geochagan.
All' Illmo. et Rmo. Monsig. la Cardinale di Como padrone nostro
Colendissmo. a Roma.
(*Miscellanea Vaticano-Hibernica,* Archivium Hibernicum 1918-
21 Vol VII p.323.)

["After our visit to the honourable V.S. we were presented to the
Duke of Guise by order of the Nuncio, who mandated us to go directly to (His Excellency) Fr. Claudio Mattheo, rector of the Jesuit
College, a man very connected to the Duke. His Excellency suggests we should leave for Scotland first, an opinion shared by the
Nuncio and the Scottish Ambassador. However, it is not up to us
to do this and we have been advised too of the grave dangers we
would be in. The journey would truly be gravely dangerous considering that most sailors catch land in England, [on their way
to?]...Scotland, that kingdom being under the control of heretical
ministers, who, as we understand, use every cruelty against
Catholics. Despite all this, God is helping us and we will not
spare the smallest detail to accomplish all that we will be
commanded, hoping to succeed for the glory of God and the good
of the Holy Church; we desire to procure this with our lives or our
deaths. The honourable Monsignor assures us strongly that the
Nuncio would order to pay for our resources here in Paris and to
avoid paying transportation taxes in Rome and from Rome to
Scotland. In the meantime we cannot leave in this need and as the
honourable V.S. was not displeased may this recommendation be
seen to [polite way of begging for money?]. And with this we
humbly kiss the hands.

From Paris, 27 May, 1584.
From V.S. Honourable and (Reverend/female??)
Most humble and most dedicated Servants.
William Nugent, Brian Geoghegan
To the Honourable and Reverend (?) Monsignor, Cardinal of
Como, our great Colendo father, in Rome."]

William Nugent and Brian Geoghegan in Paris to Cardinal Como
in Rome 4 June 1584
Vatican archives Gallia Vol 17 fol 407
LXXXIII 1584 S 123,
All' Illmo et Rmo. Monsignore lo Cardinale di Como patrono
nostro Colmo

Parigi 4 Giugno 1584

Illmo et Rmo prone nro Colmo.

Domani che sarà alli S. del presente ci mettiamo in camino per
Iscotia. Hieri capitorno qui due giovani Irlandesi, quel che ci
riferiscono del paese in generale non è altro che persecutione de
Catolici. In particolare dicono che l'Arcivescovo Cassellense, il
quale e stato prigione già sette mesi, fu dal Viserè posta a tortura
per farlo confessare cose de congiuri, delle quali presupponeva lui
esser stato consapevole, o vero rinegare la fede. La tortura fu tale,
gli fece metter in piedi con un paro di stivali nuovi conbuturo et
sale dentro, poi il fece ligare tendolo vicino al fuoco insino a tanto
che dal cuojo, il che gli si strinse intorno alli piedi, et dal cuocente
liguore gli furono tutti scorticati. Ma con tutto questo non gradag-
nò più che tanto, che l'Arcivescovo non si ridusse mai nè a confessare gli uni, né a negare l'altra. Anzi gli rispondeva che quanto
a' presupposti congiuri non se sapeva nulla et quanto alla fede
bisognava vincerlo con ragione et saldi argomenti, che per paura
di morte o tormenti non farebbe niente. Il Vescovo di Fernes il
quale si dice havere vaccillato, et per questo esser stato in qualche
riputatione apresso gli heretici, pentendosi del commesso fallo
venne all presenza del Viserè, et ivi apertamenté confessò la fede
Catolica incolpando se stresso della passata prevaricatione. Il
cavalier Giovanni Paratt si manda in Irlanda viserè: il quale
secondo che li detti giovani raccontano ha fatto tre dimande a la
Regina:
1. che durante il tempo di suo governo gli sia lecito per legge
d'armi far morire senza ordine di giustitia o processo ordinario
ogriuno di quel paese che si troverà Catolico;

2. che possa di sua propria autorità et immediatamente mutare Magistrati et Ministri di Leggi;

3. che possa tassare i vassalli come gli pare in discretione a sua posta. Vostra Signoria Illma consideri a che termini quel provero Regno si è ridotto. Iddio per sua infinita bontà proveda a questi mali. Havemo inteso dall' Imbasciatione del Re di Scotia, che Sua Maestà ha scacciato li rebelli che gli presero la terra di Sterlin [sic] (la quale ha ricuperata), et di quelli ha amazzato in un fatto d'arme, al quale si trovò in persona, fino a 500. Ha giustitiato il Conte di Gourei, quale era ill maggiore amico che haveva la Regina d'Inghilterra in quel Regno: gli altri della fattione sua si sono fuggiti chi in Inghilterra, chi a Rochell in Franza etc. di modo che (fussimo arrivati salvi) speriamo di poter star lì con manco pericolo che non pensammo primo; excetto se non fussimo adoprati in attione per servigii del Re, la qual cosa supra tutto desideriamo, avengane poi quel Iddio Vuole. Occorendo buona occasione, la quale sarebbe quando la Regina d'Ingliterra fosse un poco travagliata da qualche guerra esterna, allora Nicolao Eustacchio sarebbe da esser spedito per Irlanda Vescovo Midense con l'autorità del Primate (in absentia Primatis), ma temiamo che le cose non sono anchora venute a quella maturità: Vostra Signoria Illma n'habbia memoria a sua tempo. Dell' Arcivescovato Dublinense si sente qui qualche bisbiglio che sia per quel Frate Bazzono i ma Vostra Signoria Illustrissima sia servita di non lasciar quella, la quale è la prima dignita' di nostro Regno, cascar in mano di forestieri, quando non mancano de nostri persone che ne sono degne, si come particolarmente ci è Leonardo Fizzymon, il quale oltre alla dottrina et virtù sua è figliuolo del primo cavaglier di quella città. Hora non occurrendoci altro ci raccomandiamo humilissimamente a Vostra Signoria Illma, supplicandola che verso di noi et nostro paese continui sempre suo solito favore et gratia, et Iddio benedetto la conservi nella sua.

Di Parigi alli 4 di Giugno 1584
Di Vra Signoria Illma et Rma

Devotissimi servi
Guglielmo Nugenti – Barnaba Georhagan [sic]

(Fr Augustin Theiner, *Annales Ecclesiastici* (Rome, 1856) Vol III, p.818.)

["Tomorrow we will set off for Scotland. Yesterday, two young Irishmen were here and they informed us that the whole country has nothing but persecution of Catholics. In particular, they spoke of the Archbishop of Cashel who is already seven months in prison. He was tortured by the Viceroy to make him confess to conspiracies which he was supposed to know of, or to renounce the faith. The torture was as follows: they made him wear a pair of new boots with butter [?] and salt inside in them, then he was tied close to the fire which cooked [?] all the leather, and his two feet were tied together, and from the cooking oil they [his feet] were skinned. But all this gained nothing. The Archbishop was not beaten, he neither confessed nor admitted anything. Instead, he responded regarding the supposed conspiracies that he knew nothing, and as for the faith, he conquered with reason and solid arguments. Fear of death or torments meant nothing to him [?]. The Bishop of Ferns, who is said to have vacillated and as a result was in good standing with the heretics, repented of his fault. He went to the Viceroy and openly confessed the Catholic Faith, accusing himself of his past lapse. The cavalier John Perrot is being sent to Ireland, as Viceroy, and, according to these young men, he has made three demands of the Queen:
1. during his time of governance, that the army may be allowed to kill anyone who is Catholic, without the ordinary procedures of justice;
2. that he may have the authority to immediately change magistrates and ministers of Law;
3. that he may tax vassals as he deems fit according to their place. Consider, Your Honourable Lady, to what depths that poor Kingdom is reduced. May God, in his infinite goodness, protect us from these evils. We understand from the Ambassador to the King of Scotland that His Excellency has thrown out the rebels who took the land of Stirling (which was recovered), and of these as many as 500 have been killed by the army [?]. The Earl of Gowry judged who is the closest friend of

the Queen in that Kingdom: the others have fled, some to England, some to Rochelle in France etc. so that (if we arrive safely) we hope to stay there with as little danger to ourselves, such as we have never thought of. [Meaning they can go there safely now because the Protestant Ministers, the enemies of the Queen of Scots, have been expelled.] If we do not get to serve the King, which is what we most desire, then let God's Will come. With good luck, the Queen of England may be preoccupied with external wars, then Nicholas Eustace would be sent to Ireland (as Bishop of Meath) with the authority of Primate (in the absence of the [de jure] Primate), but we fear that things are not at that point of maturity yet: Your Honourable Lady may have her own memories [reports] in her own time. The Archbishop of Dublin is feeling some unease(?) regarding Bro. Bazzono and Your Honourable Lady would be served not to let him, who is the greatest dignity of our Kingdom, to fall into the hands of strangers, when we do not want for worthy persons of our own, in particular Leonard Fitzsimons, who besides his doctrine and his virtue is a son of the first cavalier of that city. Now, with nothing else to say, we commend ourselves most humbly to Your Honourable Lady, in supplication for your continued good favour and grace towards us and our country and may the good God protect you."]

William Nugent and Brian Geoghegan in Edinburgh to Cardinal Como in Rome 30 June 1584
Vatican archives Anglia Vol 2 fol 288
Al Medesimo Cardinale Di Como
Edinburgo 30 Giugno 1584

Illmo, et Rmo, Padrone nostro Colendissimo

Alli 12 del presente secondo la computa di costoro arrivammo in questo paese, quale trovammo un pezzo mutato dal solito. Il Re alterato quanto può essere contra li ministri universalmente, et parimente contra tutti gli nemici della Regina sua Madre, per esser stati gli uni et gli altri authori et essecutori di tutti i congiuri macchinati contra Sua Maestà in questi tempi passati. Del che conoscendosi colpevoli i ministri si sono fuggiti in Inghilterra attorno a 17 ó 20 delli principali, che si tennero per più dotti di tutti. Nell' ultimo parliamento quale è stato di questo Maggio, fu tolto a loro ogni authorità d'usare censure ecclesiastiche, et certi Catholici già scommunicati da loro, assoluti dal Re. In questo parliamento fu ordinato che non si ricevano ministri se non quelli che seranno ammessi da Vescovi, et che da essi vescovi dependano et a loro sottostiano: Furono anchora altre restrittioni poste alla libertà che godevano per lo passato: questo pure non fu delli parliamenti più solenni, ma quale chiamano corrente o corsivo. Nel primo, quale ha da incominciarsi d'Agosto, si spera, che le cose anderanno innanzi anchora un altro passo. Di questo dà grandissima speranza il procedere del Re, al quale dispiace molto quello della Regina d'Inghilterra, riducendo la religione a caso di Stato, et consequentemente facendo morire li Catolici, de' quali esso s'affida e si serve quanto di qualsivogliano de' suoi vasalli. Non vuole, et non lascia fare violenza alla coscienza di nissiuno. In corte si ragiona liberamente di religione. Di nostro paese intendiamo mancho qui che se fussimo in Roma, et perciò siamo risoluti che ol' uno di noi vada a sapere il stato. Dopo il ritorno di cui V. S. Illma. sarà avisato del tutto, si come sarà anchora di tutte l'altre occorrenze, secondo che ci verrà la commodità, se intenderemo che le nostre di qua habbiano ricapito. Quanto al nostro particolare fummo raccomandati dal Duca di Guisa al Maestro di Gray un Signore molto favorito del Re, al quale sendo lui Catholico havemo mostrato la provisione che ci da N. Sre. dicendogli che non volemo dare aggravio al Rè; ma che in ogni occorrenza saremo presti a servirgli in tutto quel che sapremo et potremo et che a questo effetto S. Stà. ci ha mandati. Al nostro partire da Parigi li Padri del Giesu ci buscarono una mesata e ci dettero una poliza per ricevere altertanto qui da un Gentilhuomo; ma questo ultimo non viene affatto perchè il gentilhuomo non corrisponde; et noi cí troviamo al fondo di nostri denari per esser stati dal tempo che partimmo di Roma in continuo moto. Intanto V. S. Illma. sia servita d'haverci raccommandati; et se le pare nel procurare che le nostre provisioni si paghino in Parigi ne' principii delli mesi che saranno ben a fine inanzi che le potremo ricevere di quà: et con questo fine basciamo humilissimamente le mani a V. S. Illma.

Di Edinburgho, alli 30 di Giugno seconda la computa di questo paese 1584
Di V. S. Illma

Humilissi. Servri
Guglielmo Nugenti – Barnaba Georhagan.
(Fr Augustin Theiner, *Annales Ecclesiastici* (Rome, 1856) Vol III, p.817 and *Miscellanea Vaticano-Hibernica* Archivium Hibernicum 1918-21 Vol VII, p.324. The latter continues the text from 'liberamente di religione', which is absent from Theiner.)

["At 12 to the second [meaning that the date is accurate? A reference to its being calculated by the continental calendar rather than the Scottish one?] we arrived in this place which we found partly changed, as usual. The King was as much against the ministers universally [entirely] as against the enemies of the Queen, his Mother, to see which were the authors and executors of all the false accusations against His Excellency in these past times. Those who knew they were guilty have fled to England, about 17 or 20 of the leaders who were the cleverest of them all. In the last parliament, held this May, every authority was taken from them to use ecclesiastical censure, and certain Catholics already excommunicated by them, were absolved by the King. In this parliament it was passed that ministers are not received unless admitted by the Bishops, on whom they depend and submit to. There were other restrictions on their freedom which they had enjoyed in the past: this was not from the more solemn parliament but what we call the current or passing one. First, to commence from August, it is hoped that things will advance another step. That which gives the greatest hope is that the King, who dislikes very much the Queen of England, will proceed reducing the Religion to a matter of state, and consequently [will take in hand] the affair of the killing of Catholics, in whom he trusts and who serve him as his vassals. He does not want and will not let violence happen to anyone's conscience. In short, freedom of Religion is argued for. Our understanding here of our own country is lacking just as if we were in Rome, and so we are all resolved to get to know the state. After the return of the Honourable V.S. she will be informed of all, if as with all the other happenings, according to which will come the commodity [?], if we will understand that ours [our things?] may be known [?]. With regard to our particulars we were recommended by the Duke of Guise to a Mr. Gray, a man very favoured by the King, believing him to be a Catholic we showed him our plans which we got from N. Sre. saying to him that we did not want to aggravate the King; but in every event we will be ready to serve him in all the ways we know and are able and it was for his purpose that we were sent by His Holiness. On our departure for Paris, the Jesuit priests gave us a message [meaning money!] and said to us to receive the same again from a Gentleman; but this didn't happen because the gentleman didn't correspond; and we found ourselves down and out for money and we were continually on the move after leaving Rome. All in all, the Honourable V.S. has been served in having recommended us; and if it seems to her that our resources can be paid for in Paris for the main months we will be there, it will be good, until we will be able to receive them over there: and with this conclusion we most humbly kiss the hands of the Honourable V.S."]

Lord Deputy Perrot to Lord Burghley 4 Dec 1584 PRONI D/3835/A/5/40
"I have laid all the baits I could to catch William Nugent but seeing myself dallied withal therin..."

Attached to the letter is William's submission, which he did under Perrot's safe conduct. Perrot had decided on this strategy because he had given up trying to catch him, as pointed out:
"Right Honours for as much as I have through an overdeep preconceived fear fallen into most undutiful and rash behaviour by joining myself to such persons as stood in rebellious actions. Whereby I have incurred her Majesty's indignation and deserved whatsoever most severe chastisement although my fault proceeded not of malice but of an inconsiderate fear. Neither was I ever in any personal action of rebellion. And that now it hath pleased your Lordship of your own noble disposition and favour-

able inclination towards men that offend rather through ignorance than of unsound intent, by giving your honour's word for my security to open way for me to implore her Majesty's mercy, which is never denied to any how great soever an offender that which humility and repentance recurreth unto it. I that acknowledge myself guilty among the deepest and worthy the most sharp correction, that is due to offenders in the highest degree, do here, most humbly prostrate myself at her Majesty's gracious feet. Beseeching with most penitent heart that I may find repose in those virtues of mildness and mercy proper and peculiar to her above all the princes in the world. And that your lordship will vouchsafe to work me the means once again to be looked upon by her most merciful and gracious eyes. Whereby this stain now abiding in my name which marks me ever loathsome unto myself may be wiped away and I made worthy to serve her Majesty in the place of a loyal subject. Which I desire the most earnestly to perform with the spending of my blood to the last drop.

The most unfortunate and odious to himself William Nugent."

Another enclosure is this letter from William to Perrot:

"Right Honourable to showed [?] it may appear unto your Lord how greatly I desire to ransom my late offence by performing in every part the duty observance and service that may be required at the hands of a loyal subject. I have, in the occurrences which at the present offer themselves, taken occasion to discharge me in that behalf by delivering unto your Lordship such intelligences in this true and simple declaration as I could come by and in my judgement might import the state to have knowledge of.

In the last Easter week Mageoghegan's son and I were sent for by the Cardinal de Como who told us that it was the Pope's pleasure we should with all speed take our journey to Paris where he said the Nuncio Apostolic and the Bishop of Glasgow should direct us in all that might occur.

After our arrival at Paris the Nuncio directed us to the Duke of Guise (who indeed procured our coming from Rome as we understood by himself), he sent us in company of certain Scottish lairds and household servants of the King of Scots into Scotland with the first shipping and gave us two letters. The one directed to the

King, which bore but ordinary commendation, the other to the Master of Grey (a person of importance and in great secrecy about the King) and that was in cipher, what it contained, other than a more effectual commendation of us the bearers than the other letter did, I cannot say for so much only did the Master of Grey disclose unto us of it.

As often as I with others of my countrymen had conference with the Cardinal Como, he would utter that the expedition for Ireland must come from the King of Spain, that the Pope was too far off to take it in hand, that from time to time he sent his direction to the Nuncio in Spain to solicit the King for it and that the King promised to proceed in the matter when opportunity should serve. I was told by some that were privy to these practises that the Pope would bear a good part of the charge and that seemeth to me likely because he hath already twice laid out of his treasure to maintain the attempt first to Stukely and after to James fitzMoris and the Italians and Spanish that landed at Dunanoir, wherefore he would not fail now when he conceive the more than a hope the business will succeed.

It was thought the expedition should have set forward by the last September, at the furthest, which might be conjectured by the haste made in the sending of my companion and me from Rome, and therefore to be looked for this next year, except it be prevented by her Majesty, interrupted by the wars of Flanders, or disturbed by the Turk or some other potentate. The Duke of Guise hath correspondence with the Pope, Spain and Scotland whereby it may be gathered that though there be no immediate nor direct dealing betwixt the King of Scots and the Pope or the King of Spain, yet he practiseth with either [meaning each of them] indirectly by the intermediation of Guise. This a man might perceive by the diligence of Como in the despatch of my fellow and me from Rome, to Paris, procured by Guise, the Nuncio and he concurring in the sending of us to Scotland.

At my being in Scotland when I had told the Master of Grey that I was to come into Ireland, he cast out these words: "We may not comprehend what God purposeth, but except what he let it. It passeth the compass of man's wit to find out how the plot laid for the relief of Ireland may fail."

I conceive upon these words that the force intended to be sent must be great and being so methinks they would rather resolve to land in England than in Ireland, the reason is that upon England depends the consequence of both realms, which once won there needs no more for Ireland. Besides that there is not in Ireland to maintain any great force, for it would not quit the cost, neither is a small force able to keep it.

More particular intelligence of these matters I could not learn for the persons upon whom they depend are not want to commit the special points of Importance to private men."
[A natural story teller isn't he?]

1587

Robert Legge to Lord Burghley 27 Jan 1586/7 PRONI D/3835/A/5/44

"A great suit depending in the Exchequer upon information of intrusion for certain lands witholden from her Majesty some time belonging to the Abbey of Fore and letten in lease to the now Lord of Delvin. The defendant pleaded not guilty, only standing upon an old deed granted from the abbot upon the dissolution of the house and inserted in an office supposed to be taken upon the succession thereof.

This matter proceeded the last term to trial by Jury who gave a special verdict referring the matter to the consideration of the Barons. But when I began to make up the verdict and record perusing the same office well I found the same office to be lately forged and written by a clerk of the Remembrancers Office at the procurement of one Mr Byse, sometime using the place I now have, as deputy in the same. And yet the office bearing date 18th March year 31 of Henry VII and the hands of Sir Thomas Cusack Knt and Robert Dillon esquire then Kings Attorney General Commissioners at that time appointed manifestly counterfeited. In which forged office the said deed was inserted greatly to the disinherison of the Queen's Majesty to the same lands [and hence claiming that she couldn't lease the lands to Delvin] if it had not been found out, a most pernicious act and now in suit in the Castle chamber."

1590

Lord Deputy and Chancellor from Kilmainham advising the steps to be taken against the Nugents 21 Sept 1590 PRONI D/3835/A/4/301

"And being of great credit through the Pale for their kinred, affinities, possesions, wits, and courage, specially the Baron and his brother, of whom we may forbear to speak. They are dangerous men to be abroad (this being time) if the Spanish do purpose anything at all against this state. And being laid up we think the enemy will be thereby both cut off from intelligence and also disappointed of great instruments, yea perhaps the head their party here ...[if they are imprisoned it will] abate the courage of the ill affected in the Pale (a kind of people easily appalled, being but laid too.)"

Attached to the above letter is a description of various Nugents added as a gloss to the [forged] Parma Latin letter of 1577 that came from the Dean of Farranan PRONI D/3835/A/4/297 [The letter emerged in the early 1590s and the notes date from that period, I think 1590.]

"This Edward Nugent [in 1577 said to be living in London. He was a student at Grays Inns and the son of Thomas Nugent of Drogheda – probably William's uncle. In 1585 he was MP for Meath where he is described as of Morton. Not to be confused with Friar Lavallin's father.] the lawyer is conjectured both a dangerous and malicious man against the state. In the last parliament when an Act entitled "An Act for provision to be made for surety of the Majesty's most royal person" etc was moved in the Lower House he used a long premeditated speech in defence of the mass and Romish religion with imputation of all good success whereunto and encounter since."

1591

William Nugent to Burghley 15 August 1591 Dublin CSPI p.414

"[A continuation of the text given in the chronology in Chapter 4...giving me hearing] I said, "My Lord, the reason that makes me hold it dangerous to allege my proofs is: Sir Robert Dillon is a man of great authority and countenance, and if he shall be seen at liberty being accused of so great matters as these are, contrary to the course holden against others of his sort, those persons who are able to prove the articles will be discouraged to stand before your Lordship to that they have informed me. Moreover, upon the examinations of those whom I should produce, some one might, peradventure, disclose what interrogatories he had been examined upon, which from one to another might come to his own knowledge, and then he being at liberty might practice with such he knows were privy to his dealings and so work that the matters should be smothered and choked up."

Then said my Lord Chancellor, "Mr. Nugent, show some proofs, or else you may hinder the service."

Then quoth I, "For some proof of the first article. The very same day that those two brethren had accused either other to Sir Robert of treason, Walter Cusack came to Clonardrane in great fear, and told Jenet Cusack the whole of that discourse, betaking unto her his lease to keep. She, the same day, told it to Patrick Bermingham. She told it also to John Plunkett, her husband, and Robert Cusack told the same Bermingham that his brother Walter had accused him of treason."

My Lord then asked me whether I had any proofs for the rest of the articles. I said I would be loathe to bring before his Lordship and that board any proof but such as should answer their expectation; and told them I doubted not to get proof of all the rest, but that the same was not yet so ripe as I thought meet to bring before their Lordships. Then my Lord, having caused the solicitor to write to certain gentlemen a commission for apprehending the two brothers, willed him to take me into the next chamber. After I had remained there towards an hour, in which mean while Sir Robert Dillon, I think, was brought before their Lordships, Mr Solicitor brought me before them again.

Then said my Lord Deputy, "We have committed this gentleman to the Castle. Now will you show your proofs?"

I said I would, and if it pleased his Lordship to respite me until the next morning I would bring them in writing. But then, I told him, I could not travel that night with the commission if I stayed to bring the proofs next morning. Then was it concluded I should bring them to the council chamber in Dublin at six in the afternoon, which I did, and there prayed that certain the brethren and servants of Sir Robert Dillon might be committed and examined for the Queen's advantage, and also lest they being at liberty might shift out of the way his money, plate, and such like, but especially any writings lying in his studies at Dublin, or at his houses in the country, which I prayed might be searched by persons of trust.

My Lord asked if I had aught to accuse them of. I answered, No. Then he thought it no reason to commit them, where nothing was laid to their charge, but his Lordship willed Simon Wilde or Wile, Sir Robert Dillon's secretary, to be stayed in town, and I caused Mr Solicitor to note another of his servants, viz., William Ivers, to be committed for that he brought a threatening message to Walter Cusack, that if he would not sell his interest in the Ross of Skryne to Sir Robert he would have his head.

Thus I departed from their Lordships and rode by night with the Commission, and within a mile or two of Sir Robert's house heard it reported that Simon Wilde was come at midnight to Lady Dillon, at Riverston. I imagined that he rode not in that extraordinary time and haste only to bring the lady tidings of her husband's committal. There having delivered the commission, the commissioner rode straight to Gerardstown to apprehend Robert Cusack, who was gone to my Lord Deputy before being, as his people told, sent for by his Lordship, which I believed not at that time, but judged that he had some secret warning sent him to prevent the commission, wherein was inhibited that he should have conference with any before he came to his Lordship. I returned with all possible speed, and arrived at Dublin that night. The next day, being Sunday, 8th August, I was before the Lord Deputy and Council at Kilmainham in the afternoon, where I told what I heard of Simon Wilde, and moved my Lords that he might be committed and examined. My Lord Deputy sent to the Lady Dillon for him, who promised to send him to his Lordship, but afterwards she sent by one of her servants to the Bishop of Meath that she had licensed Wilde to go about his harvest, and since understood that he was gotten into England. This was not only without license or passport, but also upon a stay of shipping commanded by the Lord Deputy and Council. The other of Sir Robert's servants whom I wished to be committed, William Ivers, has not yet been before their Lordships to be examined, for on Thursday last, the 12th, he was overseeing his harvest at his dwelling in the country, whereby I am moved to think that the pursuivants and others whom their Lordships trust in this business, omit some diligence. The Solicitor and Nathaniel Dillon, Clerk of the Council, took the search of his houses at Riverston and the Bective, on Saturday afternoon. Thus far of the proceedings."

Delvin and Howth to the English Privy Council Kilcarne 16 Sept 1591 PRONI D/3835/A/6/430
[In reference to the decision to release Sir Robert Dillon] "where he may speak with who he list, practice to prevent all proves, and stop men from complaint by giving rewards, good turns, and terrifying them from dealing against him by mean of his former credit and his present unexpected liberty."

William Nugent c15 Oct 1591 PRONI D/3835/A/5/53
[Outlining the difficulties the Lord Deputy is placing preventing him from continuing with the case]
"When I made scruple to show my proofs before Sir Robert were committed he said in a great rage "I am a better man than thou. I never ran away. I never went beyond the sea, by the son of God if I had treason against thee I would hang thee by the neck." And when I offered if his Lordship would give me a passport to prove the matters before the Lords of the Council in England he refused it and made me complain."

1592
Examination of Christopher Nugent of Laragh Co. Longford. 6 June 1592 PRONI D/3835/A/6/407
"Deposeth that about August last, the deponent being sheriff of Co. Longford, Cahill McCongowney served under him then sheriff as one of the kerne and he saieth the said Cahill was condemned about 4 years past at Cavan before Sir Robert Dillon, Justice there, for stealing sheep and saw the said Cahill have his book to read, as a clerk, and whether he read or not he cannot tell because he was not within hearing; but the deponent saw him

burned in the hand and heard him cry with the pain of burning and after this Deponent laboured with the gaoler to have him delivered and so upon the Deponents bonds for his fees he was enlarged and saith [that] the people there saw the said Cahill burned in face of the court."

William Nugent to Burghley Clonin 13 Sept 1592 PRONI D/3835/A/5/65
Complaining about the preference the Lord Deputy and Council are showing the Dillons:
"Thirdly his discountenancing of those who prove or profer matter for the Queen in this service.

Fourthly and lastly the fear by reason of these favours and disfavours must strike the people, that lay before their eyes the crime of sundry innocent persons compassed by the ungodly drifts of Sir Robert Dillon, some to satisfy his implacable malice and hate borne them, some for envy and some for their living, which his insatiable covetise greedily desiring persuaded him that by their falls might fall into his hands.

These mischiefs the more part conceiving to hang over their own heads in case they should open themselves and detect him whom they are persuaded to be over mightily favoured for any truth to prevail against dare not intermeddle in any matter that might provoke his revenge, so as what crimes so ever are proved they must have been very manifest or else they had lain buried from sight and knowledge of the world choosing this time that the favours which embraceth him is of sway in this realm."
...now noting his concern that the case is to be decided by Sir Henry Wallop:
"I am not any way to except to them, of whom I must think always reveretly, as becometh me, only this much in discharge of my duty. I desire that your Lordship be advised of, that before Sir Henry his going into England there was great correspondence thought to be betwixt him and Sir Robert Dillon."
...Some of the details that show Dillon was involved in fostering rebellions:
"2) Shane na Sheaghe proveth that his father Brian Mac Ferale Oge ...sent the kine to Sir Robert Dillon; that the said Brian was

in actual rebellion is proved by the head money [a reward paid for killing a rebel] paid by the inhabitants of Co. Cavan to Hugh O'-Moloy who with others, the sheriff of that county slew the said Brian within a few days after he had sent the kine to Sir Robert Dillon; that Sir Robert knew him to be in open rebellion is very clear, he being Chief Commissioner at that time, and long before, at all sessions holden in the Counties of Longford and the Cavan aforesaid, where the said Brian did continually exercise his rebellious feats.

3) The depositions taken before Sir Richard Bingham prove that Teigh Keigh O'Kelly was in action of rebellion, before, at the time, and after the time that Sir Robert Dillon by his letter assigned certain relief of money to be delivered to the said Teigh, the said letter Sir Richard sent to the Commissioners here, and I suppose is sent over by them to the Lords.

...

7) Patrick Tankard...[his] deposition to be weighed for the death of the Justice Nugent wickedly practised."

Letter of Fr Sean McCongawney formerly secretary to O'Rourke from Dublin castle to the Baron of Delvin. prob.1592 PRONI D/3835/A/5/73
"I let you well [know?] that it is for [your] sakes that I am here without cause other than that it is demanded I should charge you with matter that would be your destruction. And God be praised I have no such to accuse you of. And I tell you further there live not persons whom I do more affect than you though I fare never a whit the better for it now...
Christopher Browne [go between from Dillon to O'Rourke] sent him O'Rourke all intelligences and that he warned him O'Rourke at such times as the Commissioners went to Longford that he should in no wise come in and that he knew he should perish if he did. And I hold that he [Browne] had been in his company three days in his last rebellion...
I tell you further that they are sharply bent against you...and further that I have a great matter to open against these men which I dare not write in this letter. No more but follow Christopher

Browne well...[and if the priest can get out on bail] I will tell you things that shall be more to your satisfaction."

2nd Letter from the priest this time addressed to Delvin and Howth Oct 28 1592 PRONI D/3835/A/5/75
"...but am placed 23 foot under the earth and do lose my legs by reason of the weight of the irons or fetters which I have on me, neither am I permitted to go to the grate to beg mine alms..."

Questions that the Barons of Howth and Delvin wish asked of Sir Robert Dillon prob Oct 1592 PRONI D/3835/A/5/75
"Was it Sir Robert Dillon that sent him [O'Rourke] intelligence of them, and by whom did he send the same.
...
Hath Sir Robert Dillon written or sent to O'Rourke animating him to move war in the province of Connaught, and who was the messenger by whom he wrote or sent to such effect and did he undertake the same should be acceptable to the Lord Deputy and state."
[He would be making war against Bingham as President of Connaught. Bingham felt he was also set up by the Dillons et al.]

William and Patrick Bermingham [of Corballies] pleading before the Irish Council 13th Nov 1592 PRONI D/3835/A/5/77
"The same day after [the council meeting] the said Lords [Delvin and Howth] received intelligence from the priest Shane McCongawney how the Deane of Farranan (who had before being placed among the prisoners of within the grate) was removed from thence to the Upper rooms, and that Garrat Dillon clerk of the crown, Sir Robert's brother, had been with the said Deane at sundry times with pen ink and paper and had written a great deal which the said Shane imagined was some device forged of the said Deane and the said Garrat to discredit the informations of the Lords and to d[islike?] the service [of the Lords]."

Petition of William Nugent 15 Nov 1592 PRONI D/3835/A/5/71
"Right Honourable, William Nugent, most humbly beseecheth and on the Queen's behalf requireth your Lordships where it is a thing despaired that even her Majesty shall have justice against

Sir Robert Dillon seeing how strangely fortune supporteth not only himself, but for all these whose like bad causes have any dependence or conjunction with his case, whereby partly cometh pass that men dare not inform nor witness against him such matter as they know and do greatly import her Majesty and this state and partly for that his liberty since the 7th of September hath given him desired opportunity by all practises to prevent, direct and suppress the matters and witnesses produced and to be produced against him, to her Majesty's great prejudice.

...[Wants him jailed and close watched:] that he may have not commodity to suffocate the matters of state disclosed as he hath in a great part done the form[erly.]"

1593

Carew MSS 1593 p.75 et seq.

[These numbered paragraphs are from the published Carew volumes, with the wording sometimes modernised. Incidentally these documents, which are described as a 'book' prepared by William Nugent in cooperation with Delvin, Howth and Patrick Bermingham, were in the possession of Sir George Carew of Stratford upon Avon.]

I. "Sheane McCongawney's Relation, written by himself in Irish, and translated afterwards into English."

Delivered to the Lord Deputy and Council the 13th of August, anno '93.

"This is the service which I have opened against Sir Robert Dillon, viz., that O'Rourke sent the constable of Longford, Chr Browne, to Sir Robert Dillon and Sir Lucas Dillon, to know what course they would advise him to hold, or whether they were able to do him any good, or espy about the Lord Deputy and Council, what disposition they bare towards him; and Sir Robert sent him answer that it was hard for him to do him good, for that Sir Richard Bingham had written into England how he had made a wooden image for the Queen, and caused the same to be trailed at a horse's tail and kerne and horseboys to hurl stones at it, every day; and that therefore there was commission come from the Council of England to apprehend O'Rourke, howsoever he might be gotten, in war or peace.

And moreover Sir Robert Dillon sent him writing how the Lord Deputy said, if he were taken in peace or war, the usage meet to be holden towards him was, to bind his tail to a board, and to cram him with meat until his belly bursted. And O'Rourke was upon Lough Moiltaghar, when Chr. Browne brought him these intelligences, and he brake the letter immediately after Christopher had left it him, and I myself was present that day. And therefore it was that Sir Robert might not help him, and thus much might suffice him for intelligence, and he wished him to be assured of all that Chr. Browne should tell him. And within two days after, O'Rourke sent for the McSwines of Tirconill.

And further, when certain bands of soldiers went into McWilliam Burg's country [Mayo], Christopher sent O'R. word that he had been in Dublin, and had gotten most certain writing from those of his acquaintance, that when they had brought in that country, they would make seeming to dissolve and disperse them, but they had commandment from the Lord Deputy to invade O'Rourke, one company from Connaught and another from the country of Longfort, by reason whereof O'R. sent for Murgha na Mart, who was with Captain Bingham in Connaught.

And whatsoever other service I have disclosed to the Council, I have the copy of it; and the cause why I have written this is, for that the Council do not understand my language, and also for another reason, that I know not what the interpreter declares, and that I wot not but that he might leave some things unexpounded to the Lord Deputy or the Council which I should speak. And further, truly I will stand to all this for the Queen, here or before the Council of England, wheresoever I shall happen to be, there or here.

Johannes MacCongawney."

III. "A Relation delivered by John Garlond to the Lords of Delvin and Howth, in the Easter term, anno 1593.

When I was sent from Sir John Perrot with letters to O'Rourke by direction of the Lords of H.M. Privy Council in England, within a two months after mine arrival here, I set forward to perform that service, attended upon by my brother Patrick Garlond and my horseboy Richard Neile. And being come as far as Mr Rowyr O'Ferall's house in the Analy [Co. Longford], he sent one with me to be my guide. Having travelled so far as to the woods beyond Longfort, we overtook three men on foot, whereof one carried a bottle of acqua vitae, the other a small barrel of gunpowder, and the third, who wore a hat, bare in the skirt of his mantle some heavy thing, which to our seeming should be lead. We made no long tarrying with these fellows, misdoubting the danger of the way, by reason that O'Rourke was (not long before) fallen into rebellion. This was on Tuesday, and we held on our journey towards O'Rourke, to whom we came the morrow after and accompanied him to Loughfguire.

Upon Thursday the three footmen before mentioned arrived there, where O'Rourke, being at dinner, called for Chr. Browne's man, whereupon he that had carried the gunpowder, leaving off his mantle, stood up and answered.

Then said O'R, 'I will drink to thy master and to my friend's man there with thee. Thank thy master for the acqua vitae and munition he hath sent me; pray him to send me more, and tell him I will pay him for it to his own contentation, and (that I may not forget it) commend me to Tanckerd's daughter." At these words one of O'R.'s men that waited did shake his head, as seeming to mislike with him.

Hearing these things I rowned my brother in the ear, saying, 'Brother, what traitorly knaves be these?' Wherewith he jogged me on the elbow, and I bade him say nothing, but mark all things that should be spoken or done.

Dinner being ended, as O'R. was going forth at the door, Chr. Browne's man stepped to him, and pulling him by the cloak, for I remember he ware a long black cloak, said, 'Christopher wisheth you to give credit to anything that this messenger of Sir R. Dillon's shall tell you; and now, if you will anything with us, let us understand it, for we would fain be going.[']

Before we had come from the Lough, O'R's letter being written, his secretary, finding me and my brother together, said these words: 'O'R. marvels greatly that Sir John Perrot is so earnest in persuading him to come in and not to stand to his defence against the Lord Deputy, considering that sundry as well of Sir John's inward friends as O'R.'s friends in the English Pale, and among the rest Sir Robert Dillon, do forbid him anywise to trust the Lord Deputy or Sir Richard Bingham, affirming, if he do, that he shall lose his head; for you [i.e. Garlond] were not past a week in Ireland when Sir Robert Dillon sent him warning that he should not give credit to you nor to Sir John Perrrot's letters, for all was but to betray him.[']

My brother and the guide wished me to come in company with these messengers of Sir Robert Dillon and Chr. Browne the shortest way towards Longford, but I refused so to do, telling my brother that I would never keep company with such traitorly knaves, bidding him to note well what he saw and heard.

The messengers, driving with them a six or seven heads of cows and garans, departed, which Rowrye O'Ferall's man, that was our guide, saw as well as we.

After we were come over the Lough, and that O'R. was on horseback, I being come to take leave of him, he laid his hand upon my shoulder, and said,

"John Garlond, I thank you for your pains, and I would you had comen a six or seven days sooner, for then had I not done that which I have done; but now I am so far gone as I cannot draw back again, without the Queen will use grace towards me. [Sir Brian O'Rourke, a popular figure in Irish history well known for aiding the survivors of the Spanish Armada, was of course hung at Tyburn in October 1591. Incidentally Perrot was also sentenced to death, partly for supposedly aiding O'Rourke, and died in the Tower of London before he could be executed. You cannot help wondering that the real reason they were hung is that they knew too much, and even that they could have aided William Nugent's court case?] And you were not in Ireland a week when Sir Robert Dillon sent me warning that I should not give credit to you nor your letters, as Edmund McShane here can tell (meaning his secretary); and here is now again his messenger comen with Chr. Browne's man yonder, and he wisheth me in any wise not to come in, assuring me, if I do, that I shall lose my life.'

Which words my brother heard, and may remember, if he please."

IV. "The Relation of Patrick Garlond made to the Lords of Delvin and Howth the 8th of August 1593, at Howth.

Delivered to the Lord Deputy and Council the 13th of August in '93."

Description of the journey made by himself and his brother John to O'Rourke, similar to that in the preceding document. He then proceeds to say:

"After our return from O'R.'s country my brother sent me before him to Dublin, where I repaired to Sir Lucas Dillon's house, whom I found in his hall walking with Sir Robert Dillon.

Sir Lucas asked me, 'What news from O'R.?'

I told him he was out and would not come in, and all was long of them, as he affirmed. Sir Lucas asked of whom.

I answered, 'Of you and Sir Robert Dillon, and others his friends.' With this Sir Robert stormed, and said, 'God's body! not I; the knave lies!'

Then said Sir Lucas, 'Fear not, Sir Robert; I warrant you Pat. Garland is an honest man; he will say nothing.'

And therewith Sir Lucas and Sir Robert went from me to the window towards the garden, where they talked together in secret a little while. And after Sir Lucas put his hand into his pocket, and gave me a twenty shillings sterling in money, saying, 'Pat, stay within the house, and go not abroad, and say nothing!' And then Sir Robert, well quieted, and he went together to the Castle."

V. "The 15th of August '93, in the forenoon, Jo. Garlond, at the Castle of the Crane in Dublin, added further to his former relation, in presence of the Lords of Delvin and Howth, William Nugent, and Patrick Bermingham, this following:–

After my brother Pat. was departed from me, I took my way to Agher, where, being something diseased with a flixe, I sojourned for certain days. Sir Lucas Dillon, one day coming thither from his house of Moymet, asked whether his cousin George Garlond was at home; and being answered that he was not, he asked mine aunt whether I was there. She told him I was, and he prayed her to call me to him. When I came to the door, where I found him on horseback, he bade me welcome, and prayed me to pull on my boots, and ride with him a piece in his way. I said I could not.

'Go to! I pray you come,' quoth he.

Then I made me ready, and rode with him a part in the way towards Maynooth, where (as we rid together) he had this speech
with me, viz.,

'Cousin Garlond, your brother hath been with me at Dublin, and
told me that Chr. Browne sent certain aqua vitae, powder, and
lead to O'Rourke when you were there.'

Then said I, 'What more did he tell you?'

'Marry!' quoth he, 'he told me there were some of Sir John Perrot's friends and of O'R.'s also, who warned him not to give credit to you nor the letters you carried, and, if he did, that he should
lose his head: and I pray you who be those?'

I answered, 'The Bishop of Laighlin for one, and one Mr. White,
and you and Sir Robert Dillon.'

Then said Sir Lucas, 'I had lever he were hanged than that he
should prove that.'

And so we left at that time.

Being to return from him, he asked me when I would be at
Dublin. I said within a ten or twelve days, when I were well; and
so we departed, I returning back to mine uncle's house again,
where, when I was come, mine aunt asked.

'I pray you what great counselship was this betwixt you and Sir
Lucas Dillon? I am glad you are taken up with such great men. It
is well that Sir Lucas Dillon stays for you until you have pulled
on your boots. Nephew, there is something in the wind when such
men stay for you.'

After my recovery, when I went to Dublin, I repaired to Sir
Lucas his house, where I supped with him. Supper being done, he
commanded all his servants out of the chamber, and locked the
door himself, then fell in talk with me of Chr. Browne, of whom,
when I had said that he was a traitorly knave, Sir Lucas said,

'John Garlond, you mean to go into England shortly.'

'Yea marry do I,' said I.

Then he leaned with one elbow upon the bed, which was low, and
his knee almost laid upon the ground, with tears standing in his
eyes, lifted up his hands, saying,

'John Garland, I desire thee, for the passion of God, not to bring
Chr. Browne in question; for if you do, you undo him and me and
all my friends. I will be thy friend during thy life, and I will never

see you want anything as long as I live.'

Within a little while after he gave me forty shillings in money and a grey nag. Not long after I went into England, and returned hither back again. At my next going over, which was with the examinations of the priest Sir Dennis [O'Roughan], that I carried in a bag, Sir Lucas gave me £5 sterling in money, and said,

'John Garlond, look well this; if this were taken, it is as much as my neck is worth, and all that ever I have."

VI. "The last part disclosed by Jo. Garlond, tending to the proof of Sir R. Dillon's traitorous practice with O'Rourke; by him opened to the Lords of Delvin and Howth, William Nugent, and Pat. Bermyngham, the 11th of September 1593, and by them delivered to the Lord Deputy and Council at Killmainham the 13th of the same.

When I landed at Chester, being returned into England with the answers of O'Neill, O'Rourke, and others of the Irishry upon those letters which I brought them from Sir Jo. Perrot, there I met Sir Edward More, who delivered me a letter from Sir John, which I have forthcoming. This letter, among other things, bare special direction that I should come with Sir Thomas Cecil into Ireland, and attend upon him during his abode here, etc, which I did accordingly, sending my brother Patrick with my packet and certain hawks to Sir John. At my return into England again in company of Sir Thomas, I carried, among other letters, one from Sir Lucas Dillon, who at my leave-taking bestowed a hackney upon me.

When I was come to Sir John and delivered my letters, he commanded the rest of his servants to avoid, which done, and I having shut the chamber door, he said,

'God's wounds! Garlond, hast thou not heard how that same blind villain hath played the traitor, first with the Queen and after with me?'

I asked, 'Who, sir?'

He answered, 'That blind traitorly villain Sir R. Dillon.'

And drawing forth of his desk the packet which I had before sent him by my brother, pulling out of the packet a letter, and out of that letter another written paper, he said,

'Here is a note which O'Rourke sent me in his letter of their names who forbade him come in; and he was the only principal man, as I understand by O'Rourke; but, by God's wounds! I know who set him on. I do not marvel that he should play the traitor now, for he played the villain with me when I was in Ireland Deputy, and I knew it very well; but by God's wounds! I shall want of my will but I will hang him.'

Then said I, 'By God! Sir, if you do, you will hang another with him, whom you think very well of.'

'Why, who is that?' said he.

I said, 'Sir Lucas Dillon; for if you bring him in question you must bring Sir Lucas in question too.'

He said, 'Nay, God's wounds! I would not do that for a thousand pounds.'

I said, 'By God! then, you must let the other alone.'

Then, said Sir John, 'Garlond, how hath Sir Lucas dealt with you?'

I answered, 'Well, Sir.'

Then he nodded, smiling, and said,

'That is because thou canst tell tales of him and that blind villain: I know what thou canst say as well as thyself; but i'faith, Garlond, what did he give thee, or what did he promise thee?'

I told him he promised to keep me two horses and a boy, and that I should myself be allowed as long and as oft as I would during my life to lie and remain at his house, and that he would, under his hand and seal, bind his son and heir to give me the same allowance all the days of my life. At my next return into Ireland I told him also that he had given me five pounds and a nag at my leave-taking.

Sir John said, 'God's wounds! I think I shall let the blind villain escape for Sir Lucas Dillon's sake, for fear lest I should bring his name in question.'

At my next coming into Ireland, which was betwixt the Christmas and Shrovetide following, when I went to take leave of Sir John Perrot at Greenwich, he having written letters by me to sundry of his friends here, and having gotten me allowance of packet money, though I came but with private letters only, said to me these words,

'Garlond, commend me to Sir Lucas Dillon, for he is one of the best friends I have there, and I charge you, as you look for any good at my hand, do not touch him, for, by God's wounds! if you do, I will hang you.'

As I was taking my leave, he caused his servant Mainwareing to give me forty shillings in gold, and caused also his secretary James to write to Rise Thomas, who kept his wardrobe at York House in London, to deliver me his Irish ash-colour cloak, which was thick laid on with gold lace over the sleeves; and taking me by the hand (a thing extraordinary for him to do to any of his servants) said,

'Farewell, Garlond; commend me to all my good friends in Ireland. As for those that are not my friends, I care not that they were all hanged.'

The morning next after my landing at Dublin, which was, as I remember, a week before Shrovetide, I repaired to Sir Lucas Dillon's house in St Nicholas' Street, to whom, being in his study, I delivered Sir John Perrot's letter. He welcomed me very kindly, and after he had read the letter he said,

'Jo. Garlond, I think myself greatly beholden to you for the good report you have made of me to Sir Jo. Perrot, as I understand by his letter. Have you seen my cousin Sir Robert since your coming?'

I answered, 'No.'

Then said he, 'He is below in the garden: I pray you do so much as desire him to come up hither.'

Then went I down to the garden, where I found Sir R. Dillon and Fergus O'Ferall walking together; but Sir Robert, so soon as I came thither, brake off his talk and company with him, and coming towards me, said,

'O gentleman, are you there? You are welcome out of England.'

I thanked him, and told him Sir Lucas desired him to go up unto him.

He said, 'I will do so when I have walked half a dozen turns with you.' And then said he,

'I am sorry that Sir John Perrot is such an enemy to me; he hath undone and discredited me with the Queen and the Council there; he hathe brought me upon my knees.'

I said, 'If you had not deserved it, I am sure he would not have done so; but, by God! I know, were it not for fear lest he should bring Sir Lucas Dillon in question, he sware God's wounds he would hang you.'

'I sent him a goshawk,' said he, 'by my son Patrick Sadgrave, but he refused it, and was at defiance with me and my hawk.'

'Well,' quoth I, 'Sir John told me so much, and said he would rather see you and your hawk hanged than he would be beholden to you for a hawk; but if you had sent her by me, I think I would have used that office that would have made him to receive your hawk.'

Then went he up to Sir Lucas his study; I went up also, and stayed without in the chamber. After they two had been some quarter of an hour there together, and that Sir Lucas, as I imagined, had shown him Sir Jo. Perrot's letter, they came both together out of the study into the chamber, and Sir Lucas said,

'Cousin Sir Robert, John Garlond hath dealt honestly and like a gentleman with you and me; therefore I would have you to deal well with him, and use him like a gentleman, for he hath deserved it well at our hands.'

Then Sir Lucas willed me to call his man Shea, who being come up, Sir Lucas said,

'Shea, send for some white wine for John Garlond for his welcome.'

The wine being come Fergus O'Ferall being brought in also to drink, when we had drunken, Sir Lucas, taking Fergus with him down, said,

'Well, cousin Sir Robert, I will leave you and John Garland together, and Fergus and I will walk into the garden.'

And so they went down together, leaving Sir Robert and me in the chamber, whence Sir R. went into his study, and there remained a short while, and after anon asked,

'Who is there without?'

I answered, 'None but I, Sir.'

'O Sir,' quoth he, 'I pray you come in.'

I went in, and he said,

'John Garlond, I understand, by my cousin Sir Lucas, that you have dealt very justly and truly with him and with me, and whatsoever he hath promised you I dare undertake he will perform it;

and as for mine own part, assure yourself, if I may do you any good, I will be ready to do you a good turn as soon as any friend you have in Ireland.'

And therewith he put his hand into his pocket, and drew out, lapped in a piece of brown paper, ten angels, which he delivered me, saying,

'John Garlond here is a token of goodwill for you until a better come, and if your master were not, I should be able to give you a better;' and then embracing me, said, 'John Garlond, you are welcome, and I thank you with all my heart.'

Then he and I went down immediately to the garden, where Sir Lucas and Fergus O'Ferall walked together. Then Sir Lucas said,

'Cousin Sir R., I pray you that you will sup with me here this night, for John Garlond and we will be merry; and, cousin Fergus, I pray you, sup with us too.'

We supped there together that night, and so departed.

At my last coming into Ireland (which I trow was about a twelvemonth past), after my landing, I went late in the evening to see Sir R. Dillon, and being told at his lodging that he was gone to see Mrs Parkins, I went thither, and found him in talk with her in her garden. She having departed into her house, I walked with Sir Robert half a dozen turns, talking of the proceeding of his man Anthony Dillon in England, and thence brought him to his lodging.

At my departing he prayed me to see him the next morning, and so I did. I found him in his hall, accompanied with Mr. Fitton and one more. Sir Robert, making towards me, said,

'You are welcome, gentle John;'

whereupon Mr Fitton and the other departed. Then he said, embracing me,

'By my truth! Jo. Garland you are welcome. I heard say you have behaved yourself like a gentleman, and I am glad of it. And now tell me what news, I pray you.'

I said, 'By my troth! I have no news, but I did abide a year's imprisonment for Sir Lucas Dillon and you, for Captain Wooddhowse charged me before the Commissioners that I could accuse Sir Lucas Dillon; and you know what promise Sir Lucas made me, but now he is dead, and may not perform it; howbeit I hope, if you be out, you will remember me, and use me as I have deserved.'

Whereunto he said,

'Assure yourself, John, whensoever I am abroad you shall not want anything that I have.'

And so we departed."

VIII. "A note of such the Lord Deputy's [Sir William FitzWilliam] favours showed to Sir Robert Dillon since his coming out of England, as were open, and are by us able to be proved.

1. The morrow after his landing here he rode with the Lord Deputy to the church in great pride, familiarly conferring with him by the way.

2. When William Nugent demanded protection for Carbre O'Treawair the 2nd of August, the Lord Deputy denied it, saying Carbrey was the arrantest traitor in all Ireland. Nugent said that his Lp. had yet protected him before that time.

'Yea, Mr Nugent,' said he, 'that protection was upon letters out of England, and for a matter concerning you;' so as he thought him a meet man to be examined upon Nugent, and for that purpose twice protected him; but when he was to be examined upon Sir R. Dillon, he took exception to him. But yet after this, the 13th of August, the same demand being made again for Carbrei's protection, a full Council then being there, it was granted.

3. When Jo. Garlond, being commanded by the Council to attend at Dublin for this service, was maliciously arrested by Sir Robert Dillon's son-in-law, and the same was complained by William Nugent, who besought the Lord Deputy to give order for discharging him of that arrest, he showed discontentment that Nugent would trouble him with his importunity, saying it was reason that men should pay their debts. Nugent said he would be bound for him in any bond. The Lord Deputy said he had not to do to take sureties, and so departed out of the Council chamber; but two of the judges going forth after him, said,

'We have commanded him to stay for the Queen's service, and we will protect him.'

And so, when the Council came there again in the afternoon, there was order given for Garlond's discharge.

4. The Lord Deputy and Council having written for the party that procured the arrest of Garlond, viz., Sir Robert Dillon's son-in-law, determined to punish him for arresting Garlond, he never made appearance. The same was remembered to the Lord Deputy, yet he never punished him for that contempt.

5. The Coarb of Drumrela was a very inward man with the late O'Rourke. This man was being alighted into the hands of the sheriff of the county of Leitrim, and the agents in these matters understanding the same, moved the Lord Deputy and Council that the sheriff might be caused to send him to be examined upon Sir R. Dillon. Commandment was sent to the sheriff to that effect very peremptory. The sheriff dismissed the prisoner for certain money, and (as it was informed to the Lord Deputy) for the use, or rather the abuse, of his sister. The Lord Deputy seemed to be greatly moved hereat, and threatened to punish it severely; but yet the sheriff is now in the English Pale, and nothing said to him for this.

6. After the examinations heard and the relations seen of the priest, Carbrey O'Treawair, and both the Garlands, when all men had now in their own opinions seemed to condemn Sir Robert Dillon; the Lord Deputy, with the Lord Chancellor and others of the Council, being at the hills, of Taragh to take view of the musters of the English Pale, he graced Sir R. Dillon in the presence of all that assembly, using him as a special concillor and assistant in all public actions by him there done, to the wonder and astonishment of all those that saw him, and that night after lay at his house.

7. Where Chr. Browne was bound in recognizance to be at Dublin in the Easter term '93, and was not, yet he is not called upon for his recognizance, though the same were remembered to the Lord Deputy the last day of that term.

8. It hath been often demanded that he might be committed in respect that the priest chargeth him to his face, and the Garlonds by means, but it hath never been granted.

9. It hath likewise been often urged that the agents and the priest might be brought face to face before the Lord Deputy and Council, whereby no doubt there would practices appear that as yet be hidden, but it is ever avoided.

10. Where there was direction sent from the Lord Deputy and Council to Sir John Norris to send O'Rourke's secretary to them, and a protection also sent to him, the same was delivered to the Lord of Delvin, who sent his footman to seek for the secretary in Munster. He could not find him, but yet hath heard where he hath been the very night before his own arrival in the same place. After the return of the messenger, when the Lord of Delvin told what success he had, the Lord Deputy said,

'Why, I understand the secretary was gone into Spain a quarter of a year since.'

11. Sir R. Dillon sat in Council not past three or four days before his going into England now last, which by some of the Council was thought strange.

12. Richard Neile, who was with John Garland at O'Rourke's, was not examined, and yet the same was demanded."

Signed C. Delvin, H. Howth, William Nugent, P. Bermingham.

1599

Lord Delvin from Clonin (Delvin) to the Lord Justices and Council in Dublin 22 Nov 1599 PRONI D/3835/A/5/109

"My Lords I am in the greatest extremity that may be, being environed with Tyrone's forces between me and Trim, the Leinster forces on the other quarter between Athboy and Portlester and the great [O']More and O'Rourke's forces being in the next part of the County of Longford ready to enter this country and draw forward ready to meet about my house here, which is made rather for pleasure than defence. I posted one with a letter to the Navan not doubting but my Lord Lieutenant [Earl of Ormond] had been there, with forces able to relieve me, but this day the whole country being on fire, my boy returned with my own letters from the Navan and told me that there were no forces but a few for the defence of the town, and that his Lord returned to Dublin, which was a cold comfort for me, whose person is the most desired by them of any in this kingdom. Therefore I beseech your lords direct me with all speed what course to hold, whither I shall steal away if I can to your lords and so save one that may hereafter serve the Queen in a better time, or stay here subject to all adventures of fortune in a weak house, not possible long to be kept the country being already overrun. I sent away part of my children yesterday towards Maynooth, which I fear are taken by the rebels. I mistrust a great part of the country will revolt, some according to their lewd disposition, as I formerly wrote unto your lords, and others in respect they have no defence. And so in haste I humbly take leave."

[He stayed and bought time by sending ambassadors to Tyrone, with the permission of Ormond, and posting his small army at Killua to await the outcome of the negotiations held at Crossakiel Co. Meath.]

24 Nov 1599 PRONI D/3835/A/4/403
"Upon Tuesday last Christopher Fitz Oliver (Nugent) a gentleman of Westmeath, nearly allied to O'Reilly's wife, and having certain intelligence of the enemy's purpose to overun the country, met them by the way, and of himself demanded the cause of this great envy towards the Lord of Delvin. Tyrone [Hugh O'Neill] answered him that the Lord of Delvin was the only block that hindered him overrunning the whole kingdom, and vowed that he would never leave Westmeath until he had overrun him."

Instructions given to ambassadors from the Baron of Delvin to the Earl of Tyrone enclosed in a letter of 28 Nov 1599 PRONI D/3835/A/4/410
"Item you are to tell him [Tyrone] if he pretend as he doth the same list [?jist] for the advancement of the Catholic religion, as commonly he giveth out: That all of the inhabitants of the English Pale for the most part, and specially myself, are Catholic, and were so when he was thought not to be one. And many of us having heard and read a good deal more than he did could never find in scripture, General Councils, by the Fathers, or any other authentical authority, that subjects ought to carry arms against their anoint[ed] Christian prince for religion or any other cause; and especially against so gracious a prince as we have, whose bounty and special favour we have ever found, and he himself most of any. Therefore this gross and inexcusable ignorance is not sufficient for him to seek our destruction...[asking that he put any

claims he wants properly before the Council]...

which if he deny let him understand that the world in general must judge that he useth the pretence of religion but as a cloak for tyranny, for which he may expect no other reward in this world, or in the world to come, than every other [person] persevering in like purpose have had."

1600

Delvin to the same 27 Jan 1600 PRONI D/3835/A/5/109
He is constantly being slandered as having joined up with O'Neill:
"...yet the devices and idle plots of every runaway fellow of them [rebels] will be heard with greater attention than mine who's whole study is with the hazard of my life, and loss of my blood, to further her Majesty's service, by cutting of many of the rebels daily in the counties and borders towards me, wherefore I could wish that actions were preferred in her Majesty's service before the brabblings of such as never yield any other fruit..."

Sir Francis Shane writing to Sir Robert Cecil 8 April 1600 CSPI p.85
"Duty to God inciteth me to disclose unto your Honour another thing, which in my knowledge hath always not only hatched these our rebellions from time to time, but also withdrawn the hearts of the subjects from obedience; I mean the friars of Multyfarnham in Westmeath; the nursey of all mischevious practices, the subversion whereof hath been often moved to the State here, but the fear of offending the lord of Delvin hath always the let, having a more interest in some than ought, which doth draw upon us the wrath of God, whereby their endeavours take so small effect, in that they prefer the fear of men before the service of God."

Instructions from the Queen to her Deputy in Ireland June 1600 CSPI p.272
[She wants him to deal severely with the growth of the Catholic religion, despite the times and will not] "suffer friaries to stand, when we have an army of 17,000 men to fight withal.
Likewise in the diocese of Meath, which is in the heart of the

English Pale, there is suffered to stand untouched a house of friars, called Multyfarnham [the only specific place mentioned in the letter], the only place of assembly and conventicle of all the traitorous Jesuits of the realm, and where was the first conspiracy and plotting of this great rebellion.

This of all the rest is most lamentable and worthy of reprehension in the Bishop, for that the friars, and all other popish adversaries to Her Majesty's government, have their recourse and passage to and fro thither, in as open and public manner as if their idolatrous profession were justified by the authority of the clergy.

That the Lord Deputy charge the Bishop of Meath, in her Majesty's name, to see how this house may be demolished, or at least the friars expelled, and the house converted to a place of garrison."

1607

A list of grievances compiled by the Earl of Tyrconnell c.1607 PRONI D/3835/A/4/576
no.33 "Ferighe O'Reille [?Kelly] being condemned to be hanged at Athlone for some crime, by a messenger secretly sent by the Lord Deputy who arrived just as the said Ferigh was to be hanged and offered him his life and large rewards if he would charge the Earl [of Tyrconnell] with treason which he promised to do. And thereupon he was taken back and privately examinat. But finding his examination to halt (and no wonder because since it was forged at the same instant) resent him to the prison to "remain there until he had performed somewhat of that he had promised" if he could not do it that he was to be hanged and there he continued until the Earl last departed from Ireland."

Lady Delvin's (née Mary Fitzgerald) letter to her son the Baron of Delvin c.1607/8 (before 19 April 1608) PRONI D/3835/A/4/565
A lot of commentators forget that Ireland has always been a matriarchal society! So its not surprising to see that it was probably Delvin's mother that forced him to submit:
"Dear son, as God hath made me the mother to give you life, so your being now in the state to lose the same life, which is no less dear to me than mine own life, I must in this extremity advise you

(as well by the bonds of nature, as by what other obligation either of love or duty I may challenge at your hands) to yield to make your submission to our most gracious prince, the which I am assured safety and to the preservation of your house and ancient honour which without the same will I fear be utterly lost (yet for that it shall appear that I advise you hereunto for no other respect so much, as for the natural care, or more than so, if it maybe that I have of your person and state.) I intend once more to press your honourable friend the Lord Deputy for some other particulars and would therefore have you not to fail to be ready to make your submission, whereunto I would have you to agree before I engage or endanger myself further for you, or else absolutely to resolve me of your purposes by the bearer. Thus praying God to guide you I remain etc.

My love could not admit this persuasion if I and the rest of your best friends had not assured ourselves, it to be your only best and safest course, from which upon my blessing no discontented person or persons dissuade you."

[It is interesting to note that this Mary Fitzgerald, William's sister-in-law, was a first cousin once removed of the 3rd Earl of Southampton, from Cockatrice op.cit. inside cover.]

Chichester to Earl of Salisbury Dec 10 1607 PRONI D/3835/A/4/584-583

Chichester says that Delvin rebelled because he felt he would never find any justice from Salisbury in England, who is also supposed to have insulted him. Salisbury denies this in a marginal note on the letter: "...but true it is I know he hated me, for fear I was likest to discover him, and for his talk, he was never true, yet never openly a traitor, so his own malice to the state multiplied only his passion to me for I never used that word."

[Of course its probably the other way around. Salisbury probably paid off the Baron of Howth to hype up and partly manufacture the whole Flight of the Earls episode which conveniently made way for the Plantation of Ulster. (Thomas Nugent of Coolamber found out while hunting with the Baron of Howth, his first cousin once removed, that he had got 1,000 pounds from the state at this time, although he was defrauded of 300 pounds of it by the Lord

Treasurer. Dec 10 1607 PRONI D/3835/A/4/556. See also references to the Gunpowder plot etc in *Orwellian Ireland*, chapter 4 at footnote 104.) So it is more likely that Salisbury was afraid of Delvin finding him out and was getting in the early slander to confuse people. The reference to malice clarifies what was meant by the phrase, which was frequently used to describe the Nugents.]

Lord Chancellor Archbishop of Dublin to Salisbury (same date and reference as above)
About Delvin: "but it is truly said that that which is bred in the bone will show itself in the flesh, and the offspring of men which have been disloyal commonly inclineth to like course."

Sir Oliver St John to Salisbury 11 Dec 1607 PRONI D/3835/A/4/581
Baron of Delvin "is a dangerous young man and one if it please God he may be cut off it will be a happy turn for this country for he is composed of the malice of the Nugents and the pride of the Geraldines."

Chichester to the Lords of the Council 11 Dec 1607 Dublin Castle PRONI D/3835/A/4/582
"...The Proclamation lately published upon Delvin's flight, against him and his abettors, together with the sudden and sound prosecution of him with our forces have done this good effect, that such persons of sort and quality, as should otherwise undoubtedly have adhered unto him, are therewith stayed from flocking to him. And finding himself thus disappointed that way, he returned to Cloghoughter in the County of Cavan, with some of his servants and 40 kerne, and I forseeing that this would be his retreat and refuge for default of sufficient strength abroad, I sent Sir Garret Moore to the Cavan a town within 3 or 4 miles of the Castle and Lough of Cloghoughter with 200 foot and some horse and kerne, which I put under his charge for this service. Whilst the Marshall lay in Delvin's country, and near the mountain of Slewcarbery to keep him from comforts and assistance that way.

On Sunday last at night Delvin sent out part of his men to

snatch up some cows and sheep from the neighbours adjoining for his relief, and being met withal by some of our men, who lay in wait for them, there were 2 or 3 of them killed and the cattle rescued by our men. Whereupon the rest fled and escaped into the Lough by means of their codles [sic]. Delvin being much dismayed thereunto and withal standing in want of victuals, went out of the Lough, the next night after, himself and most of his men. And having passed a small way into the country to gather he told them he meant not to return to the castle anymore, but would take another course. And so bidding them all shift for themselves, he departed from them, accompanied with one gentleman of his own name and a poor slave for his guide. This is all I have yet heard of him, since his escape hence whereunto I thought fit to advertise your lordship.

I have directed the Marshall and Sir Garret Moore to take in the castle in any wise, his child and nurse and such as were parties or privy to his escape hence, being left there. And I imagine that having that [sic] made a short turn and will lurk there, being now diffident of every man."

1608
Chichester 4 June 1608 PRONI D/3835/A/4/559
The baron of Delvin is so poor at this point that Chichester has to pay for his journey to see the King in England.

1618
Revd Thomas Dease, titled Doctor of the Sorbonne later Bishop of Meath of course, writing from the Irish College in Paris to Fr Francis [Lavallin] Nugent in Rome 5 Feb 1618, describing those Irish who tried to stand up for the Catholic faith:
"Talis erat Desmoniae Comes, talis MacCartorum Comes et Princeps, talis Vicecomes Baltinglassiae, talis Jacobus Mauritii ex amplissima Geraldinorum stirpe cum innumeris magni nominis optimatibus quibus cum Gulielmo Nugentio cognato tuo se ab haereseos tyranide asserere molientibus proindeque ob fidem Catholicam capite redum possessionum ac dominiorum multa plexis, Baro Nugentius suspendii martyrio gloriosissimae est extinctus."

(Fr Robert O'Connell O.F.M. (Cap.), *Commentarii de Missione Hibernica Capuccinorum* (Charleville, c.1654), p.29 (38) from the transcript in the Capuchin Archives Dublin.)

["Of such a kind was the Earl of Desmond, and the Earl and Prince of the MacCarthys, and the Viscount of Baltinglass, and James Maurice, the most distinguished of all the stock of the Geraldines, and innumerable other great names and nobles (with many rents, possessions and dominions) who alongwith your relation William Nugent attempted to assert, by interwoven struggles, the Catholic faith from the capital tyranny of heresy, and Baron Nugent who was killed, by hanging, in a most glorious martyrdom."]

1624

Lord Deputy to Secretary Conway Dublin Castle March 31 1624
PRONI D/3835/A/4/513-4
"...I can but observe his [Earl of Westmeath's] ways, to find something said or done by himself might give me just ground to question him, of whose inclination I confess myself the most jealous of any man in this kingdom. But without that, he might challenge me of doing him wrong and colour his discontentments upon my errors which I shall careful to prevent.
...His nature is very busy and ambitious, and his way very popular appearing in all occasions wherein his country may seem entitled to any interest, and eager in the public representation and pressing of grievances, often enforcing some to be such which are indeed none at all, for which I have given him gentle check, and some private admonitions of a friend whereof I find the effects rather more wariness than chastity.
He is the minion of the Jesuits and priests who labour to R[?]inett him in the opinion of the people of the popish party, who have all their eyes fixed upon him, as for them the principal person of consequence in this kingdom. And to him have the discontented persons for plantations great relation...He [John Fitzpatrick brother of the Lord of Upper Ossory] had married the Lady of Inchiquin and sister unto that party [Westmeath] who stands out against all reason, as if animated to that obstinacy in

despite of duty."

[He also warned the people of Connaught about the possible plantation there, much to the Lord Deputy's annoyance.]

Lord Deputy to Secretary Conway H.G. May 13 1624 Dublin Castle. PRONI D/3835/A/4/509

"Right Honourable sir you have now the Lord of Westmeath with you. I assure myself you are satisfied in his loyalty and will use him fairly to his contentment; and yet not return him over suddenly. His being there keeps all those who had fixed their eyes upon him at a gaze and for this time hath amused their imaginations; which might unhappily have wrought his hurt in the way of their own ends, without his Privity, had he stayed still. His friends now give it forth that the Papists are jealous of him for the affection which he bear the state, and that great suspicions are conceived of him, lest he will be drawn to change his resolution in religion, who lately was the most presumed upon of any man in that land for being well grounded. Their sudden mutations of voices I hold it necessary to acquaint you to judge what is meet to be done. I love his person and am most careful of his well doing, yet my duty to our master is the supreme one which doeth and must sway me above all second respects. And yet I presume this is the way to preserve him, and will in the end prove to have been the office of a friend."

[Translated what that means is that the Deputy wants the government to hold Westmeath in England longer so that they can spread rumours that he had become a Protestant and so weaken and divide the Catholic party in Ireland. They had already put it about that Westmeath wanted to become King of Ireland in order to get him into trouble with the King (April 24 1624 PRONI D/3835/A/4/509). The King himself rejected these slanders and wrote back to the Irish Council (PRONI D/3835/A/4/508) on June 28th of that year refuting it and wanting the people who spread the slander dealt with. One of them was named as Thomas le Strange.]

1625

Propositions for securing Ireland (in the handwriting of Sir Francis Annesley) c.1625 or 1626 PRONI D/3835/A/5/218

"4. The Earl of Westmeath is a vehement papist and of a popular carriage amongst the Irish both for matters concerning religion and the commonwealth in so much that none of that religion appears in more eminence upon all occasions for the papists, he is well known to this and that state [prob. England and Ireland] and it is offered to consideration whether he may not be sent for upon some pretence to make his repair to his Majesty and upon his coming hither be kept here for the furtherance of this Majesty's service."

List of 'chief men reckoned dangerous' to the British administration in Ireland. CSPI 1615-25 p.75

Only these listed:

Munster – Lord Kerry a Papist and fights with his son

Florence McCarthy, brought the Spaniards to Kinsale. Should be secured.

Antrim – Earl of, should be sent for and treated kindly. Has friends at court. [Still he remained a Catholic and was not liked by the government because of that. He was closely allied to Westmeath, who's son had married Antrim's daughter, and Westmeath frequently used Antrim's proxy vote in the Irish House of Lords because Antrim was more interested anyway in Scottish politics. (See the biography of Antrim's son by Ohlmeyer)]

Eastmeath [sic] – Earl of Westmeath "heretofore fair dipped in treason".

Sir Arthur Magenny, Tyrone's son in law and others.

1641

Fr Patrick Hackett O.P., *Aphorismical Discovery of Treasonable Faction* (Louvain, 1652), Vol I under 1641 first published in John Gilbert ed., *A Contemporary History of Affairs in Ireland from 1641-1652* (Dublin, 1879-80), Vol I p.35.

[For the identification of Hackett as the author of this work see http://www.indymedia.ie/article/84054 footnote 19.]

"Others to follow this recent dogmatist [Thomas Dease, Bishop of Meath], and especially the Earl of Westmeath, being thereunto the only champion in Ireland for religion, was now deluded by this poor prelate dwelling in his house, this brave nobleman was very sickly and old, and not able to do any business abroad, and for those respects was easily induced to this ungodly scene [in not joining the 1641 rebellion], notwithstanding if not for the surmishes and erronious infusions of this degenerate pastor, he would join and unite his own name the Nugents to the rest of the gentry of that county, for the defence of religion, king and county [error for country no doubt], whereof he was ever very tender, by which disunion the Nugents were shamefully divided in several parties or vandos, the Baron of Delvin heir apparent of this old earl, and married to Sir Thomas Nugent's daughter, was gone for England. Sir Thomas [of Moyrath] himself was tepid, neither hot nor cold. Robert Nugent [Carlinstown] more generous than venturous, Andrew [Donore] more wise than potent, others more loyal than hardy, others neither fish or flesh, so that by the means of this prelate, in crubbing the Earl, all the service of that brave family of the Nugents (otherwise a brave support for the now affairs) did mar, not only in his [the Earl's] particular honour, and temporality but also was like to run a desperate and bemoaning course in the behalf of his soul, after acting so many heroic and unparalleled deeds in the behalf of holy religion and native soil at home and abroad, that his mate, in the undergoing of very difficulty, if not desperate in pursuance of the said ends, was not to be had, "non est inventus similis illi," but was amused by this zeudoprelate.

The Divine Providence very tender of this subject, so well deserving of his church, moved my lord primate of Ireland, Hugh Reilly, a godly and upright prelate, to send one Fr James Nugent a young monk of St Bernard's order to the earl, to insinuate unto him, in what a dangerous plight his lordship was in, adhering unto the bishop [Dr Thomas Dease Bishop of Meath who lived with the Earl and opposed the rebellion], himself already excommunicated, "caesus caecum ducens, ambo in foveam cadent," and his lordship's no less, what would he expect but the compliance of our Saviour's sentence, expounding unto his lordship all the particulars thereof the very bishop in place [the bishop listening to the discourse]. The monk told his lordship the cause of his coming, his delegation from my lord primate, to absolve his lordship, if penitent and desired it, promising a recantation in what passed, and amendment for the future. His lordship was very attentive unto this discourse, and persuaded of the verity thereof grew mighty angry and offended with the seducing prelate who to colour his own actions, said that his lordship should not be so sensible of it as not of that consequence as the monk did paint it. Whereupon the earl enraged, with the fervour of true zeal, answered the prelate,

"avoid Satan, trouble me no more, let me adhere unto my mother the holy church, who ever yet cherished me and I served her, that now in my drooping days I should become a prodigal child, ever obedient unto her, in my flourishing and blossoming years."

"Father," said he to the monk, "for God's sake reconcile me presently to my mother and get a whip a absolve me after the manner of an excommunicated person, as I am," which was done incontinently.

The earl thus reconciled with mighty comfort, but because the bishop would not imitate that good example, would never admit him afterwards. The heir apparent of this earl married as aforesaid, with Sir Thomas Nugent's daughter, dowager of Dunsany's eldest son, of tender years was now in England, so was viscount Dillon and viscount Taafe, of whose party I do not know, but young Westmeath was not of capacity to serve any, and withal was in walls the matter of 14 weeks in a kind of restraint, that he was not admitted to come for Ireland, whereby is averred he served neither party in England. The old age of Westmeath, the minority and absence of his said heir, and the public and private working of the said prelate [Bishop Dease], did minister fuel unto the distraction of that noble family, and consequently of the raising of Sir James Dillon to the government of that county whereof they are most sensible unto this very day." [They disliked this because of their ancient feud with the Dillons.]

1667

John Lynch, *Supplementum Alithinologiae* (St Omer, 1667), translated at PRONI D/3835/A/1/82

[At the time of the Desmond rebellion of James FitzMaurice Fitzgerald:] "some also of the chief families in Leinster and several of English origin began to conspire from a desire for the Roman religion. Of whom the most celebrated was 1. Nugent, Baron of the Exchequer, a man of excellent life and reputation deceived (as the Irish relate) by the fraud of those who were envious of him. And he secure in his innocence, when the Viceroy solemnly promised him his life if he would acknowledge himself guilty preferred to undergo an infamous punishment rather than live with his innocence dishonoured. But the Earl of Kildare and his son-in-law the Baron of Delvin having fallen under the suspicions of the Viceroy for having entered into an alliance with Desmond were brought into England and imprisoned in the Tower of London.

...

[Fr Richard O'Ferrall in his pro Rinucinni pamphlet] accuses among others Fr Robert Nugent of plotting Rinucinni's downfall while "feigning themselves to be faithful to him" [quoting the pamphlet.]...Fr Robert Nugent who had long before joined the Society, ruled in a most praiseworthy manner in Ireland, not without distinction but with supreme power, and that not for less space than 20 years, and would without doubt have held that office to the close of his life if his Holiness had not abridged all the offices of the Society, except the General, to three years. ...

But I will pass over in silence the pre-eminent knowlege of the Revd. Fr Robert Nugent in Theology, and Mathematics, and his wonderful activity in recalling wicked men to reformation of character, his unceasing labours in preaching and his memorable unselfishness (which shone in him above all his other virtues.) As I learned from him who knew him intimately (and having been familiar with him by dwelling with him for a lengthened period) [who] declared [that] to me assuredly. While he governed the Society of Jesus the condition of the Society flourished very much. For the Fathers...zealously gave their attention with fair success to the heretic people to be brought over to the Catholic religion. Would that that Father was as fortunate in receiving that sum from him or his heirs as he was liberal in giving to the Nuncio 12,000 Tyrone pounds. Which I have heard he received from his relation the Countess of Kildare for laying the foundation of a house to receive the novices of the Society. [He leant a lot of money to Rinucinni that he never recovered.] In truth the very opportuness of [lending] so much money ought to be an argument rather of his liking for the Lord Nuncio than of any perfidy undertaken against him...

But for example the same refutation [of the pamphlet by 'a certain father of that society'] states that the same Fr Robert Nugent entertained for 20 days together – with splendid and magnificent hospitality, at his own or rather the Society's expense, in the castle of Kildare [Kilkea], which the said Countess on her deathbed had left by will, alongwith all the household furniture, to the fathers of the Society – the Lord Nuncio, who had set out to urge on the siege of Dublin, and the large number of attendants among whom were several prelates...

Furthermore besides (those mentioned in the next work by O'-Sullivan and others) it appears that many of the same recent Irish fought for the sake of their religion; for most reliable documents are forthcoming, which prove that the Nugents burned with a glowing ardour to preserve and follow the Catholic religion.

Christopher Nugent Baron of Delvin, as we learn from Hooker p.172, was a companion to his father-in-law the Earl of Kildare, who was committed to custody in the Tower of London, as well on the journey as in prison. And it is related in the Alithinologia p.39 following his statement, that both feared to lend aid to the Earl of Desmond – who took up arms for the sake of preserving the Catholic religion from being extinguished. They are said to have suffered the penalty of incarceration for the desire, by which they were influenced, that the Catholic faith might not suffer detriment. The Earl of Kildare died and his son in law [the Baron of Delvin] remained long in prison and sent and took his eldest son and his other children of his wife Mary [with him into prison?] Who as he became melancholy through his long abode in prison, so he sought to soften it a little, and cultivated music, till he gained a great proficiency in it. We have often heard his celebrated song on liberty lost sung to the harp, the violin and the harpsichord.

Walter Nugent, whom Christopher appointed to the Lieutenancy of his permanent band [of soldiers], snatched the Franciscans of the Monastery of Multyfarnham out of the clutches of the soldiers who hauled rather than led them to Dublin that they might be plagued with those torments which were usually inflicted on ecclesiastics at the time when persecution raged; on which occasion several of his band were severely wounded amongst whom Walter Nugent lord of Dromcree who was so lamed by a wound in the thigh that he could only walk with his legs bowed out and could not take a single step without a contortion of his whole body. He ultimately restored the convent to the monks. Christopher as he spent the greater portion of his life in prison so he ended his days in captivity. Furthermore we learn from Landers 'de Scismate' that on the 19th of June 1580 the roll of Irish nobles confined in the Tower of London included the Archbishop of Armagh, the Earls of Kildare and Clanricard, the Baron Delvin and our Nugent. ['Nugentium item Meuumque' maybe "and also Nugent of Meath", meaning Justice Nicholas no doubt.]

Attempt of William Nugent and the rest to set up the Catholic religion.
Now William Nugent, Baron of Skryne in issue of his wife, the brother of the aforesaid Christopher, took into his confidence 50 nobles born in the English Province. [They planned] that they would secretly get possession of Dublin Castle and hold it to themselves, and would restore the open profession of the Catholic Religion which the storm of persecution then springing up had not so entirely depressed. But the design being betrayed by the wife of one of them (who having found a letter in her husband's pocket, which detailed the whole plot of the matter, through the frailty of her sex let the matter out to others.) Those of them who could be caught were subjected to capital punishment near Dublin, having been accused of high treason before the one eyed Justice Dillon. Among them were Cusack of Cusintowne and a certain Netterville but I have not heard the names of the rest. William escaped punishment by flight first into Ulster then into Scotland and ultimately into Italy.

He was an eminent poet in various languages.
Then he learnt the more difficult niceties of the Italian language and carried his proficiency to that point that he could write Italian poetry with elegance. Before that however he had been very suc-

242

cessful in writing poetry in Latin, English and Irish and would yield to none in the precision and excellence of his verses in each of these languages. His poems which speak for themselves are still extant.

The First Earl of Westmeath born in prison
The circumstances that Richard Nugent, the heir of the above Christopher and afterwards the 1st Earl of Westmeath, was born in prison was a certain presage of his future constancy in adhering to the Catholic faith, of sedulously encouraging it within the boundaries of his country and advancing it with his ability. This Earl came to Maynooth, the chief residence of the Earl of Kildare, to attend the Council held in 1605 with the Earls of Tyrone and Tyrconnell, in which it was determined by unanimous consent that they should take up arms to shield religion from the point of threatened ruin. [However] when they made some one of their order privy to their enterprise, with a confident hope that he would be won over so that he would be induced to protect the religion, their projects vanished away like smoke, he relating the intended designs to the Privy Council. Which when the Earls of Tyrone and Tyrconnell heard they consulted their safety by taking to flight.

He is taken and committed to custody and sentenced to death.
Richard alone was taken and thrust into the Tower of Dublin [Dublin Castle] and in the end sentenced to death. But the day before that day on which he should have been brought to be beheaded on the fatal scaffold he received from some friend a wicker basket filled with golden apples. In one of which [baskets] he let himself down into the ditch beneath, with a gentle fall, and passed over to his servants who were waiting on the opposite side of the ditch to mask his coming over. And presently leaping to horse reached the same day his strong castle of Clochuchtair in the Co. of Cavan, having ridden his horses at a most rapid pace. But when he had abode there a very little while he departed thence to various hiding places. During which time Sir Richard Wingfield Knt, Marshal of Ireland, spent much time and labour in investing it [Clogh Oughter castle], but to no purpose. He also, with no better success, proffered large gifts to such men as should

take him; for Richard had secretly made his way over to England and obtained from King James a pardon for his faults; whence he returned to his country for his country's great good. Whence frequently, when great tempest of persecution against the Catholics began to rage, he would quickly pass into England, not dreading to commit himself to the peril of crossing in an open fishing boat if there was no other vessel in which he might be carried over. He was said by King James to have spanned the sea with an arch. Nor was any one such journey undertaken by him barren of fruit; for as often as he visited England for the sake of freeing his country from misery, so often he took back commandments from the King that the storms of persecution should be delayed.

He, while he was yet only Baron of Delvin (O'Sullevan p.231), advocated in a noble manner the cause of the Catholics before the King in the year of salvation 1517 [recte 1617?] and is said with heroic courage to have concluded his harangue in these words:

"You O most noble King I prefer before all human things, but you will grant me this one concession, that I should esteem God before you." (Relation of Gerald p.298 et seq.)

Then also was added the most ardent spirited study of the Catholic religion, by Sir Christopher Nugent, who informed the King that the Catholic religion had never at any time been abolished by decree of the Parliament of Ireland, and that he should beseech his Majesty, that he would not make a beginning of the abolition of it.

He gave a large portion of his inheritance that he might obtain immunity for the Religious of Multyfarnham.

It is indeed worthy of record that the religious of Multyfarnham, placed in the possession of Richard, clad in no other habit than that of their order while residing openly in that monastery after the Catholic religion had been proscribed in Ireland. The religious of Ulster for the most part inhabited it, and when some happened to be accused of some crime Richard, that he might obtain immunity from punishment for them from the Viceroy Chichester, bribed him with a large portion of his inheritance, viz the ample territories of Ballyshannon and Killybegs which are enjoyed by

Chichester's heirs to this very day. This Richard moreover offered so great worship to the Blessed Virgin that he attributed to her all his fortunate success, and for the sake of showing her the greatest reverence he established a fast on Saturdays, for ever to be observed by himself and household. Which custom is even now rigidly observed by his heirs and other Earls and is called by others the Nugent's fasts. His piety towards the Blessed Virgin increased to that degree of fervour that when he was blind he went to Loretto and thence to Rome, whence he departed laden with the favouring prayers of Urban VIII and with gold and silver monies or a gift of medals.

Andrew Nugent
Andrew Nugent of Donore an opulent man whose annual revenue almost reached the sum of 1000 pounds sterling or 100,000 in the money of Tyrone; nor was he more abundant in wealth than ingenerous in the pious uses of it. For he collected a number of poor countrymen that they might dig a deep and broad moat into which he led channels from the neighbouring lake. And so constructed a fish-pond, and a lofty island in the midst of it, around which the waters flowed so that fish might live in it and swans might swim in it.

How he spent his wealth.
And so that to this island the swans might retire from time to time, and when there was any danger the inhabitants of the neighbourhood might retire to it also and might find a refuge and protection. He caused the said countrymen to enclose a vast space of land with a hedge, which should form a preserve for deer. Not that he at all cared to labour to prepare deer and swans to stock either his preserve or fish pond with, but only that he might supply the poor countrymen with fitting means of livelihood.

Hospitable to needy nobles.
To the stranger likewise, and especially to such as were of noble birth whether men or women, if they should happen to be in need he showed himself particularly courteous and liberal. He founded a hospital at Multyfarnham in which old gentlemen of

straightened circumstances could receive bread and board.

He imposed on himself a restraint in every way
Thirdly he joined himself to the Order of St Francis. He was led
by an earnest desire of mind to trace out histories of what kind soever, and to restrain this passion (for the sake of God) he both de-
prived himself of that delight and severely denied to himself all
reading of history.

How free from vainglory
He also bound himself by a religious promise that he would never
do anything for the sake of ostentation. He undertook to say a certain formula of prayers daily throughout the week and to each of
them he added a more earnest entreaty for something of greater
moment.

His custom in prayer
On Thursday he used to recite the office of the most Blessed Sac-
rament and would complete it with this little crowning request:
that the ancient splendour of the church of Ireland might be restored, [even] if in the accomplishment of that wish he himself
should be compelled to suffer the loss of all his fortunes. Yes and
it was with no vain prayer that he besought God. Before the last
day of his life [no doubt having also seen the Confederation of
Kilkenny restore the Catholic faith], having suffered the loss of
all his goods, he was compelled to beg from door to door. For
having experienced the fulfilment of his wish, he was dragged
about in a little cart through various places.
    I should never make an end if I should endeavour to produce
in this discourse all the Nugents, even of one family of the Nugents, who displayed not merely their own steadfastness in the
Catholic religion but further an example of the greatest piety.
From these three or four the reader may form a conjecture of the
rest. For "in the mouth of two or three witnesses every word is established."

Their firmness in the Catholic Religion
This only I will add that the most vehement tempests of persecu-

tion which have now agitated Ireland for a hundred years have not dashed any of the Nugents of any note, or scarcely one out of all the families of Nugents, onto the rocks of heresy or given his name over to the adversary. So that no man but a most brazen faced calumniator will attempt to snatch away the title of Catholic from them who have not only shown themselves sincere in the practice of the Catholic religion, but brave in defending it. And still further so sedulous and fervent have they been in embracing piety that of their own accord, directing themselves [away from ?] the most ample fortunes, they have given their names to religious orders.

Oliver Nugent
Oliver Nugent of Dromcree while not yet out of his youth passed 18 years as a horseman under the care of the Baron of Delvin, 18 years in matrimony, and his last 18 years as a Franciscan.

Lavallin Nugent, refusing the opulent inheritance of Dysert which came to him on his brother's death, associated himself with the Order of the Capuchins. He was so pious that he became the institutor of the Capuchin missions to Germany and Ireland. And at the consecration of the host, which he exhalted as was his custom while performing his office, Our Saviour having put on the form of a little child manifested himself visibly to a woman who was a heretic. [This] so influenced her mind that having adjured her heresy she joined herself to the Catholics. [A miracle attributed to Friar Lavallin, see his biography by F X Martin.] He was of so great estimation that Paul V was willing with the purpled fathers [Cardinals] to become his auditor and gave much praise to his discourse. He was so powerful a preacher that when in Germany he was attended by many of the nobility who came to hear his preaching in Latin or French, which they greatly affected. And it was only on account of his deep aversion to their vices and heresy that he left that country. He was so admirably skilled in controversies of the faith that very many [became] convinced by the arguments addressed by him, and having given up the heretic messenger betook themselves to the bosom of the church. Nor should Lord Nicholas Nugent, long Chief Justice of the Common

Pleas, be passed over in silence, who half strangled on the gibbet, was cut down, and torn into four parts on account of a suspicion of his having entered into a secret confederacy with the Viscount Baltinglass. [He was accused of] countenancing [joining Baltinglass'] War of the Catholic Religion, then just commenced, alongwith the noblemen David and John Sutton brothers, and the heir of David, William Ougano [?] of Rathcoffey, Robert Scurlock, Lord Clench (Lynch) of Skryne, Lord Netterville and Robert Gerald bachelor of Theology...

[In 1641] The Earl of Westmeath, who was about to support Athboy with a guard, while the enemy was holding Trim with a garrison, checked the sortie. Those who were irritated by that affair, in order that they might churn the stomach of the Earl, and bring on his forfeiture, made a sally into Delvin, his most powerful dominion, and took away huge spoils from hence. But the Earl, proceeding on his way with those who were returning, snatched away both all booty and life from those that you might refer to as emissaries, by number 260. James Nugent's sons from Dromcree repeatedly drove off from that place, oftimes by force, the unjust occupiers of their ancestral domain, and by these means rescued the castle of Drumcree."

(Nugent entries translated from the Latin at PRONI D/3835/A/1/82 apart from the last paragraph:

Westmediae Comes Athboyam praesidio firmabat, ut hostium, qui Trimmiam praesidio tenebant, eruptiones coerceret. Qua illi re irritari, ut stomachum Comiti mouerent, et damnum inferrent, excursione in Deluiniam potissimam Comitis ditionem facta, ingentes inde praedae abegerunt. Sed Comes reuertentibus obuiam procedens, et praedam iis omnem et ex emissariorum istorum numero duce[n]tis et sexaginta vitam eripuit. Filii Jacobi Nugentii de Dromeryh iniquos paternae ditionis occupatores crebro inde abegerunt, quibus firmum castellum de Dromcryh per vim saepius eripuerunt.")

Index

1

1641 rebellion.........43, 84, 145, 151, 237

A

A Passionate Pilgrim (published 1599)..58
A Yorkshire Tragedy (play of 1608)......58
Annesley, Sir Francis...........................236
Aphorismical Discovery28, 136, 152, 163, 170, 237
Asquith, Claire.....................................55
Athboy (Co.Meath)......................228, 248
Attainder, Act of (passed against William Nugent).......56, 68, 69, 101-104, 108-110, 125-129, 137
Aylmer family.....................................115
Aylmer, Julia.....................................69

B

Ballaknock (Co.Westmeath)................176
Ballina (Co.Meath)..............2, 26, 27, 100
Ballinvalley (near Oldcastle Co.Meath)
....185
Ballyshannon (Co.Donegal).................244
Baltinglass (Viscount of) see under Eustace
Bathe S.J., Fr William.....................66, 96
Beglin, Fr Patrick (hermit of Fore)......155
Bermingham, Patrick....41, 162, 209, 214, 215, 219
Bingham, Sir Richard. .160, 162, 213-216, 218
Bismarck, Otto von....................................6
Book of Howth...........30, 86, 89, 116, 161
Borlace, Sir John.........................152, 166
Broadgates Hall (Oxford)......................90
Browne, Christopher...142, 150, 162, 181, 213, 215-218, 220, 227
Burghley, see William Cecil
Burke, Fr William...........................60, 94
Burke, Ulick (1st Marquess of Clanricard)
....145, 161, 168, 242
Butler, James (1st Duke of Ormond)...152
Butler, Thomas ('black tom' Earl of Ormond)..228
Byers, Sir John..............................61, 94

C

Cade, John (his rebellion in Henry VI pt 2)..47
Caleno custurame.................................18
Cambridge. 32, 68, 70, 76, 82, 92, 96, 122, 155, 157, 158
Campion S.J., Fr Edmund............6, 32, 70
Capuchin Order.....4, 28, 29, 85, 135, 151, 154-156, 234, 247
Carew, Sir George (President of Munster later Earl of Totness)57, 59, 63, 86-90, 92, 96, 117, 136, 158, 162, 170, 215
Carey, John...73
Carlinstown (Co.Westmeath)85, 152, 154, 181, 238
Cassidy, Daniel...............................62, 95
Cecil, Sir Robert (Earl of Salisbury).....83, 88, 92, 149, 162, 230, 232, 233
Cecil, Sir Thomas...............................221
Cecil, William (Lord Burghley)..6, 31, 37, 41, 88, 99, 100, 106, 110, 131, 133, 146, 150, 155, 158, 159, 162, 174, 193, 194, 204, 207, 208, 212
Celtic mythology............................15, 74
Cess (controversial tax)...33, 93, 137, 138, 140, 141, 147, 161, 173
Chettle, Henry.......................................58
Chichester, Sir Arthur. .139, 166, 232-234, 244
Clare Hall (Cambridge)...................32, 92
Clogh Oughter castle (Co.Cavan). 42, 233, 243
Clonardrane (Co.Meath).....................209
Clonin (Co.Westmeath)......158, 177, 179-181, 212, 228
Clopton House (Stratford upon Avon)..89, 90
Como, Cardinal de. 35, 195-198, 201, 205, 206
Conegan, Piers....................140, 181, 190
Confederation of Kilkenny......27, 43, 170, 246
Cook, James.......................................120
Coote, Sir Charles..............................150
Crossakiel (Co.Meath).......................229
Crosse, Richard...........................184, 188
Cusack, Fr Christopher.......................154
Cusack, Edward...............................38, 87
Cusack, John. .35, 132, 140, 151, 161-163, 179, 182-185, 187, 190-192
Cusack, Robert.................40, 64, 209, 210
Cusack, Sir Thomas............114, 157, 207
Cusack, Walter.........40, 64, 154, 209, 210
Cynthia (poetic title for Queen Elizabeth

and poem of 1604). .24, 25, 29, 52, 53, 65, 66, 80, 81, 84, 91, 92, 106, 111

D

Dalkey (Co.Dublin)..................20, 21, 78
Dating problem of the First Folio........118
Davies, John (of Hereford)..........124, 125
Davison, William..............................36
de Lacy family.............................90, 147
Dease, Fr Thomas (Bishop of Meath)...28, 84, 85, 155, 234, 237, 238
Delahide, Edward..............................181
Delvin (Barons of) also see under Nugent 22, 33, 41, 104, 131, 187
Dillon, Anthony..................................225
Dillon, Garrat......................................214
Dillon, Sir James.................................239
Dillon, Sir Lucas (chief Baron of the Exchequer).......164, 165, 171, 181, 194, 215, 219-223, 225
Dillon, Nathaniel..................................211
Dillon, Sir Robert (chief Justice of the Common Bench)....38-40, 46, 47, 91, 143, 144, 151, 160, 207-215, 217-220, 226, 227
Dillon, Theobald.................................192
Don Quixote.................................57, 81
Donadea (Co. Kildare)....................69, 96
Donore (near Multyfarnham Co.Westmeath)......29, 34, 80, 81, 86, 93, 138, 140, 172, 181, 238, 245
Donsoghly (Co.Dublin)........116, 162, 167
Dowling, John.....................................20
Drumcree (Co.Westmeath). 181, 185, 241, 247, 248
Dublin Castle.....27, 29, 34, 41, 42, 44, 86, 132, 135, 152, 175, 180, 188, 213, 233, 235, 236, 242, 243
ducdame..17, 18
dump (a style of music)...................17, 74
Dun an Oir (Co.Kerry)........................206
Dungannon (Baron of) see Hugh O'Neill
Dungimmon (Co.Cavan)......................84
Dysert (Co.Westmeath)..........29, 107, 247

E

Earls of Tyrconnell (O'Donnells). 97, 140, 231, 243
Elsinore...20, 21
Eustace, Roland (2nd Viscount Baltinglass)....................34, 141, 173, 235, 247

F

Fagan, Patrick............................27, 84, 85
Falstaff...14, 115
Famous History of Captain Stukely (apocryphal play)...18
Farranan, Dean of...............143, 208, 214
Fay, Hubert...................................185, 186
Fay, Robert..186
Fenton, Geoffrey. .159, 187, 188, 192, 194
First Folio.................57-59, 93, 121, 122
Fitzgerald, Gerald 'the bard'.................15
Fitzgerald, Gerald ('wizard' Earl of Kildare)..173
Fitzgerald, Gerald (15th Earl of Desmond) 15, 33, 138, 235, 241
Fitzgerald, Mary (wife of Christopher Baron of Delvin).........................231, 232
Fitzgerald, Sir John.............................186
Fitzgerald, Sir Luke............................150
Fitzmaurice, Capt. James....19, 63, 75, 77, 96, 174, 186, 206, 239
Fitzpatrick, John.................................235
Fitzsimons, Leonard............................201
Fitzwilliam, Sir William24, 155, 175, 181, 226
Fleming, Thomas.................................176
Flight of the Earls.................42, 232, 243
Florence, Duke Francesco of.....35, 70, 71
Fore abbey (Co.Westmeath)....43, 67, 102, 135, 139, 186, 207
French, Dr Nicholas (Bishop of Ferns) 168, 170

G

Garlond, John......216, 218, 220, 221, 224, 225
Garlond, Patrick..........................216, 218
Gerard, Sir William..............................88
Gerardstown (Co.Meath)....................210
Glenconkeine..37
Gray's Inn..............................56, 66, 92
Greene, Robert......8, 9, 11, 31, 58, 72, 92, 124, 127-130
Grey, Master of (Scottish Minister)....149, 206
Groat's Worth of Wit.............56, 58, 124
Guise, Duke of......6, 36, 64, 70, 148, 197, 204-206

H

Hackett O.P., Fr Patrick (author of Aphorismical Discovery)....................170, 237
Hall, Dr John.....................................120

Hall, Joseph..126
Hall's Chronicle...............................30, 86
Hart Hall (Oxford)...........................32, 90
Hickey, Elizabeth 4, 21, 32, 43, 52, 56, 65, 73, 79, 80, 87, 88, 92, 95, 96, 113, 127, 145, 154, 161
Hickey, Raymond............................95, 96
Holy League.....................................148
Howth (Barons of) see St.Lawrence
Hume, Rev Abraham........................59, 93
Hussey, Walter...................................116

I

Irish Masque at Court...................74, 126
Irving, Sir Henry...................................60
Italy...............................6, 19, 43, 53, 242
Ivers, William.....................................210

J

Jaggard, William....................................58
Jones, Thomas (Bishop of Meath). 39, 157
Jonson, Ben...8, 18, 69, 73, 103, 104, 126, 129

K

Kilkarne (Co.Meath)........21, 80, 185, 186
Kilkea castle (Co.Kildare).............26, 241
Killiagh (Co.Meath)....................142, 160
Killua (Co.Westmeath)................184, 229
Killybegs (Co.Donegal).......................244
Kilmainham (Co.Dublin)............207, 210
Kiltomb (Co.Westmeath)...............84, 178
Knockdoe (battle of)...........................116

L

Lench (Worcestershire).........................53
Leon, Bishop of....................................36
LeStrange, Thomas.....................175, 236
Leyburn, Dr George...................165, 169
Lismullen (Co.Meath)...................87, 115
London Prodigal (play of 1605).............58
Loretto (Italy)....................................245
Lough Derg (Co.Donegal)....................62
Loughcrew (Co.Meath).......................185
Lynch, Fr John. .23, 26, 27, 30, 43, 79, 84, 86, 93, 131, 135, 155, 156, 166, 239, 248

M

Macmorris (Capt. James Fitzmaurice?) 19, 63, 77
Magdalen College (Oxford)..................53
Maguire clan (Fermanagh).............32, 97
Malby, Sir Nicholas............................187
Malone, Edmund....................................6

Marward, Jenet 25, 32, 111, 140, 143, 180, 189, 190
Matthew, Fr Claud.......................196, 197
Maynooth (Co.Kildare)...4, 156, 219, 228, 243
McCongawney, Fr Shane......142, 214-216
McCongawney, Melaghlin Moyle.........40
McDonnell, Randal (1st Marquess of Antrim).......................................164
McGeoghegan, Brian......................34, 35
McLynn, Pauline.......................13, 62, 73
McMahon, Brian McHugh Oge.............40
McMaster, Anew...................................62
Millar, William...................................186
Moore, Sir Edward.......176, 181, 185, 221
Moore, Sir Garret........................233, 234
Mullingar...................4, 35, 135, 156, 176
Multyfarnham friary (Co.Westmeath). .67, 135, 136, 157, 158, 230, 241, 244, 245

N

Nalson MP, Dr John...................168, 170
Nash, Thomas........................11, 72, 127
Navarre...36
Neile, Richard.............................216, 228
Nicholls, William..................................53
Norris, Sir John...................................227
Nugent, Andrew of Donore....93, 238, 245
Nugent OFM (Cap.), Fr Anthony.........156
Nugent, Catherine.......................155, 156
Nugent, Christopher (9th Baron of Delvin) passim et...........23, 131, 150, 241
Nugent, Christopher (of Laragh)....91, 211
Nugent, Christopher FitzOliver...........229
Nugent SJ, Fr Christopher...................156
Nugent, Sir Christopher (of Corbetstown) 158, 244
Nugent SJ, Fr Dominic........................156
Nugent, Edmund......34, 67, 181, 182, 192
Nugent, Edward (William's first cousin, student of Gray's Inns).....66, 92, 159, 208
Nugent, Elizabeth (Countess of Kildare) 26, 240
Nugent OFM (Cap.), Fr Francis...........155
Nugent, Gerald.....................................25
Nugent SJ, Fr Gerard..........................156
Nugent, Gerrott...........................186, 189
Nugent, James (of Drumcree).............248
Nugent, James FitzChristopher (William's uncle)............................34, 174, 193, 248
Nugent, John (of Skurlockstown)...38, 54, 132, 137, 156, 162, 180, 187, 189, 191

Nugent SJ, Fr John..........................156
Nugent, Lavallin (of Drumcree)....34, 138, 172
Nugent OFM (Cap.), Fr Lavallin....28, 29, 155, 247
Nugent OFM (Cap.), Fr Lawrence.......155
Nugent OFM (Cap.), Fr Luke.............155
Nugent, Nicholas (2nd Baron of the Exchequer).....33-35, 38, 137, 140, 141, 151, 156, 159, 171, 175, 180, 181, 184, 185, 187, 188, 191, 194, 239, 247
Nugent SJ, Fr Nicholas.........................27
Nugent SJ, Fr Nicholas (jailed in Wexford in 1671)..156
Nugent, Oliver......................26, 100, 176
Nugent OFM (Cap.), Fr Peter.............156
Nugent, Richard (10th Baron of Delvin later 1st Earl of Westmeath)25, 28, 29, 43, 80, 85, 92, 131, 135, 144, 145, 151-156, 170, 235-237, 243, 248
Nugent, Richard (2nd Earl of Westmeath) 'black baron'..................................92, 145
Nugent, Richard (5th Baron of Delvin)..22
Nugent, Richard (7th Baron of Delvin)117
Nugent, Richard (8th Baron of Delvin).22, 30, 31, 127
Nugent, Richard (author of Cynthia)....24, 42, 80
Nugent, Richard (historian, uncle of WWI general).......................................154, 160
Nugent, Richard of Donore. 29, 34, 80, 81, 86, 138, 140, 172, 181
Nugent SJ, Fr Robert.......26, 28, 100, 156, 240, 241
Nugent, Robert Bán............................181
Nugent, Thomas (lawyer, William's uncle).......34, 85, 138, 140, 147, 161, 171, 172, 175, 176, 181, 208
Nugent, Thomas (of Coolamber).........232
Nugent, Walter....................................241
Nugent, William..
    a legal expert..................................44
    as Laertes................................99, 100
    Catholic controversialist..................42
    Catholic idealist............................136
    courageous....................................137
    famous poet....................................30
    friend of Fr Lavallin Nugent............29
    his submission...............................204
    in exile in Europe...................35, 205
    Italian poem by................................80
jailed in 1575...................................33
kidnaps his wife..........................32, 90
launches a political court case in 1591 ....39, 212
modesty a characteristic of his family 93, 171
owner of Gaelic poem book............91
political career................................32
rebels in 1581................175, 180, 242
receives coded letters..............54, 187

O

O'Coffey family.....................................22
O'Connor (of Sligo)..............................40
O'Conor, Fr Charles.....24, 79, 84, 93, 154
O'Daly, Tadhg......................................89
O'Donnell, Red Hugh...........................97
O'Ferall, Fergus...........................223-225
O'Ferrall OFM (Cap.), Fr Richard......151, 163, 169, 240
O'Hurley, Dermot (Archbishop of Cashel) 200
O'Hussey OFM, Fr Bonaventura....25, 27, 31, 107, 112
Oldcastle, Sir John (play).....................75
O'Muirithe, Diarmuid...............62, 73, 94
O'Neill, Art...............................186, 189
O'Neill, Hugh....24, 33, 40, 42, 75, 97, 98, 100, 101, 104, 106, 110, 112, 134, 151, 162, 163, 193, 228, 229, 237, 240, 243, 245
O'Neill, Prior.....................................186
O'Neill, Turlough Luineach 33, 34, 36, 97, 162
O'Reilly, Myles McEdmond ('the slasher')...79
O'Reilly, Thomas McShane...............185
O'Roghan, Fr Denis...........................221
O'Rourke, Sir Brian. .35, 37, 41, 142, 150, 160, 178, 182, 213-221, 227, 228
O'Treawair, Fr Carbrey..............226, 227
Oxford.....5, 32, 44, 53, 55, 74, 77, 89, 91, 96, 115, 122, 130, 161

P

Pale (area of English rule in Ireland)....30, 32-35, 37, 38, 64, 66, 67, 97, 98, 110, 113, 115, 125, 134, 137, 139, 146, 147, 153, 154, 162, 163, 182, 183, 186, 189, 191, 192, 194, 208, 217, 227, 229, 230
Paris.....28, 29, 35, 36, 44, 70, 88, 99, 132, 155, 195-198, 204-206, 234

Parsons, Sir William......40, 151, 153, 166
Peele, George.................................8, 9, 71
Perrot, Sir John (reputed son of Henry VIII) 37, 89, 125, 162, 200, 204, 205, 216-218, 220-224
Persons SJ, Fr Robert.................32, 40, 70
Plunkett family...............33, 116, 143, 169
Plunkett, Alexander......................160, 162
Plunkett, Christopher............................38
Plunkett, Ellen..............115, 180, 183-189
Plunkett, Sir John.........115, 176, 185, 209
Plunkett, Nicholas of Donsoghly. 162, 167
Porter, Walter......................................184
Portlester (Co.Meath)..........................228
Preston, Christopher (4th Viscount Gormanston)..33, 162
Price, Diane.......................................7, 71
Primer (phrasebook presented to Queen Elizabeth I)......................................23, 65

Q

Queen Maeve...12

R

Radcliffe, Robert (5th Earl of Sussex)...31
Radcliffe, Thomas (3rd Earl of Sussex) 31, 32, 86, 99, 100, 162
Reilly, Hugh (Lord Chancellor of Ireland 1693)....................................168, 170, 238
Richard II pt 1 (anonymous play)....75, 76
Richelieu, Cardinal..............................152
Rider, Dean (of St Patrick's Cathedral). 42
Rinuccini, Archbishop Giovanni Battista (Papal Nuncio to Ireland).............240, 241
Riverstown (near Tara Co.Meath)210, 211
Robinstown (Co.Westmeath).................34
Rome.....35, 36, 44, 60, 77, 163, 186, 189, 195-199, 201, 203-206, 234, 245
Ross (near Skryne Co.Meath).............210
Ross castle (Co.Meath)..................21, 112
Rouen...19
Ruthven, William (1st Earl of Gowry).200

S

Savoy, Duke of.....................................35
Scotland.....19, 35, 36, 42, 43, 64, 80, 125, 148, 149, 157, 195, 197, 200, 205, 206, 242
Scurlock, Robert..................................248
Sedgrave, Patrick.................................224
Shakespeare, William..............................
    absence of contemporary references to his work as a playwright...................7
    clues to his identity from his works.....
        knowledge of Italian...................6
        knowledge of the Law................6
    contemporary   allusions   to Shakespeare as a pseudonym.............9
    Irish references in works.................11
Plays..
    A Midsummer Night's Dream...12
    A Winter's Tale.................17, 114
    Anthony and Cleopatra.............95
    As You Like It.........13, 15, 18, 94
    Coriolanus.....................12, 13, 95
    Cymbeline.........................12, 114
    Hamlet. .13, 19, 20, 60, 62, 67, 77, 93, 97-101
    Henry IV pt 1.....13, 14, 68, 80, 93
    Henry IV pt 2..............68, 95, 114
    Henry V......17, 19, 63, 77, 93, 94, 123
    Henry VI pt 1...........................19
    Henry VI pt 2.........46, 47, 63, 122
    Julius Caesar...........................12
    King Lear. 17, 20, 67, 93, 121, 193
    Macbeth. 14-16, 19, 20, 60, 73, 94, 121
    Measure for Measure...67, 70, 121
    Merry Wives of Windsor....17, 31, 74, 88, 92, 122
    Much Ado About Nothing.........94
    Othello. .14, 20, 60, 62, 67, 71, 94, 119-122
    Pericles............................13, 120
    Richard II. 75, 76, 80, 93, 103, 113
    Richard III.....80, 93, 95, 119, 122
    Romeo and Juliet....12, 14, 17, 61, 65, 67, 93, 94, 96, 114, 121
    Taming of the Shrew....13, 89, 90, 94
    Tempest.................65, 88, 94, 95
    The Merchant of Venice 14, 71, 93
    Titus Andronicus..................9, 71
    Troilus and Cressida....12, 94, 120
    Twelfth Night...............17, 70, 95
    Two Gentlemen of Verona. 13, 17, 65, 95
Poems..
    A Lover's Complaint..............112
    Rape of Lucrece.......107, 109, 114
    Sonnet no.135....................45
    Sonnet no.136.................46, 107
    The Passionate Pilgrim...........112

Venus and Adonis.............67, 111
traditions of Irish origin of...............20
Shallow (Justice)...........................114-116
Shane, Sir Francis................139, 159, 230
Shelton, Thomas.........................56, 81, 92
Sidney, Sir Philip.............................31, 52
Silence (Justice)...........................115, 116
Simpson, Richard..11, 18, 72-74, 128, 129
Skryne, Baron of..................................242
Skyrne (Co.Meath)...........30, 32, 104, 146
Slewcarbery..233
Sligo..40
Southampton (Earl of) see under Wrio-
thesley
Spain..24, 36, 42, 53, 64, 66, 80, 125, 148,
152, 167, 206, 228
Spenser, Edmund..8, 52, 91, 126, 129, 130
St.Lawrence, Sir Christopher (Baron of
Howth)..30, 39, 41, 86, 89, 116, 147, 160-
162, 211, 214-216, 218, 219, 221, 228,
232
Stanihurst, Richard................................30
Stanihurst, Walter.............................30, 42
Sterling Castle (Scotland)....................199
Stuart, James VI of Scotland, I of England
....148
Stuart, Mary (Queen of Scots)......78, 110,
148, 201
Stukely, Capt. Thomas.............18, 75, 206
Sussex (Earl of) see under Radcliffe
Sutton, David.......................................248
Sutton, John...248

T
Tadee, Nowland.................36, 86, 87, 185

Tara (Co.Meath) 4, 22, 41, 79, 88, 96, 111,
115, 227
Trim (Co.Meath)....35, 105, 147, 228, 248
Tudor, Queen Elizabeth 23, 24, 52, 54, 99,
109, 111, 148, 173
Tuite, William..............................176, 179
Tyrone (Earl of) see under Hugh O'Neill
.33, 40, 42, 75, 97, 98, 100, 163, 228, 229,
237, 240, 243, 245

U
uisce beatha..18
Uisneach (Co.Westmeath)....................22
Use (a legal trust)................................105

V
Vatican...........43, 148, 195, 196, 198, 201

W
Wadding OFM, Fr Luke........................74
Wakely, Thomas..................................106
Wallop, Sir Henry. 41, 134, 150, 162, 192,
212
Walsh OFM, Fr Peter...........................168
Walsh, James J................................61, 94
Walsingham, Sir Francis...36, 37, 87, 134,
141, 146-148, 150, 151, 160, 162, 172,
173, 192, 193
Westmeath (Earl of) see under Richard
Nugent
White, Nicholas (Master of the Rolls). .88,
162, 174
Wilde, Simon.......................................210
Wingfield, Sir Richard.........................243
Wriothesley, Henry (3rd Earl of
Southampton)...........................31, 57, 232

John Shakespeare = Mary Arden

William Shakespeare

"Loving countryman,

I am bold of you as of a friend, craving your help with 30 pounds upon Mr. Bushel's and my security, or Mr. Milton's with me. Mr. Roswell is not come to London as yet and I have especial cause. You shall friend me much in helping me out of all the debts I owe in London, I thank God, and much quiet my mind which would not be indebted. I am now towards the Court in hope of answer for the dispatch of my business. You shall neither lose credit nor money by me, the Lord willing, and now but persuade yourself so, as I hope, and you shall not need to fear but with all hearty thankfulness I will hold my time and content your friend, and if we bargain further you shall be paymaster yourself. My time bids me hasten to an end, and so I commit this to your care and hope of your help. I fear I shall not be back this night from the Court. Haste. The Lord be with you and with us all, Amen.

From the Bell in Carter Lane, the 25th of October 1598.

Yours in all kindness,

Richard Quiney"

The above represents the full total of letters/correspondence ever found going to or from William Shakespeare the actor, this letter to him which was possibly not sent.

Susanna Shakespeare	=	Dr John Hall
Although a signature of Susanna exists, nonetheless when the eventual publisher of her husband's medical notes visited her in 1643, she seemed unable to read.		A doctor, and Puritan, whose Latin medical notes were published and translated in 1657

(John Hall, edited and translated from the Latin by James Cooke, *Select observations on English bodies, or, Cures both empericall and historicall performed upon very eminent persons in desperate disease* (London, 1657), p.3-4.)

Thomas Quiney	=	Judith Shakespeare
A vintner, he had some knowledge of French, and his brother Richard had Latin even as an 11 year old.		

John Shakespeare

Glover, wool dealer, merchant and money lender

1568 mayor of Stratford and justice of the peace

1596 awarded a coat of arms

In 1592 he was reported by the Church Commissioners for not attending the Anglican Church, but his name was in a list with 8 others who only did so "for feare of processe for Debtte."

1757, a bricklayer transcribed a "Spiritual last Will and Testament of John Shakespeare" which he sent to Edmond Malone, the Irish Shakespeare scholar, that he claimed was discovered among the rafters of John's house in Stratford. This much disputed document, now lost, is a copy of a popular 1570s spiritual testimony of Cardinal Carlo Borromeo.

William Shakespeare

1613 Buys the gatehouse of Blackfriars in London. Blackfriars was then used as a theatre but earlier it was a site of the Dominicans in London and is thought to have retained some Catholic connections. The gatehouse was leased to John Robinson, whose brother was a Catholic priest.

Went from Stratford to London and returned on his retirement from the stage, certainly no foreign travel or involvement in wars or politics.

Susanna Shakespeare

In 1606 Susanna was one of 21 people charged with not taking Holy Communion in the Anglican Church in Stratford on Easter Sunday.

POLITICAL/MILITARY/TRAVEL/CATHOLIC CONNECTIONS OF WILLIAM SHAKESPEARE THE ACTOR AND HIS MILIEU

Sir Thomas Nugent=Elizabeth Fleming   Christopher Nugent

Richard Eleanor
Dease = Nugent

Dr Thomas Dease
Gaelic Poet
Author in Latin in 1618 of "Letters printed from Paris to the persecuted Catholiques in Ireland concerning the presenting of Recusants and other points."
Bishop of Meath

William Nugent

Oliver Nugent

Richard Nugent=Elizabeth Preston
8th Baron of Delvin, patron of a school of Gaelic poets

Seamus Dubh Nugent
Gaelic Poet

Fr Robert Nugent S. J.
Latin Poet also frequent correspondent in that language, with also surviving letters by or to him in English and Irish.

William Nugent
Gaelic, English, Latin and Italian poet

"...he could write Italian poetry with elegance. Before that however he had been very successful in writing poetry in Latin, English and Irish and would yield to none in the precision and excellence of his verses in each of these languages."
– Fr John Lynch, *Supplementum Alithinologiae* (1664)

Richard Nugent
English Poet
Also a close friend of Thomas Sheldon, the first translator of Don Quixote from the Spanish
Author of 'Cynthia' (London, 1604)

Gerald Nugent
Gaelic Poet

Christopher Nugent
Latin Poet
and author of two Highly regarded works, firstly on politics and secondly a phrase book in Irish, English and Latin.
9th Baron of Delvin

Eleanor Preston = John Bathe

Fr William Bathe S.J.
Author in English of two books on music
Author in Latin of Janua Linguarum which was translated into 9 languages within 20 years.
Including an English translation published in London in 1617, by Richard Field of Stratford-upon-Avon

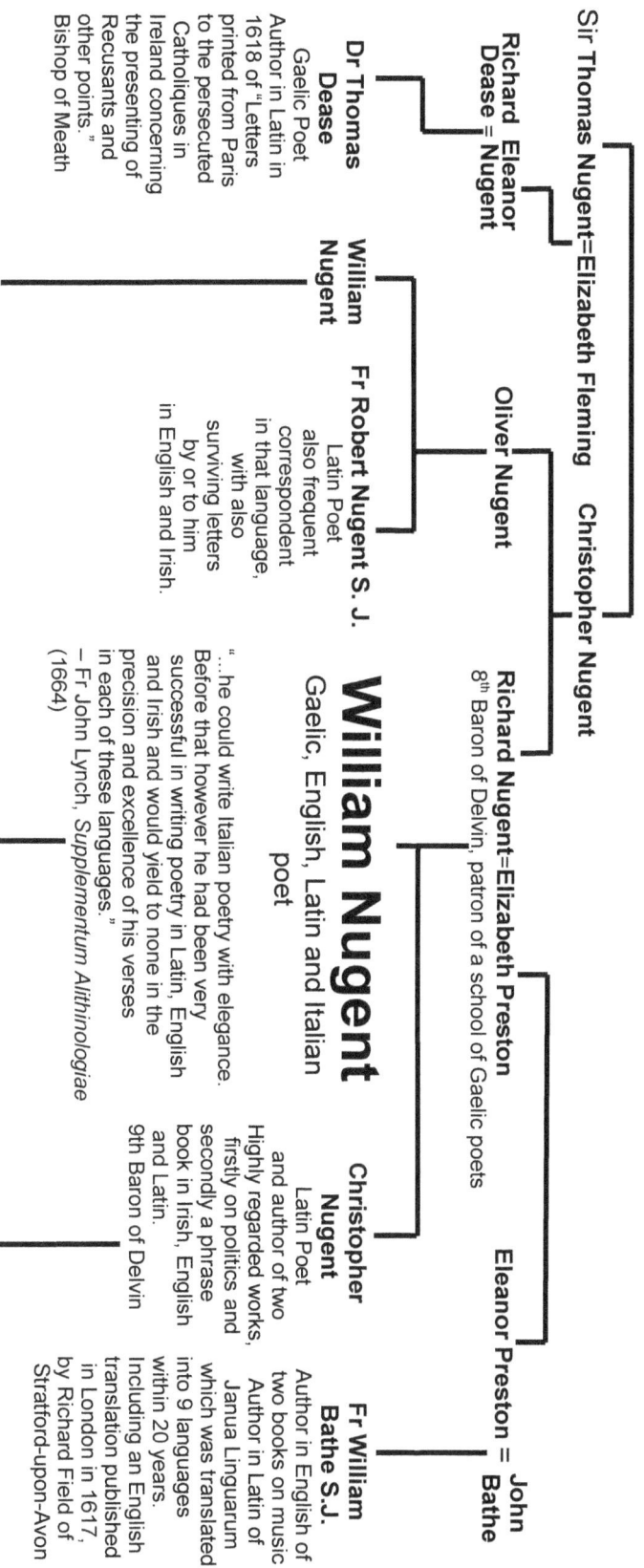

POETIC/LITERARY ACCOMPLISHMENTS OF WILLIAM NUGENT AND HIS MILIEU

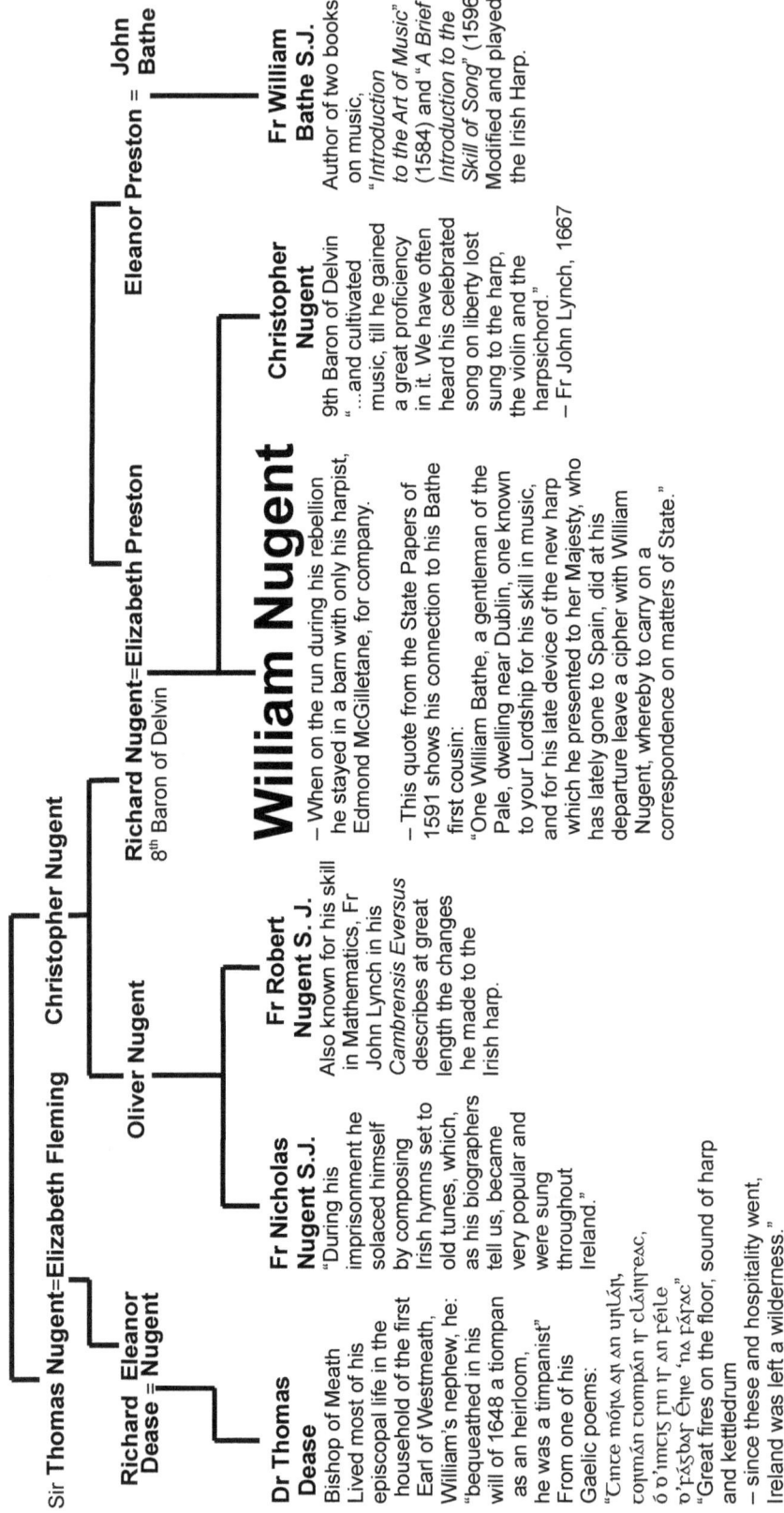

MUSICAL CONNECTIONS OF WILLIAM NUGENT AND HIS MILIEU

Sir Thomas Nugent = Elizabeth Fleming

Christopher Nugent

Richard Dease = Eleanor Nugent

Oliver Nugent

Richard Nugent = Elizabeth Preston
8th Baron of Delvin

Eleanor Preston = John Bathe

Dr Thomas Dease
Bishop of Meath
Lived most of his episcopal life in the household of the first Earl of Westmeath, William's nephew, he: "bequeathed in his will of 1648 a tiompan as an heirloom, he was a timpanist"
From one of his Gaelic poems:

"Cince móɾᴀ ᴀɿ ᴀn uɿlᴀɿ,
coɿmᴀn cɿiompᴀn iɾ clᴀiɿɾeᴀc,
ó ᴑ'imcᴐɿ ɾin iɿ ᴀn ɾéile
ᴑ'ɾᴀ́ɾbᴀɿ Éɿne 'nᴀ ɾᴀ́ɾᴀc"
"Great fires on the floor, sound of harp and kettledrum
– since these and hospitality went, Ireland was left a wilderness."

Fr Nicholas Nugent S.J.
"During his imprisonment he solaced himself by composing Irish hymns set to old tunes, which, as his biographers tell us, became very popular and were sung throughout Ireland."

Fr Robert Nugent S. J.
Also known for his skill in Mathematics, Fr John Lynch in his *Cambrensis Eversus* describes at great length the changes he made to the Irish harp.

William Nugent

– When on the run during his rebellion he stayed in a barn with only his harpist, Edmond McGilletane, for company.

– This quote from the State Papers of 1591 shows his connection to his Bathe first cousin:

"One William Bathe, a gentleman of the Pale, dwelling near Dublin, one known to your Lordship for his skill in music, and for his late device of the new harp which he presented to her Majesty, who has lately gone to Spain, did at his departure leave a cipher with William Nugent, whereby to carry on a correspondence on matters of State."

Christopher Nugent
9th Baron of Delvin
"...and cultivated music, till he gained a great proficiency in it. We have often heard his celebrated song on liberty lost sung to the harp, the violin and the harpsichord."
– Fr John Lynch, 1667

Fr William Bathe S.J.
Author of two books on music, "*Introduction to the Art of Music*" (1584) and "*A Brief Introduction to the Skill of Song*" (1596). Modified and played the Irish Harp.

Justice Sir Thomas Cusack = (fourth husband) Jenet Sarsfield (fifth husband) = Justice Sir John Plunkett   Justice James Bathe
Lord Chancellor of Ireland   Chief Justice of the Queen's Bench   Chief Baron of the Irish Exchequer

Justice Robert Cusack = Catherine Nugent
2nd Baron of the Exchequer

Edward Nugent,
A lawyer educated at Gray's Inns in London during which he acted as William Nugent's agent during his court case 1590-94.
His father Thomas, of Drogheda, was also very interested in the law, as a 1575 letter of his indicated. In it he quotes, in the original Latin, authorities as diverse as the Magna Carta and Bracton, "one of the ancient fathers of the law," and further states:
"good my lord be not offended that I do seek the benefit of the law for your honour are bound to maintain it, as I a free subject inheritable to have it, and without it I know not how I may live."

Thomas Nugent
2nd Baron of the Exchequer, and later Chief Justice of the Common Pleas, only Irish Judge ever executed, "learned sober and wise"

Justice Nicholas Nugent,
Had wardship of William's later wife and married William's widowed mother in law, William and his wife seemed to live mostly in his house at Kilcarne near Navan.

Richard Nugent = Elizabeth Preston
8th Baron of Delvin

William Nugent = Jenet Marward

– Hosted a Gaelic scribe writing Brehon law tracts, the *Seanchas Mór.*
"ⱥn beurⱪí vom a vⱪíᵹ Uⱳⱡeam oíᵹ ⱬ velbnⱥ"
"I am in Dergthi in the house of young William in Delvin."
(Scribe named MacEgan writing in a copy of the *Seanchas Mór,* TCD Ms 1337, p.377, last line second column, see *The Green Cockatrice* p.28 and 187.)
– Described as learned in the law in an intercepted 1584 letter
– Writes all the legal documents in a dramatic and involved court case taken against Justice Robert Dillon in 1590-94.

Walter Marward = **Ellen Plunkett**

Eleanor Preston = **Justice John Bathe**
Attorney General, Chancellor of the Exchequer

Christopher Nugent
9th Baron of Delvin

Sir Christopher Nugent
A lawyer of Corbetstown

LEGAL KNOWLEDGE OF WILLIAM NUGENT AND HIS MILIEU

CATHOLICITY OF WILLIAM NUGENT AND HIS MILIEU

Catherine Nugent=Robert Cusack

Their son, Fr Christopher Cusack, was the "founder and promoter of the Irish Colleges...at Lille, St. Omer, Antwerp, Douai, and Tournai."

Thomas Nugent

Oliver Nugent

Richard Nugent
8th Baron of Delvin

Christopher Nugent

Richard Nugent = Elinor Handcock

Richard Elinor Nugent = Handcock

"Richard Nugent, brother to the last Baron of Delvin, and one Boothe that married the widow of Goghe of Dublin and dwells at Drum Conrathe, a mile from Dublin...have undertaken the printing of Papistical books"
(Sir William Wade to the Earl of Salisbury, 10 August 1605)
His widow started a riot in 1629 in Dublin, trying to protect a Franciscan Chapel.

Christopher Nugent

9th Baron of Delvin
– 1580, Lord Deputy: "...whose obstinate affection to Popery hath now approved him unsafe to himself, unsound to friend, disloyal to prince, and false to God, such is the yield of such seed."
– 1583, Lord Deputy: "The cancerdest and most malicious man, both for religion and English government (I think) that Ireland then bare."
– Converted the traveller and diarist Henry Piers to Catholicism.

William Nugent

– From one of his Gaelic poems:
"ᚔᚱ ᚉᚏᚓᚐᚈ ᚁᚐᚔᚏᚈᚓᚋ ᚁᚐᚅ ᚋᚐᚅᚐᚉ
ᚑ'ᚐᚔᚏᚈᚒᚅᚑᚌ ᚔ ᚅ-ᚐᚌᚈ ᚐᚋᚐᚋᚐᚌ."
"in my dream it was a troop of slender-handed white monks that I saw in conflict with the foreigners."
– Launched a rebellion in 1581, partly to assert the Catholic faith.
– Witnessed, with his brother Christopher, a Eucharistic miracle in Delvin Church.
– In 1600 he launched a religious controversy in Dublin in defence of the Catholic faith.
– His son, Fr Christopher Nugent, a Franciscan priest, in Louvain in 1617.

Edward Nugent

"...one Edward Nugent, a lawyer, to come into the lower house with a premediated speech in defence of the Mass and Romish religion, declaring the good success her majesty's progenitors had whilst they embraced the Mass and the Catholic religion, as he termed it, and the bad success which pursued the rejecting thereof."

(Adam Loftus writing in 1590 with respect to the parliament of a few years earlier.)

Fr Robert Nugent S. J.

– Was for seven years: "continually being looked after by the pursuivants, whom he only beguiled by night-travelling and various disguises. All this time, however, he never ceased preaching to crowds of eager listeners."
– For c.25 years head of the Jesuits in Ireland.
– His brother Nicholas, also a Jesuit, described in 1618/19: "Prisoner in Dublin for the Catholicke faith."

Richard Nugent, Earl of Westmeath

"an obstinate recusant",
c.1617: "In audience with King James he gave the "most ardent, spirited study of the Catholic religion," and "informed the King that the Catholic religion had never...been abolished by...the Parliament of Ireland."

Sir Christopher Nugent
of Corbetstown

– 1625: "A vehement Papist...in so much that none of that religion appears in more eminence upon all occasions for the Papists."
– 1641: "being thereunto the only champion in Ireland for religion."

Elizabeth Nugent,
Countess of Kildare

"Her castle became not only the asylum of the neighbouring Catholics, but a sort of head-quarters for the Catholic clergy..."
(Cardinal Patrick Moran, *History of the Catholic Archbishops of Dublin* (1864)).

Justice Nicholas Nugent

Executed by the Irish government for involvement in his nephew William's rebellion in 1581.

Richard Nugent

8th Baron of Delvin. A member of the Irish Privy Council, he died on campaign against the Irish rebels in Ulster. He was a close friend of the Lord Deputy for Ireland, the 3rd Earl of Sussex.

James Nugent

Arrested for his involvement in William's rebellion, escaped from Dublin Castle, went to London and was interrogated there in the Tower of London. Attacked by William's illegitimate brother Edmund.

Edmund Nugent

Rebelled alongside his legitimate half brother William, but was caught and assisted the government, particularly by attacking his uncle James Nugent. He died in the attempt

William Nugent

1577 Jailed in connection with the cess controversy

1581 Launched his own rebellion at Robinstown on the eastern shore of Lough Ennell in Co. Westmeath. Stated that he was the official Papal agent in this rebellion, via Captain James FitzMaurice Fitzgerald.

1582-4 Exiled to Scotland, France, Rome and Spain where he had dealings with the monarchs of all those countries.

1590-4 Conducted a major court case accusing a politically well connected Irish judge of corruption, particularly of secretly fostering rebellions. Consulted the Queen as part of this and stated that he was acting on her behalf.

Richard Nugent

c. 1600 Alongwith Captain Richard Tyrrell, he was Hugh O'Neill's principal lieutenant in the Pale during his rebellion, i.e. the Nine Years War.

Richard Nugent

10th Baron of Delvin, 1st Earl of Westmeath

1607 Rebelled after he escaped from Dublin Castle, where he was jailed because of his involvement in the Flight of the Earls.

1625 In a list of "chief men reckoned dangerous" to the Irish government described as "heretofore fair dipped in treason."

1627 Fought with the Duke of Buckingham at the Isle of Rhé in France.

c.1610-1640 Arguably the principal Catholic/Irish Nationalist politician in Ireland

Christopher Nugent

9th Baron of Delvin

Frequently military commander of the Pale forces.

Regularly jailed by the government for political/religious reasons, and died in Dublin Castle in 1602 while facing a treason charge.

Gilbert Nugent

Negotiated with the King of Spain on behalf of the Irish Catholic leaders in 1640, seeking an island where Irish Catholics could migrate to.

POLITICAL/MILITARY ACTIVITIES OF WILLIAM NUGENT AND HIS MILIEU

If you liked this book you might like to read some of the author's other works, including:

A Guide to the 18ᵗʰ Century Land Records in the Irish Registry of Deeds

The Registry of Deeds in Dublin contains a vast repository of summaries of Irish land transactions for the 18th century. This collection is particularly important, to genealogists among others, because of the destruction of other historical records in Ireland for the same period, especially since the Four Courts fire of 1922. In this guide you will find a description of the records held there, an explanation of the different Irish land and currency units used, and a wide ranging discussion of Irish land transactions and registries of the period and somewhat later. This includes the influence of the Penal Laws, the nature of Irish marriage settlements and the economic climate and prices prevailing in Ireland in that century.

978-0-9556812-9-5

An Cᴦeᴦoeᴀṁ

This book seeks to illustrate the type of literature that shaped and influenced the Irish people's faith over the centuries, a cornucopia of Catholic writing, a skirl around the kind of books and journals that graced Irish priest's libraries over the years. Outlined in chronological order it gives the full text of the Confession of St. Patrick, the Life of St. Columbanus, an ancient Irish tract on the mass; extracts from the Confessions of St. Augustine, the Irish Annals, and the fiction of Canon Sheehan; some theology from St. Thomas Aquinas, from 'A Handbook of Moral Theology', and the doctrine of Purgatory from an old Maynooth theologian; historical or contemporary accounts from all centuries, all the way from Tertullian, through Lough Derg in the 15th century, the Cromwellian Wars of the 17th century, to the social and economic teachings of the Church in the 19th and early 20th centuries.

978-0-9556812-3-3

Slí nᴀ Fírinne

This English language book puts the traditional Catholic proofs of God's existence into a modern context. It covers most of the arguments raging in the theism v atheism debate and also includes quotes on the nature of God and his existence from c.80 philosophers and scientists.

978-0-9556812-8-8

The Irish Invented Chess!

For over three centuries a controversy has raged as to the exact origins of 'fidchell' – in modern Irish 'ficheall' – or Irish chess, a game played in Ireland from biblical times. This book argues that that game of fidchell, or brannaimh, was recognisably our modern chess. It also raises disturbing questions about the real history surrounding the Lewis Chess find.

978-0-9556812-6-4

www.ingramcontent.com/pod-product-compliance
Lightning Source LLC
Chambersburg PA
CBHW031948080426
42735CB00007B/312